From England to Arkell: The story of two pioneer settlers, Lewis & Thomas King who left Suffolk England for the wilds of Upper Canada in 1831

A genealogy to 4 generations of their descendants in Ontario, Alberta, Australia & Michigan

by Lorine McGinnis Schulze

ISBN: 978-0-9680744-4-2

Copyright 2009
Reprinted 2016

Cover Image Credit: Library and Archives Canada, Acc. No. 1970-188-718 W.H.
Coverdale Collection of Canadiana

Table of Contents

Origins of the King Family

Origins of the King Family in Suffolk England

Wenhaston is a small village situated to the south of the River Blyth in north-eastern Suffolk, England. Roman coins, pottery and building materials unearthed in local fields indicate the existence of a settlement at Wenhaston from the first century AD, and this was probably a market of some importance between 80 and 350AD. The first written record of its existence is found in the Domesday survey of 1086, when it was noted that the village of **Wenadestuna** [sic] possessed a mill, a church, and woodland sufficient to feed 16 hogs.

Lewis and Thomas King were brothers who were born and baptised in Wenhaston Suffolk England. Their parents were James King and Hannah (Ann) Blanden.

Lewis who was born in May 1793 married Elizabeth Smith in Wenhaston in 1817. Thomas who was born in April 1796 married Harriet Dawson in Frostenden in 1817.

Sometime around 1831 or slightly earlier, the brothers left England for America. They were among the first pioneers to settle in Arkell Ontario.

St. Peter's Church, Wenhaston

Uggeshall is a village in Suffolk, England, located approximately 6 miles (10km) south of Beccles and 4 miles (6½km) north east of Halesworth. Above is St. Mary's Churchyard in Uggeshall

Thomas King's wife Harriet Dawson was born 14 March 1797 in Frostenden and baptised in the church 3 days later. Her parents were William Dawson and Sarah Smith.

Harriet had 3 brothers - David born 1795, George born 1799 and James born 1804. Her 3 sisters were Elizabeth born 1801, Sarah born 1809 and Mary born 1812. All were baptised in the local church.

She also had 2 half-brothers (James and William) born to her father and his first wife Elizabeth Baldry. Elizabeth died at the age of 32 and was buried in the Churchyard in December 1793.

William and his second wife Sarah Smith of Uggeshall, were married in the Frostenden church in 1794. William died in APril 1837 at the age of 81 and is buried in the Frostenden churchyard.

Frostenden is a small village in Suffolk, England. Its church, All Saints, is one of 38 existing round-tower churches in Suffolk

Lewis & Thomas King's father James King was living in Chediston Suffolk England in July 1791. On the 6th of July 1791 he was recorded as a husbandman and was served with a bastardy maintenance order for the female child of Hannah BLANDON. On that same day, Hannah Blandon, residing in Holton, singlewoman, underwent a bastardy examination

Source: FC189/G5/1 & FC189/G3/36 Suffolk Record Office, Ipswich Branch

Holton, in Suffolk, England, is a small village near town of Halesworth. Holton is split into two parts, Upper Holton and Holton. It often referred to as Holton St. Peter, to prevent confusion with Holton St Mary. The church of Holton St Peter is one of 38 existing round-tower churches in Suffolk built by the Normans in the 11th century. Holton also boasts a post mill, parts of which date back to the 18th century. The post mill is the earliest type of European windmill.

Chediston, Linstead Magna and Linstead Parva are three villages in North Suffolk linked by a grouped parish council. The church at Chediston lies in the heart of the village, on a slight incline overlooking the river Blyth. Recent excavations just outside Chediston churchyard led to the discovery of a burial, possibly Saxon. Remains of a minor Roman settlement lie near the river and were excavated some years ago. There is a dispersed settlement at Chediston Green lying about half a mile away from the church to the north. Many of the houses are listed as being of historic interest and are timber framed and some have large moats surrounding them.

Hannah Blandon's grandfather may be the THOMAS BLANDING, of WENHASTON who was served with a bastardy maintenance order on 26 OCTOBER 1741 for support of the female child of ELIZABETH BARLEY, otherwise BARTLET, singlewoman. Source: FC189/G5/2 Suffolk Record Office, Ipswich Branch

On 18 MAY 1778, a Removal Order was served on THOMAS BLANDON, DRUMMER in the Western Battalion Militia of Suffolk. Thomas, Mary, his wife, and their children Mary, Elizabeth, Ann, Thomas & Susannah were ordered removed from St. James, Bury St. Edmunds and sent to Wenhaston.

Source: Removal Order FC189/G4/14. Suffolk, Ipswich Branch, WENHASTON PARISH RECORDS Date: 1778.

St. James Church, Bury St. Edmunds

Hannah Blandon's father THOMAS BLANDEN alias THOMAS BLANDON born WENERSTON [Wenhaston] Suffolk received his Discharge Papers as a Chelsea Pensioner in 1787

Served in Suffolk Militia and was discharged at age 48 after 28 years of service. Date: 1787.

Source: Royal Hospital, Chelsea: Discharge Documents of Pensioners WO 121/1/38. The Catalogue of The National Archives. held at The National Archives, Kew

A Chelsea pensioner is now an in-pensioner at the Royal Hospital Chelsea, a retirement home and nursing home for former members of the British Army located in Chelsea, London. Historically, however, the phrase referred to both in-pensioners and out-pensioners.

During the reign of King James II, the Royal Hospital was under construction, so he introduced a system for distribution of army pensions in 1689. The pension was to be made available to all former soldiers who had been injured in service, or who had served for more than 20 years.

By the time the Hospital was completed, there were more pensioners than places available in the Hospital. Eligible ex-soldiers who could not be housed in the Hospital were termed out-pensioners, receiving their pension from the Royal Hospital but living outside it. In-pensioners, by contrast, surrender their army pension and live within the Royal Hospital.

In 1703, there were only 51 out-pensioners. By 1815 this figure had risen to 36,757.

In 1662 England an Act of Settlement was passed to define which parish had responsibility for a poor person. A child's birthplace was its place of settlement, unless its mother had a settlement certificate from somewhere else stating that the unborn child was included on the certificate. From the age of 7 the child could have been apprenticed and gained a settlement for himself or he could have obtained settlement for himself by service by the time he was 16.

After 1697, the poor were allowed to enter any parish in search of work, as long as they had a Settlement Certificate signed by the church wardens and overseers of their place of settlement and two magistrates guaranteeing to receive them back should they become chargeable. No one was allowed to move from town to town without the appropriate documentation.

If a person entered a parish in which he did not have official settlement, and if it seemed likely he might become chargeable to the new parish, then an examination would be made by the justices or parish overseers. From this examination on oath, the justices would determine if that person had the means to sustain himself and, if not, which was that person's parish of settlement. As a result of the examination the intruder would then either be allowed to stay, or would be removed by means of what was known as a Removal Order.

A Removal Order was sometimes accompanied by a written pass to the parish of settlement showing the route to be taken. This would apply even within a city or town which consisted of more than one parish. Your parish of settlement was obliged to take you back.

Removal Orders would often take a person or a family back to a place of settlement miles across the country, sometimes to a parish they had only known briefly as a small child. It was not uncommon for a husband and wife to have their children taken from them, each being removed to separate scattered parishes

Suffolk. The Examination of Hannah Blandon now
residing in the parish of Holton in the said County
within the Hundred of Blything Single woman
taken upon oath before us two of his majesty's
Justices of the Peace acting in and for the said County
the sixth Day of July 1791 ——————————

Who upon her oath saith That on Thursday the
fourteenth Day of October now last past at the House
of Ephraim Lockwood in the Parish of Holton
aforesaid in the Hundred and County aforesaid she the
said Hannah Blandon was delivered of a Female
Bastard Child which Child is now living and is become
Chargeable to the said Parish of Holton and thereby to
the Guardians of the Poor with in the said Hundred of
Blything, And that Samuel King late of Chediston in
the said County Husbandman did get her with Child
of the said Bastard Child ——————

Sworn and Subscribed
before us

E Davy.
Curtis

Hannah Blandon
her ✗ mark

Bastardy Examination of Hannah Blandon 6 July 1791. Under Oath Hannah states that on Thursday 14 October 1790 she gave birth to female bastard child at Ephraim Lockwood's house in Holton Parish, Blything Hundred, Suffolk Co. James King, husbandman, late of Chediston is the father. Hannah makes a stylized "H" as her mark

SUFFOLK,
to wit.

THE Order of *Eloazar Davy and Charles Purvis Esquires* two of his Majeſty's Juſtices of the Peace, in and for the ſaid County, one whereof is of the Quorum, and both reſiding next unto the Limits of the Pariſh Church within the Pariſh of *Holton* within the Hundred of *Blything* in the ſaid County of Suffolk, made the *Sixth* Day of *July* in the Year of our Lord One thouſand Seven hundred and Ninety *one* Concerning a *Female* Baſtard Child, lately born in the Pariſh of *Holton* within the Hundred of *Blything* aforeſaid, in the County aforeſaid, of the Body of *Hannah Blandon* Single-woman.

E Davy

WHEREAS it hath appeared unto Us the ſaid Juſtices, as well upon the Complaint of *Robert Smith one of the acting Guardians of the poor with in the said hundred* as upon the Oath of the ſaid *Hannah Blandon* that ſhe the ſaid *Hannah Blandon* on the *fourteenth* Day of *October now last past* was delivered of a *Female* Baſtard Child at the *House of Ephraim Lockwood* in the Pariſh of *Holton* aforeſaid, within the ſaid Hundred of *Blything* in the County aforeſaid; And that the ſaid Baſtard Child is now living and is *become* chargeable to the ſaid Pariſh of *Holton* and thereby to the Guardians of the Poor within the ſaid Hundred of *Blything* in the County aforeſaid. And further that *James King late* of the Pariſh of *Chediston* in the County of *Suffolk husbandman* did beget the ſaid Baſtard Child on the Body of her the ſaid *Hannah Blandon*

Purvis

And whereas *the said James King hath appeared before us in pursuance of our Summons for that purpose but hath not shewed any sufficient cause why the said James King shall not be the reputed Father of the said bastard child*

We therefore upon Examination of the Cauſe and Circumſtances of the Premiſes, as well upon the Oath of the ſaid *Hannah Blandon* as otherwiſe, do hereby adjudge him the ſaid *James King* to be the reputed Father of the ſaid Baſtard Child. And thereupon we do Order as well for the better Relief of the ſaid Pariſh of *Holton* and Guardians aforeſaid, as for the Suſtentation and Relief of the ſaid Baſtard Child, that the ſaid *James King* ſhall and do forthwith upon Notice of this our Order, pay, or cauſe to be paid to *John Robinson of Southwold* in the ſaid County of Suffolk Treaſurer to the ſaid Guardians the ſum of *Forty Shillings* for and towards the Lying-in of the ſaid *Hannah Blandon* and the Maintenance of the ſaid Baſtard Child to the Time of making this our Order. And we do alſo hereby further Order that the ſaid *James King* ſhall likewiſe pay, or cauſe to be paid to the ſaid *John Robinson* or to the Treaſurer of the ſaid Guardians (for the Time being) the Sum of *one* Shilling and ~~Pence~~ weekly and every Week, from this preſent Time, for and towards the Keeping, Suſtentation, and Maintenance of the ſaid Baſtard Child, and for and during ſo long Time as the ſaid Baſtard Child ſhall be chargeable to the ſaid Pariſh of *Holton* or Guardians aforeſaid. And we do further Order that the ſaid *Hannah Blandon* ſhall alſo pay, or cauſe to be paid to the ſaid *John Robinson* or to the Treaſurer to the ſaid Guardians (for the Time being) the Sum of *Six* Pence weekly and every Week, ſo long as the ſaid Baſtard Child ſhall be chargeable to the ſaid Pariſh of *Holton* or Guardians aforeſaid, in Caſe ſhe ſhall not nurſe and take Care of the ſaid Child herſelf.

Given under our Hands and Seals the Day and Year firſt above-written.

Bastardy Order James King & Hannah Blandon 6 July 1791. Justices of Peace Eloazar Davy and Charles Purvis in Parish of Holton, Hundred of Blything, County of Sufoolk hear the case brought by Robert Smith, Guardian of the Poor in Blything. James to pay 1 shilling per week to John Robinson of Southwald or to Treasurer of the Poor, for maintanance of child as long as living in the parish. Hannah to pay 6 pence weekly.

No. 38.

R. B.

To the Church-wardens and Overseers of the Poor of the
Parish of *Saint James* in the said ~~County of~~ Borough
and to the Church-wardens and Overseers of the Poor
of the Parish of *Wenhaston* in the County of
Suffolk aforesaid and to each, and every of them.
UPON the complaint of the Church-wardens and Overseers, of the
Poor of the Parish of *Saint James* aforesaid, in the
said ~~County of~~ Borough unto us whose Names are hereunto
set, and Seals affixed, being two of his Majesty's Justices of the Peace in
and for the said ~~County of~~ Borough and one of us of the
Quorum, that *Thomas Blandon* *Drummer in the Western Battalion of the Suffolk
Militia and Mary his wife Mary their eldest Daughter of the age of 13 years or thereabouts,
Elizabeth their infant Daughter of the age of Years or thereabouts, Ann their infant Daughter of the
age of Years or thereabouts, Thomas Blandon their infant Son, and Susannah their infant and
Susannah their infant Daughter of the said Thomas there abouts both their children not named*
have come to inhabit in the said Parish of *Saint James* not
having gained a legal Settlement there, nor produced any certificate owning *them*
to be settled elsewhere, and that the said *Elizabeth the Wife of the said Thomas
Blandon, & Mary, Elizabeth, Ann, Thomas and Susannah their
Infant Children are become*
~~likely to be~~ chargeable to the said Parish of *Saint James*
We the said Justices, upon due proof thereof, as well upon the Examination of the said *Thomas Blandon* upon Oath, as otherwise
and likewise upon due Consideration had of the Premisses, Do adjudge
the same to be true ; and We do likewise adjudge, that the lawful Settlement of the said *Thomas Blandon & Mary his Wife & Mary, Elizabeth,
Ann, Thomas and Susannah their Infant Children*
is in the said Parish of *Wenhaston*
in the said County of *Suffolk* We do therefore require
you the said Church-wardens and Overseers of the Poor of the said Parish
of *Saint James* or some, or one of you, to convey the
said *Mary the Wife of the said Thomas Blandon, & Mary, Elizabeth,
Ann, Thomas and Susannah their Infant Children*
from and out of your said Parish of *Saint James* to the said
Parish of *Wenhaston* and them to deliver to the Church-
wardens and Overseers of the Poor there, or to some, or one of them, together with this our Order, or a true Copy thereof, at the same time shew-
ing to them the Original ; And we do also hereby require you the said
Church-wardens and Overseers of the Poor, of the said Parish of
Wenhaston to receive and provide for them as inhabitants of
your Parish.
Given under our Hands and Seals, the *eighteenth* Day of
May in the *eighteenth* Year of the Reign of
his said Majesty King George the Third.

Jos. Macculloch

James Oakes

FC189/C4/14
1443/3

Removal Order Thomas Blandon, wife Mary & children Mary 13, Elizabeth 9, Ann (Hannah) 7,
Thomas 4 and Susannah 2. 18 May 1787

His Majesty's *Western* Regiment of *Suffolk Militia* whereof *The Earl of Euston* is Colonel.

THESE are to certify, That the Bearer hereof *Thomas Blanden Drummer* in *Captn Q Burch's Company* — — of the aforesaid Regiment, born in the Parish of *Wrentham* — — in or near the Market Town of *Halesworth* — — in the County of *Suffolk* — — Aged *68 Years* and by Trade a *Labourer* — — hath served honestly and faithfully in the said Regiment *28* — — Years: But by *being afflicted with bad Eyes & worn out in the Service*

is hereby discharged, and humbly recommended as a proper Object of his Majesty's Royal Bounty of CHELSEA HOSPITAL. He having first received all just Demands of Pay, Cloathing, &c. from his Entry into the said Regiment to the Date of this Discharge, as appears by his Receipt on the Back hereof.

GIVEN under my Hand, and ~~the Seal of the Regiment~~, at this *12th* Day of *January* 1757.

Reuben Thurgood Surgeon
Michl Wm Scheup
Jas Oakes | *Deputy Lieut*

Euston Cole
Grafton
his Majesty's Lieut of Suffolk

N.B. When a Soldier is discharged his Wounds and Disorders must be particularly mentioned, *when*, *where*, and *how* they were contracted; and the Surgeon must sign the Certificates as well as the Field Officer.

Sold by C. Fourdrinier, No. 20, Charing-Cross, where may be had Stamps for Leases, Bonds, Notes, Receipts, &c. and all Sorts of Stationary Wares.

Thomas Blanden in Chelsea Pensioners Records

I _____ do acknowledge that I have received all my Cloathing, Pay, Arrears of Pay, and all Demands whatsoever, from the Time of my enlisting in the Regiment and Company mentioned on the other Side, to this present, Day of my Discharge, as Witness my Hand this ____ Day of January 17__

Thomas B Lewis

Royal Hospital, Chelsea: Discharge Documents of Pensioners

THOMAS BLANDEN alias THOMAS BLANDON Born WENERSTON, Suffolk

Served in Suffolk Militia Discharged aged 48 after 28 years of service Certificates of service (disability or reason for discharge, length of service, rank, regiment, Date: 1787)

Source: The Catalogue of The National Archives. held at The National Archives, Kew. WO 121/1/38. Images 171, 172

Western Suffolk Militia
Earl of Easton's
Thomas Blandon Drummer
28 years [service]
Aged 48
Bad Eyes & Worn Out
Halesworth E Suffolk
A labourer

I Thomas Blandon do acknowledge that I have received all my Cloathing [sic], Pay, Arrears of Pay and all Demands.....(etc) 2nd January 1787.

His Majesty's Western Regiment of Suffolk Militia whereof The Earl of Easton is Colonel

These are to certify that the Bearer hereof, Thomas Blandon, Drummer in Capt. Burche's? Company, of the aforesaid Regiment, born in the Parish f Weneston, in or near the Market Town of Halesworth, in the County of Suffolk, aged 48 years and by Trade a labouer hath served honestly and faithfully in the said Regiment 28 years, but by being afflicted with bad eyes and worn out in his Service, is hereby discharged (etc)

12 January 1787

The King Family in Upper Canada

Lewis and Thomas King were brothers born in Wenhaston Suffolk England to parents James King and Hannah Blanden aka Blanding. In October 1830 when Lewis was 37 and Thomas was 34, the brothers joined a group of men and sailed from England to New York. According to written histories, the men arrived in November 1830.

The trip across the Atlantic would have been quite horrendous at that time of year, with storms and bad weather. Although passenger lists of ships arriving in USA ports were collected and archived as early as 1820, many of the manifests for ships arriving in New York 1828-1830 have been lost. Thus it is no surprise that the names of this group of settlers cannot be found.

The men were intent on forming a settlement in Upper Canada and after wintering in New York they set out in May 1831 for what would become Arkell Ontario. A list of men said to be in the party includes Thomas and John Arkell, for whom the settlement was named, James Hewer (whose son William married Lewis King's daughter Sarah), John Outin, James Carter, Joseph Dory, Charles Willoughby and Peter Bell (whose daughter Mary married Thomas King's son David).

It is not known if their families came with them in 1831 or joined them later, but in April 1834, Lewis and his wife Elizabeth had a son born in the wilds of Upper Canada. Since Lewis' daughter Sarah later stated that she arrived in 1831 presumably the entire family group left England together.

In 1831 Lewis and his wife Elizabeth had 4 children between the ages of 6 and 14 (Sarah, George, Louisa and Hannah), while Thomas and his wife Harriet had one known child - their son David age 14. After wintering in New York the group set out for Upper Canada. They had a few travel options available to them, because in 1828 with the arrival of more and more immigrants, transportation began to change. 1830 was a huge emigration year to Canada and the USA from England. Over 7000 English immigrants arrived in America that year, many planning on going on to Upper Canada.

By 1831 settlers could not only travel up the Hudson River in New York to Albany fairly inexpensively, but since 1824 the Erie Canal took them all the way to Buffalo with easy trek to Niagara. From Buffalo to Niagara they had choices. They could continue on foot or by stagecoach, and part of the journey could be by Lake steamer.

This is a typical ad which the group may have seen in a local newspaper.

Once in Upper Canada, the families had a more challenging journey to Arkell. There were some rough roads they could use for part of the trip, but they would also have had to make their way through forest to reach their final destination.

Ad courtesy of TheShipsList.com at http://theshipslist.com/

The Canada Company conveyed immigrants into remote sections of Upper Canada. One ad stated that *"…two good covered Stage Wagons with Teams of good Horses each, are to be constantly kept traveling between Hamilton and through Wilmot to Goderich in the Huron Territory"* The fare was $3.00.

Following is an ad the Canada Company placed in newspapers in 1828 to try to encourage immigrants to settle near the new town of Guelph, which is quite near Arkell

Ad courtesy of TheShipsList.com at http://theshipslist.com/

After arriving at the proposed settlement area, Thomas and Lewis, their families and the other newly arrived settlers had to start clearing land and building homes. Often settlers built a shanty as their first home. A shanty was a "make-do" dwelling until a settler could build something bigger and better. It was a rough assembly of wood and whatever materials could be easily found, converted to a small one-room dwelling. Often it had no floor, as it was constructed level to the ground. So dirt was the inside flooring of many shanties. Over time a settler with the help of other men would cut logs to build a bigger and better constructed log cabin. But the shanty would keep his family warm and dry during the first winter if he had not had time to build a proper cabin. We do not know if Thomas and Lewis built shanties or if they perhaps worked together with their older sons to build one substantial home to be shared until separate homes could be built.

The following letter was written by John Arkell in 1831 from Farnham Plains (later called Arkell) to his brother Thomas in England. It describes the conditions in the new settlement and province. It provides a wonderful glimpse into the daily lives of the newly arrived settlers from May until December. We should note that since the letter was written in February 1831 the arrival of the settlers had to be in May 1830 rather than May 1831 as is most often given.

Farnham Plains,
Township of Puslinch,
Guelph,
Upper Canada
4/2/1831

To Mr. Thomas Arkell
Donnington Mills
Stow-on-the-wold
Glos. Old England

Dear Brother,

I received your note of March last by the hand of James Hewer, who came up from New Jersey in August last, and was sorry you had so little time to write to me..... <edited for brevity> Father, in his letter of August last, requests me to inform him what sort of climate generally prevails in Upper Canada both in the winter season and the summer season.

The climate varies much in Upper Canada, the province being situated in many degrees of West longitude, and of North Latitude. <edited for brevity> From a great portion of the lands being surrounded by Lakes Ontario, Erie and Huron, the climate is genial, as changeable as in England, but the heat in summer and the cold in winter are both more intense than with you except for the few days in unusually extreme seasons that sometimes happen in England. The Spring is reasonably short: the Summer breaks out all at once some time in the latter part of May. In that month the mosquitoes and black flies in the weeds begin their havoc among the pale-faced Englishmen, who dare not venture at that season of the year to chop down wood in the forest. In the open parts of the country where the trees have been cut down for a few years very few nests of the men tormenters, the mosquitoes and black flies are to be seen, but on the new lands they are a complete pest and torment to the human race, as well as to the poor cattle and horses.

The black flies take their leave in about a month after the Summer has set in and at their heels comes a remarkable small fly called in the country a "knat fly" which settles upon and crawls over the wearied labourer in the evening after his days toil, just as the sun disappears in the evening, and again in the morning for about an hour just after the sun has risen over the tops of the trees. The general tormentors, the mosquitoes, continue their plunder on the human frame throughout the whole summer. They are sometimes more troublesome than usual, and their favourites are bog-land and swampy ground, which is generally covered with cedars and balsam fir trees.

On the lands where we have formed our village and selected our farms, very fine strawberries grow all over the surface of the earth when it has been bared of timber, and in many places raspberries are to be plucked into baskets with as little trouble as if an Englishman's farm here was a gentleman's garden in the old Country. Plums hang overhead as thick on the branches as damsons are with you, but I must tell you that if the day be dull and damp the raspberries and plums shall go hanging so far as I am concerned, nor will I set out to gather them for the pleasure of the present enjoyment of eating them for if my face is not well covered all the time I should have the marks of the venomous little beasts boring instruments for weeks after.

As to wild animals, we have bears, wolves, foxes, raccoons, squirrels (brown, black and striped), deer and hares. We have likewise of the feathered tribes, turkeys (very large ones), pheasants (rather larger than the English partridge), woodpeckers, robins, will-o-wisps, katydids and many others. Bears, foxes and raccoons are not really common. Wolves we hear now and then, but do not often see them, although they swiftly make great havoc with the farmer's sheep if he neglects to bring them up near home at night. A pig or two is now and then also lost when Bruin is pushed for food, as in the fall of the year before he takes to his winter quarters. Great numbers of deer are shot by the settlers in the course of the year.

Your cousins Thomas and Frederick Stone tell me that within the last few days they have seen a herd of 20, but although we are in the middle of things we have both of us had bad luck in shooting them, and but little time to spare to ramble after them as we have been engaged for the most part on our own farms. We have three haunches at the present time in our chimney, and as it has been salted, it remains remarkable firm and good. The deer are larger than those in England, but they do not get as fat. I believe that this is due to the way the flies hunt them about in the summer and to the different food they have to eat in the winter.

The Canadian hare is rather larger than the ordinary rabbit; they change their colour in fall from brown to white. Their chief haunts are in the cedar swamps and their manners are more like those of the rabbit than the English hare. Turkeys are scarce in this part of the province, but I have heard of several being in the township this winter and of one being shot. They are generally very fat when taken. Pheasants are rather numerous and after being followed by the hunter for a few days become wild and fly very rapidly, more so, I think than the ones used to do at home, even after a disturbed season. The flocks of long-tailed pigeons [passenger pigeons, now extinct] which arrive here in spring and leave again in the fall are beyond description. Their resort for the winter is in the southern part of the continent, which is warmer than here.

To return to the climate, I know no better way of describing it to you than be me telling how we felt ourselves in the work of the settlement, and by recollection from memory, as we have not always time to keep our journals as we should wish to do so.

We arrived at Guelph on the 26 of May in very fine and warm weather, mosquitoes and flies just beginning to move out of the black earth and swampy places. I believe it was on the 28th of the month that we commenced our search for the spot or district (then unsurveyed land) where we hoped to settle. Exceedingly warm weather then set in and we were pestered very much while cutting down trees and digging the foundations in a bank to build this house. A few days after my second trip to New York and back again, made under a parching sun and in spite of the boring implements of thousands of mosquitoes, these having accompanied me for the whole distance of 132 miles, we had the pleasure of a few cooling showers of rain from thunder clouds. During the first night Thomas Arkell and James Carter remained on the plain sheltered only by a few boards. Very heavy rain fell, but it did not injure them, the weather being so warm in the day-time. We had no continuance of the dry time after this enough to injure any crops of hay or grain, but throughout the summer afterwards we had plenty of intervening showers to cool the earth and to push any vegetation in all of its natural and violent forms. After the turn of the days, as we say in England, we had more rain than we wished for although it did not fall in any large quantities. Through August and September we had much rain and many heavy dull days, but although the latter end of the summer was considered by the natives to be a very cold, wet time, yet there plenty of drying winds for the industrious farmer to use to the advantage of his harvest crops, and as to the haymaking, the former part of the season being dry and fine, it was only for him to cut down grass and hay and carry it as hay the next day or so fatter one turn and swath.

After building our house and shingling it with shingles made and split out of pine trees, which is the general way of covering houses in N. America, we set to and cleared of weeds and ploughed up and planted about 10 acres of wheat lands for ourselves, and by the end of the month the rest of the settlers, our countrymen, had sown about the same amount as ourselves. Very heavy rain fell three or four days in each week through the end of September and the first half of October when a [--] time came and lasted for about a month. Rainy weather then followed until the end of November, when we had it very cold while I shingled my new farm hay house, and several heavy falls of snow came on before we had finished it.

On the 3ʳᵈ of December we moved James Carter and his wife and 4 children from the cabin we were living in to my new one, by which time winter had set in and the frosty nights began to be rather severe, which occasioned the newly put up "lags" to pop and bounce as they do standing in the forest, so that old dame Carter was of the opinion that ghosts came there nights and that someone had been killed somewhere about there. However, we laughed at the foolish idea and the ghost disappeared in a few nights, so that they have been tolerably comfortable until about a fortnight ago when one of the oxen licked the door with his rough tongue and frightened their young dog so that he barked out and ran under the bed and howled out, which under the circumstance all at once (in the old dame's mind), brought a wolf or bear into the house and she and her young ones shrieked and squalled so much that old Jimmy was half inclined to think that one would take hold of him while he was hunting for the old dame's wolf or bear. However all has been quiet and comfortable since. The wolf and bear story serves us for a laugh often, as well as the ghost shooting off his cannons, in descriptions of which she said "Old Love dam's cannon were nothing to the noise in my new home"

[---] severe and intense cold in the month of December and I see by the paper that on December 4 the thermometer stood at 10 degrees below zero. River navigation was stopped on December 10 and on the 15 the Delaware was passed over with horses. Last year and in other years I understand winter had not set in until Christmas Day and to my knowledge it did not set in last year in New York until the first week in January. From astronomical observations I once saw in an inn at stow, and from the extreme changes from heat to cold, I believe that all over this continent, as the astronomer called it, the sun is at a much greater distance than it is in England and also nearer to us in the daytime than in your country. We had a "spel" as the Yankees called it, that is, a few days of beautiful weather in the first part of last month, which was followed by several frosts, some of them very severe indeed. On Wednesday night last, it commenced raining and a thaw set in, but last night again we had a tolerable sharp bit, and today it is a very pleasant time.

In fact, the American winter altogether is more preferable to work in than the English one, the ground and air being more dry and steady. Chopping down trees in the forest is done principally at this season of the year, and I might say on fine days all winter long. The snow was very deep sometimes, but even then the large trees receive the woodsman's tap, tap, tap, until great is the fall thereof, and the neighbours immediately shrug their shoulders and say "A fine crashing however, Joe or Jack or Tom is tumbling them down at a good rate today"

As Mary wished to know how we lived, tell her by the help of good bread, beef, mutton, pork, venison, tea, coffee, sugar, potatoes, Swedish turnips (excellent), common turnip0s, carrots and parsnips. From the great quantity of rain in the fall, and the getting of the house James Carter and James Hewer live in, we had not time to put our own home in good order so well as we could have wished to do so, but thanks to God, we have now made it rather more comfortable, and as this seems to be a tolerably healthy neighbourhood, I hope we shall get through the winter pretty well.

But in a rather more polite way you can tell Polly that we live like two old, long-bearded and grave old bachelors, sometimes laughing and joking with one another and our fellow settlers. Thomas made one stool, and is preparing to make his farmhouse. We allow Mrs. Carter to wash our clothes for us and make our bread. We cook the food we eat nearly every day with the exception of meat, which we boil or fry, two, three or four times a week as occasion may demand. Being without good beer, and the means of obtaining it at present, we boil our tea kettle or coffee pot three times a day, at Breakfast, Dinner, and Supper. Thomas vows that if none of the English girls will return with him to America when he goes home, he will have an Irish, Dutch or Yankee wife before long. James Hewer is likewise very impatient to receive his wife and four children in America.

James has sent to his son William to come over and take a farm near him, and should you hear of, or see, any working farmers likely to come over here, tell them to be sure to bring with them a good boiling pot and many other kinds of brass, copper and iron household goods, such as fire irons, tea kettles, washing and brewing kettles and coppers, in fact all descriptions of goods and implements of husbandry except what is made of wood is useful in this country, and common English ox plough harness, as what you get here is nearly useless. A good lugging chain is useful enough for American farmers, but as the oxen are in yoke and the horses in pairs with light or gig cart harness, anything heavier is not wanted.

An English farmer coming to Canada should leave all his nice farming behind him, but, at the same time, must be strong as Hercules in resisting the many idle and extravagant ways which exist among people of this province. The everlasting whiskey bottle must not be known at all in his house, even if it be a log one. I have seen many young married couples from England who bid fair to do well in this country, they being industrious, earnest looking people from Yorkshire. But as the colony is so little known to the people of England in general, and from the many vicious persecutions of the Borough villains at home and their tools out here in the land, few farmers of capital have come here, although from information and facts which I have gathered this is a far more preferable country for a farmer to reside in than the United States.

Hoping you are in as good health as we are, I remain your affectionate brother,

John Arkell

PS. If any young industrious and deserving young farmers' servants with a little money, and not given to drink, want to come to Upper Canada, do not dishearten them, as they might bring a good industrious wife with them to this country without their being considered a pest to society and without dread of their having more children than they can maintain. When you write to me again do not send blue bank small note-paper so far with so little information in it, but give us a long description of past and passing events, and likewise tell if James Hewer's wife and family are coming here or not. I should have said more to you but the boy is waiting without for the letter. Tell the Blacksmith's "Jack" that I do not advise him to come to Upper Canada if he is doing well, but if not tell him also that blacksmith's work is some of the best paid out here.

Feb. 4, 12 o'clock. J.A.A. All's well in Upper Canada

[Source: originally published in full in The Gloucestershire Standard, October 8, 1932. With thanks to Ronnie Martin for sending it to me]

This letter gives us a wonderful image of the conditions that Thomas and Lewis faced on arrival at Farnham Plains. We also see that some men came with their families while others (like James Hewer) sent for wives and children later.

From the letter we know that the following men were certainly in Farnham Plains by February 1831 – Frederick Stone, Thomas Stone, Thomas Arkell, John Arkell, James Carter and James Hewer. It has been reported that Lewis and Thomas King and others arrived in May 1831, but since many of the ships passenger lists from those early years have been lost or are damaged and almost unreadable, we may never know with certainty.

Some of the men sent for their families later, some brought their families with them and some appear to have made more than one voyage back to England and then returned to Upper Canada. Although a history of the settlement of Arkell is not my intent in this book, my research into the King family turned up several records of some of these first settlers arriving in New York on board ships, and I feel I should share those here.

Ships Passenger List for the Ship Bristol sailing from Bristol England to New York 10 November 1834 with the Hewer family: James Hewer 67, Sarah Hewer 43, William Hewer 16 and John Hewer 11. The notation "2" in the column "Deaths on the Voyage" seems to indicate that 2 of the Hewer party may have died en route

Ships Passenger List for Catherine sailing from London England to New York 15 April 1840 carried James Hewer, 45, his father John Hewer 70, Robert Thatcher 25 & Peter 11

Robert Thatcher was another first settler of Arkell and his wife Ann Hewer was on board the same ship. Ann was a daughter of the Arkell pioneer James Hewer and his wife Sarah Hill, and she and Robert married in England in 1839. Ann is listed as age 23 on the passenger list, followed by Jane Thatcher age 7 and Jemima Hewer 68. Jemima was the wife of John Hewer and mother of James.

The passenger list for the *Catherine* is puzzling as there are many names of Arkell pioneer families but they are not recorded as family groups and some I cannot place with certainty. But it certainly appears that many of these first settlers traveled back and forth between England and Upper Canada with ease.

Both Thomas and Lewis King are recorded on the 1840 "Census", the 1842 Census and an 1843 Assessment Record, with Thomas owning 100 acres on Concession 10, Lot 6 and Lewis living beside him on another 100 acres on Lot 5. These records do not give details of the homes they had built. We have no record of Thomas or Lewis' homes until 1851 when the census which was taken records Lewis and his family living in a one-storey log cabin. Thomas does not appear in the 1851 census, although he was certainly living there. The first page of the census for Puslinch for 1851 is missing and it is possible that Thomas and family were recorded on that missing page. Thomas' son David, married with a family of 6 young children in 1851 is recorded as living in a 1 ½ storey log home that year.

The land Thomas and Lewis purchased was good farm land and the families prospered and did well. Lewis and his wife Elizabeth had 7 known children, the last 3 born in Upper Canada. Elizabeth died in 1871, Lewis died 2 years later in 1873. Both were buried in the Arkell United Church Cemetery.

Thomas and his wife Harriet had one known son born in England and a possible daughter born in Upper Canada. Harriet died in 1854 at the age of 57, and she was the first burial in the new Arkell United Church Cemetery. Thomas remarried a younger woman, Elizabeth Gow, and had 2 more sons before his death in 1863. He too is buried in Arkell United Church Cemetery.

I suggest you find your direct line of ancestors in **Part One**, and circle or mark their numbers. Then go to **Part Two** and look for your ancestors by number (which you found in **Part One**). The individuals are in numerical order so as long as you know your ancestors' numbers, you can easily find the pages which tell the stories of your ancestors.

Genealogy Report

5 Generations of Descendants
starting from James King & Hannah (Ann) Blanden,
parents of Lewis King & Thomas King

Generation No. 1

1. James[1] King He married **Hannah (Ann) Blanden**, daughter of Thomas Blanden and Mary Jackson. She was born 26 Dec 1770 in St. James, bury St. Edmunds, Suffolk, Eng.

Children of James King and Hannah Blanden are:

+   2   i.   Lewis[2] King, born 05 May 1793 in Wenhaston, Suffolk, Eng.; died 29 Nov 1873 in Arkell, Puslinch Tp. Wellington Co. Ontario.

+   3   ii.   Thomas King, born 08 Apr 1796 in Wenhaston, Suffolk, Eng; died 18 Jun 1863 in Arkell, Puslinch Tp. Wellington Co. Ontario.

Generation No. 2

2. Lewis[2] King (James[1]) was born 05 May 1793 in Wenhaston, Suffolk, Eng., and died 29 Nov 1873 in Arkell, Puslinch Tp. Wellington Co. Ontario. He married **Elizabeth Smith** 15 Jan 1817 in Wenhaston, Suffolk, Eng.. She was born Abt. 1800 in Suffolk, Eng., and died 03 Sep 1871 in Arkell, Puslinch Tp. Wellington Co. Ontario.

Notes for Lewis King:
1831: Lewis' daughter Sarah showed her year of immgration as 1831 in the 1901 census. (She would have been 9 years old]

April 3, 1834: Lewis is shown as the owner of the Crown Lands front half Lot 5 Conc 6, Arkell, Puslinch Tp. Wellington Co. Ontario. ID 5, Sale Clergy Land 01 C1113 001 008

1840 Census Puslinch tp Wellington Co
Heads of Families/ Males under 10/Males over 10/ Females under 10/ Females over 10/ Deaf and Dumb/ Insane / Total in family / Church of England
William Hewer -/1/-/1/-/-/2/2
James Hewer 1/3/-/2/-/-/6/6/
Robert Cook
Lues [sic] King 2/2/2/1/-/-/7/7/
Thomas King -/2/1/1/-/-/4/4
Peter Bell 1/2/-/2/-/-/5/5/

1842 census Puslinch Tp. Gore District [MS 700-2]:
Lues [sic] King, head of a family of 7, consisting of 2 males over 16, 2 males under 16, 2 females under 16 and 1 female over 16. They are all Church of England. Lewis is living

beside his brother Thomas.

This family group means he had one son born before 1826 (George?), 2 sons born 1826-1842 (Thomas & unknown), 2 daughters born 1826-1842 (unknown)

1851 census C 11743 Puslinch Tp
Lewis King, farmer b Eng WM, 55
Elizabeth King, b Eng, WM 52
James King labourer b C.W Wm 14
Jane King b CW WM 9

" . . . Minutes of the yearly school meeting held at the school house on Wednesday the 13th day of January, 1858. Moved by Mr. John Caulfield, Seconded by Mr. Henry Haines, that Mr. John Iles be appointed Chairman. Moved by Mr. John Caulfield, Seconded by Mr. James Hewer, that James Coleman be appointed Secretary. Moved by Mr. Thomas Carter, Seconded by Mr. Louis King, that Mr. James Fulton be appointed trustee. Moved by Mr. Adam Hume, Seconded by Mr. William Scott, that Mr. James Orme be appointed trustee. On a show of hands being called for, it was decided that Mr. James Fulton had the majority; he was therefore declared elected. Moved by Mr. Peter Orme, Seconded by Mr. Robert Cook, that the school be conducted in the free system for this year. Carried unanimously."

1861 census for Arkell p 16: Lewis age 63, farmer and "Mrs." age 55 are living with their son Thomas, age 25 and his wife "Mrs"] and their son Lewis age 2 months. Also living with them is Lewis' daughter Jane aged 18.

1871 census for Arkell: Lewis and Elizabeth are living with their grandson George, age 27 and his wife Jane, on Lot 5, Conc 10, Arkell.

District:	WELLINGTON SOUTH (033)
Sub-district:	Puslinch (A)
Division:	4
Page:	24
Microfilm reel:	C-9945

Lewis King, 75 b England WM
Elizabeth 71 b Eng
George 27 b Canada, C. Presbyterian, farmer
Jane 24, b Canada, C. Presbyterian

1873: Lewis' gravestone in Arkell shows a date of death of 29 Nov. 1873 but his will at the Archives in Ontario [Reel 6-705 Surrogate Court records Wellington Co.] shows he died on or about 1 Dec. 1873.

Obit in Guelph Evening Mercury of Sat. Nov. 29, 1873:
Obits. KING: In Puslinch on 29th inst, Mr. Lewis King age 78 years. Deceased was one of the earliest settlers in Puslinch and was widely known and respected. His death was hastened by the bite of a dog on his hand a few days ago.

Arkell United Church Cemetery, Arkell Ontario, In memory of Lewis King who died Nov. 29, 1873, 78 years. A native of Suffolk England.

Notes for Elizabeth Smith:
Arkell United Church Cemetery, Arkell Ontario, Sacred to the memory of _____, wife of Louis King, who died Sept. 3, 1871, age 51 [71?] years.

Children of Lewis King and Elizabeth Smith are:

+	4	i.	Hannah[3] King, born 28 Feb 1828 in England; died 10 Jun 1904 in Kilbride, Halton Co. Ontario.
+	5	ii.	Sarah Catherine King, born 07 Aug 1817 in Bain, Suffolk Eng; died 11 Jan 1910 in Guelph, Wellington Co. Ontario.
+	6	iii.	George A. King, born Bet. 1817 - 1819 in Suffolk, England; died 17 Nov 1881 in Guelph, Wellington Co. Ontario.
+	7	iv.	Louisa King, born 10 Apr 1825 in England?; died 13 Oct 1917 in Guelph, Wellington Co Ontario.
+	8	v.	Thomas William King, born Apr 1834 in Ontario; died Aft. 1910 in Possibly Huron Co. Michigan.
	9	vi.	James King, born 1837 in Canada West.

Notes for James King:
Ploughing Matches 1853

The Puslinch match took place on Friday last on the farm of Mr. Arkell when the following were successful competitors:

Ploughmen
1st — Joseph Kirby, in the employment of Mr. Stone
2nd — Thomas Waters, in the employment of D. Stirton
3rd — John Wakefield, in the employment of Thomas Arkell
4th — Henry Iles, son of John Iles

Ploughboys
1st — Alex Gow, in the employment of D. Stirton
2nd — W. Dory, in the employment of H. Haines
3rd — Peter Arkell, son of T. Arkell
4th — Robert Thompson, son of W. Thompson
5th — J. King, son of L. King

from the Guelph Advertiser newspaper Thursday November 10th 1853

1881   Census Place: Amaranth, Wellington North, Ontario,

Canada

Source:FHL Film 1375896 NAC C-13260 Dist 153 SubDist I Page 20 Family 87

	Sex	Marr	Age	Origin	Birthplace
James KING	M	M	45	English	Ontario
Occ: Farmer	Religion:		P M		
Marey KING	F	M	45	English	Ontario
	Religion:		P M		
Minney KING	F		21	English	Ontario
	Religion:		P M		
Henery KING	M		18	English	Ontario
Occ: Son	Religion:		P M		
Elisabeth KING	F		16	English	Ontario
	Religion:		P M		
Bethea KING	F		13	English	Ontario
	Religion:		P M		
Marey KING	F		11	English	Ontario
	Religion:		P M		
Charles KING	M		4	English	Ontario
	Religion:		P M		

+ 10   vii.   Harriet Jane (Jane) King, born 31 May 1842 in Puslinch Tp. Wellington Co. Ontario; died Aft. 1901 in Possibly London Ontario.

3. Thomas² King (James¹) was born 08 Apr 1796 in Wenhaston, Suffolk, Eng, and died 18 Jun 1863 in Arkell, Puslinch Tp. Wellington Co. Ontario. He married **(1) Harriet Dawson** 19 May 1817 in Frostenden, Suffolk Eng, daughter of William Dawson and Sarah Smith. She was born 14 Mar 1797 in Frostenden, Suffolk Eng, and died 14 Apr 1854 in Arkell, Puslinch Tp. Wellington Co. Ontario. He married **(2) Elizabeth Gow** Bef. 1856 in Arkell, Puslinch Tp. Wellington Co. Ontario, daughter of James Gow and Christina Ferguson. She was born Abt. 1834 in Canada.

Notes for Thomas King:
Frostenden Parish Registers. Thomas King, single man, married Harriet Dawson, single woman, 19 May 1817 with consent of parents. Witnesses Sarah Jisk & John Harvey.

No baptism of Thomas King.

Baptism Harriet Dawson 17 Mar 1797 [born 14 Mar 1797] d/o William & Sarah [late Smith]. They had 6 more children ; David bap 19 Mar 1795 born 9 Mar 1795 George bap 13 Apr 1799 born 9 Apr 1799 Elizabeth bap 19 Nov 1801 born 15 Nov 1801
James bap 18 Apr 1804 Sarah bap 17 Apr 1809 born 16 Apr 1809 Mary bap 20 Dec 1812 born 11 Dec 1812

No marriage of William & Sarah in Frostenden but Banns were read on 27 Apr, 4 May & 11 May 1794 as follows - William Dawson widower otp & Sarah Smith, single of

Uggeshall.

Burial 19 Dec 1793 Elizabeth Dawson [late Baldry] age 32 wife of William.

No marriage of William Dawson & Elizabeth Baldry..
No baptism of William Dawson.
William & Elizabeth had 2 children -
James bap 20 Nov 1791 born 30 Sep 1791 [mother's name spelt Bauldry] William bap 18 Dec 1785 [mother's name spelt Boldry]

In passing we found 4 children bap to John & Frances Dawson- Amos, Rebecca & William all bap 5 Jun 1814 Samuel 30 Apr 1815 No marriage of John & Frances

Burials
29 Aug 1817 Harriet Dawson age 3 weeks
19 Jul 1820 David Dawson age 25
9 Apr 1837 William age 81
25 Feb 1878 David age 61

Thomas King
Gender: Male
Age: 31
Occupation: Farmer
Country of Origin: Great Britain
Country of Destination: United States of America
Ship Name: Ship Columbia
Port of Departure: London
Port of Arrival: New York
Arrival Date: Apr 17, 1827
Nat'l Archives Series No.: M237
Microfilm Number: 9
List Number: 178

1840 Census Puslinch tp Wellington Co
Heads of Families/ Males under 10/Males over 10/ Females under 10/ Females over 10/ Deaf and Dumb/ Insane / Total in family / Church of England
William Hewer -/1/-/1/-/-/2/2
James Hewer 1/3/-/2/-/-/6/6/
Robert Cook
Lues King 2/2/2/1/-/-/7/7/
Thomas King -/2/1/1/-/-/4/4
Peter Bell 1/2/-/2/-/-/5/5/

Thomas has 2 males over 10, 1 female under 10, 1 female over 10 for a total of 4 in the house. This is himself, wife Harriet, son David and an unknown daughter

1842 census Puslinch Tp., in the Gore District [MS 700-2] shows Thomas King as the head of a house of 4 people total - 2 males over 16, one female under 16, and one female over 16. All 4 are Church of England. This would seem to indicate that Thomas and wife Mary had a daughter born between 1826 and 1842 - the first evidence we have seen of another child other than their son David born 1817.

Thomas is living right beside his brother Lewis, shown as "Lues" King on the same census.

Jan. 8, 1847: Thomas is shown as the owner of the Crown Land on front half, Conc. 10, Lot 6, Arkell, Puslinch Tp. Wellington Couny, Ontario.
ID 6, Sale, Clergy Land 01 C1113 002 212

1861 census Puslinch twp Wellington Co. ward #5
King, Thomas, innkeeper b Eng, 65
Elizabeth 27
Thomas 6
James 4

Arkell Pioneer Cemetery: "In memory of Thomas King, who died 18 June 1863, aged 62 years"

Guelph Mercury April 1994
HEWERS OF ARKELL MADE THEIR MARK
..the Hewer family who settled at Arkell in the 1830s..
Mr. James Hewer was one of a company of men from England who arrived at the present site of Arkell in 1831. These pioneers had travelled on foot all the way from the Port of New York, much of the distance through virgin forest. In addtion to James Hewer, the following men are known to have been in that party:
John and Thomas Arkell
F.W. Stone
John Outin
Henry Haines
James Carter
Joseph Dory
Charles Willoughby
Peter Bell
Louis King
and others from Farnham England. Thomas Arkell's acreage was known as Farnham Plains. The Arkell United Church stands on a plot of gourd donated by Charles Willoughby. Rev. Douglas Rudd

Frostenden Parish Records post 1840:
There was a son to a Elizabeth and Henry KING in 1840.
 another son to a Emily and George KING in 1838.
Another son to a Henry and Anna in 1859.
A daughter to a Robert and Hannah 1864

Notes for Harriet Dawson:
Arkell Pioneer Cemetery, Puslinch Tp. Wellington Co. Ontario: "In memory of Harriet, wife of Thomas King, who died Apr. 14, 1851 [4?], aged 57 years"

The first recorded burial in the cemetery was on April 11, 1851, when Harriet, the wife of Thomas King was laid to rest in her 37th [sic] year.

Children of Thomas King and Harriet Dawson are:

+ 11   i.   David[3] King, born 25 Dec 1817 in Frostenden, Suffolk Eng; died 24 May 1907 in Johnson, Algoma District, Ontario.

   12   ii.   daughter King, born Bet. 1826 - 1842.

Notes for daughter King:
Name: John James Kemp
Birth Place: Canada
Age: 34
Father Name: John Kemp
Mother Name: Tennie Totten
Estimated Birth Year: abt 1854
Spouse Name: Hannah Bird
Spouse's Age: 24
Spouse Birth Place: Canada
Spouse Father Name: George Bird
Spouse Mother Name : Charlotte King
Marriage Date: 12 Sep 1888
Marriage Place: Wellington
Marriage County: Wellington
Source: Indexed by: Ancestry.com

Name: William Hartley
Birth Place: Oxford
Age: 55
Father Name: Ralph Hartley
Mother Name: Jane King
Estimated Birth Year: abt 1847
Spouse Name: Martha Tyson
Spouse's Age: 47
Spouse Birth Place: Arkell
Spouse Father Name: Charles Willoughby
Spouse Mother Name : Mary Wilkins
Marriage Date: 23 May 1902
Marriage Place: Wellington
Marriage County: Wellington
Source: Indexed by: Ancestry.com

Name: Mark French
Birth Place: England
Age: 25
Father Name: James French
Mother Name: Hannah King
Estimated Birth Year: abt 1844
Spouse Name: Sarah Maddock
Spouse's Age: 21
Spouse Birth Place: Canada
Spouse Father Name: John Maddock
Spouse Mother Name : ?? Ann Ward Maddock
Marriage Date: 17 Nov 1869
Marriage Place: Wellington
Marriage County: Wellington
Source: Indexed by: Ancestry.com

Children of Thomas King and Elizabeth Gow are:

13 i. Thomas³ King, born Abt. 1856.

Notes for Thomas King:
KING , THOMAS
  Sex: Male
  Age: 16
  Birthplace: ONT
  Religion: Canada Presbyterian/C. Presb.
  Occupation: FARM LAB
  District: WELLINGTON SOUTH (033)
  Sub-district: Puslinch (A)
  Division: 3
  Note: Schedule Two: deaths in the preceding twelve months ending 2 April 1871
  Microfilm reel: C-9945

14 ii. James King, born Abt. 1858.

Notes for James King:
KING , JAMES
  Stray: Individual bears a different surname than the head of the family
  Sex: Male
  Age: 13
  Birthplace: ONT
  Religion: Canada Presbyterian/C. Presb.

Origin: ENGLISH
Occupation: SERVANT
District: WELLINGTON SOUTH (033)
Sub-district: Puslinch (A)
Division: 3
Page: 8
Microfilm reel: C-9945

Name: James King
Titles:
Death date: 08 Mar 1913
Estimated death year:
Age at death: 54 years
Death place: Toronto, York, Ontario
Birth date: 1859
Estimated birth year: 1859
Birth place: Canada
Gender: Male
Marital status: Married
Race or color (expanded):
Race:
Ethnicity:
Spouse name:
Spouse titles:
Father name:
Father titles:
Mother name:
Mother titles:
GSU film number: 1854930
Digital GS number: 4033087
Image number: 592
Reference number: yr 1913 cn 2454
Collection: Ontario Deaths 1869-1947

Generation No. 3

4. Hannah³ King (Lewis², James¹) was born 28 Feb 1828 in England, and died 10 Jun 1904 in Kilbride, Halton Co. Ontario. She married **James Ford**.

Notes for Hannah King:
1881 Census Place: Flamborough East, Wentworth North, Ontario, Canada
 Source: FHL Film 1375892 NAC C-13256 Dist 148 SubDist B Div 2 Page 53
Family 247
 Sex Marr Age Origin Birthplace
James FORD M M 64 English   England

```
Occ:        Labourer      Religion:     E. Methodist
Hannah FORD        F      M    53    English        England
            Religion:     E. Methodist
Alice FORD    F      20    English        Ontario
            Religion:     E. Methodist
Louise FORD  F      16    English        Ontario
            Religion:     E. Methodist
George FORD M       9     English        Ontario
            Religion:     E. Methodist
```

Source Information: 1901 Census of Canada
9 8   100 Ford Lousia F   Head S May 18 1866 34
9 9   100 Ford Hannah F   Mother W Feb 28 1828 73
9 10 100 Ford Beatrice F   Sister S Jul 1 1885 15
9 11 100 Ford George M   Brother M Mar 26 1872 29
9 12 100 Ford Elizabeth F   Broth Wife M Nov 10 1880 20
Subdistrict: Nelson, HALTON, ONTARIO
District Number: 68
Subdistrict Number: g-3
Archives Microfilm: T-6471

Halton County Death Registrations,

Children of Hannah King and James Ford are:

15	i.	Alice[4] Ford, born Abt. 1861 in Ontario.
16	ii.	Louisa Ford, born 18 May 1866 in Ontario.
17	iii.	George Ford, born 26 Mar 1872 in Ontario.
18	iv.	Beatrice Ford, born 01 Jul 1885 in Ontario.

5. Sarah Catherine[3] King (Lewis[2], James[1]) was born 07 Aug 1817 in Bain, Suffolk Eng, and died 11 Jan 1910 in Guelph, Wellington Co. Ontario. She married **William Hewer** Bef. 1842, son of James Hewer and Elizabeth. He was born Abt. 1810 in England, and died 07 Apr 1888 in Guelph, Wellington Co. Ontario.

Notes for Sarah Catherine King:
1861 census Puslinch Tp
William Hwere, Miller, b England, 41
Mrs. Hewer b Eng 31
John Hewer, labourer b Canada 17
Elizabeth Hewer b Canada 15
Jane Hewer b Canada 13
James Hewer b Canada 7
Jemima Hewer b Canada 5
Johanna Hewer b Canada 3
Richard Hewer b Canada 1

1871 censuss
William Hewer, 52 b Engl farmer and shoemaker
Sarah 50 b England
William 17 b Ont. farmer [I believe he is James on 1861 census]
Richard 10 b On
Henery 9 b On
Thomas 2 b on
Jane 22 b On
Jemima 15 b On
Joanna 13 b On
Margret Jane 4 b On

1901 census City of Guelph
124 Paisley Rd
Sarah C Hewer, head, 78, b. England, 7 Aug. 1822, immigration 1831, Religion Salvation
Army. [note that dob does not agree with death cert]

Sarah Catherine King's grandchildren, (From Elizabeth and John Marriott....Sarah
was living with them when she died) were the Marriott Twins of the Downie Bros.
circus They were famous trapeze artists. Sarah Catherine Kings's in-law, Christina
Hewer McPhee, owned the Downie Bros. circus with her husband. She, too, was in the
circus as a trapeze artist.

Ontario Death Certificate, #023010 p 339 Div. of Guelph, Co. of Wellington, Ontario
Death Certificate, #023010 p 339 Div. of Guelph, Co. of Wellington, Sarah Catherine
HEWER, female, English, d Jan 11, 1910 b Aug 7 1817 in "Bain" in Suffolk, Eng, 92 years,
5 mos, 4 days, lived 406 Paisley Rd Guelph. Retired, Widowed. Father Louis King of
Suffolk England Mother Elizabeth Smith England. Dr. Savage, notified by Mrs. Joan
Marriott (daughter) 406 Paisley Rd died of arterio-sclerosis/apoplexy, 3 days, Guelph.
Dr. Savage, notified by Mrs. Joan Marriott (daughter) 406 Paisley Rd died of arterio-
sclerosis/apoplexy, 3 days, Guelph.

Notes for William Hewer:
William Hewer came over with his parents, James Hewer and Sarah Hill, and father
John. William was 16 yrs old.

Name of Vessel   Ship Bristol
Port of Embarkation   Bristol
Date of Arrival   November 10, 1834
Number 923

HEWER
James C 9 L6 Free
William C 9 L 10 Householder

1871 census index HEWER , WILLIAM

Sex: Male
Age: 52
Birthplace: ENGLAND
Religion: I. Meth. E.
Origin: ENGLISH
Occupation: FARMER & SHOEMAKER
District: WELLINGTON SOUTH (033)
Sub-district: Puslinch (A)
Division: 4
Page: 6
Microfilm reel: C-9945

William Hewer, 52, b England, Methodist, farmer/shoemaker
Sarah King Hewer, 52 b England Church of England
William 17
Jane 22
Jemima 15
Johanna 13
Richard 10
Henery [sic] 8
Margaret Jane 4
Thomas 2
James Hewer, 77 (father), b England Methodist, farmer
Elizabeth Hewer, 71

1881   Census Place: Guelph, Wellington South, Ontario, Canada
   Source: FHL Film 1375894 NAC C-13258 Dist 151 SubDist C Div 4 Page 77
Family 370

	Sex	Marr	Age	Origin	Birthplace
William HEWER	M	M	63	English	England
Occ: Shoemaker	Religion:	Church of England			
Sarah HEWER	F	M	58	English	England
Religion:	C. Methodist				
Richard HEWER	M		20	English	Ontario
Occ: Laborer	Religion:	C. Methodist			
Henry HEWER	M		18	English	Ontario
Occ: Laborer	Religion:	C. Methodist			
Margaret HEWER	F		14	English	Ontario
Religion:	C. Methodist				
Thomas HEWER	M		12	English	Ontario
Religion:	C. Methodist				

Descendant is
Ronnie Elliott Martin
4985 Via Del Cerro
Yorba Linda, Cal. 92887 USA

Children of Sarah King and William Hewer are:

    19   i.   James[4] Hewer, born 23 Feb 1842.

    20   ii.   John Hewer, born Abt. 1844.

+ 21   iii.   William J. L. Hewer, born 07 Mar 1845 in England; died 17 May 1917 in Guelph Twp., Wellington, Ontario.

+ 22   iv.   Elizabeth Hewer, born 22 Nov 1847; died Aft. 1901.

    23   v.   Jane Hewer, born Abt. 1849.

    24   vi.   James William Hewer, born Abt. 1854.

    25   vii.   Jemima Hewer, born Abt. 1856.

    26   viii.   Johanna Hewer, born Abt. 1858.

    27   ix.   Richard Hewer, born Abt. 1860.

    28   x.   Henry Hewer, born Abt. 1863.

    29   xi.   Margaret Jane Hewer, born Abt. 1867.

    30   xii.   Thomas Hewer, born Abt. 1869.

6. George A.[3] King (Lewis[2], James[1]) was born Bet. 1817 - 1819 in Suffolk, England, and died 17 Nov 1881 in Guelph, Wellington Co. Ontario. He married **(1) Mary Anne Harrison** 1841, daughter of Edward Harrison. She was born Abt. 1815 in Yorkshire, England, and died 12 Mar 1858 in Nelson Twp, Halton Co. Ontario. He married **(2) Sarah Thompson** 16 Dec 1859 in Barton Twp Wentworth Co. Ontario, daughter of Thomas Thompson and Isabella. She was born Sep 1841 in Canada, and died 25 Aug 1864 in Arkell, Wellington Co. Ontario. He married **(3) Elizabeth Parker** 27 Sep 1865 in Wellington Co. Ontario, daughter of Francis Parker and Rachel. She was born Aug 1835 in England, and died Bet. 1900 - 1910 in probably Detroit, Wayne Co. Michigan.

Notes for George A. King:
1851 census Puslinch Tp C 11743
beside Lewis and Elizabeth King and family

George King farmer b England WM 34
Mary Ann King b Eng 37
George King b CW 8
Francis King b CW 6
Lewis King b CW 5
Elizabeth King b CW 2

1858 Barton Twp Assessment Roll - Conc 5, Pl 13 25 acres, dairyman

Name: George King
Birth Place: England
Residence: Puslinch Township
Age: 46
Father Name: Lewis King
Mother Name: Elizabeth King
Estimated Birth Year: 1819

Spouse Name: Elizabeth Parker
Spouse's Age: 30
Spouse Birth Place: England
Spouse Residence: Puslinch Township
Spouse Estimated Birth Year: 1835
Spouse Father Name: Francis Parker
Spouse Mother Name : Rachel Parker
Marriage Date: 27 Sep 1865
Marriage Place: Guelph
Marriage County: Wellington
Family History Library Microfilm: 1030067
Source: Indexed by: Genealogical Research Library

County Marriage Registers of Wentworth, 1858-1869, Ref 25. George King, 36, of Barton, b England s/o Lewis & Elizabeth King, m Sarah Thompson, 20, of Barton, b Canada d/o Thomas dec 16, 1859 Rev Geroge A Bull Church of England Wit A J Glen of Hamilton.

County Marriage Register 1858-1869 Vol. 1 Wellington Co., Ref 1: 165
George King, 46 of Puslinch b Eng s/o Lewis and Elizabeth King to Elizabeth parker, 30 of Puslinch b England d/o Francis and Rachel Parker. married 27 Sept 1865 by Rev William Newton of Guelph, Primitive Methodist. Wit Thomas Parker of Puslinch.

Directory of Wellington County, 1867
1867 Puslinch Tp. Residents
KING
David C 10 L 56 Free
George C 10 L5 Free
Thomas W. C 9 L 7 Householder
BELL
Joseph C 10 L7 Free
Richard C 8 L17 Free

1871 Guelph, south ward
George KING, 52 b Eng WM, milkman
Elizabeth 36 b Eng
Lewis 23 b Ontario
Martha 19 b Ont
Albert 10 b Ont
female (name not clear) 9 b Ont
Thomas 7 b Ont
James 4 b ont
Mary L. 1 b Ont

1881   Census Place: Guelph, Wellington South, Ontario, Canada
       Source: FHL Film 1375894 NAC C-13258 Dist 151 SubDist C Div 4 Page 75
Family 362
       Sex Marr   Age   Origin Birthplace

George KING M M 62 English England
Occ: Farmer Religion: C. Methodist
Elisabeth KING F M 45 English England
Religion: C. Methodist
Lewis KING M 30 English Ontario Occ: Laborer
Religion: C. Methodist
Albert KING M 20 English Ontario Occ: Laborer
Religion: C. Methodist
Thomas KING M 17 English Ontario Occ: Moulder
Religion: C. Methodist
James KING M 14 English Ontario Religion: C. Methodist
Louisa KING F 11 English Ontario Religion: C. Methodist
William KING M 9 English Ontario Religion: C. Methodist
Frederick KING M 6 English Ontario Religion: C. Methodist
Charles KING M 3 English Ontario Religion: C. Methodist

Notes for Mary Anne Harrison:
"Christian Guardian," Death Notices 1851-1860, Mrs. George A. King, d/o Mr. and Mrs Edward Harrison b Yorkshire England. Came to Canada at age 10. Married Mr. King in 1841. Died in Nelson Tp March 12 1858 in 37th year. Pre deceased by child in 1852. Survived by husband, 1 daughter and 3 sons. (May 12 1858 p 126 obits).

Notes for Elizabeth Parker:
PARKER Elizabeth Francis Rachel b 1834 England Puslinch (1851) attending school

1891 census City of Guelph Div 5 p 57
N 1/5, 263
King Elizabeth 55 widow b Eng father and mother b Eng Meth
William 19 b Ontario father and mother b England, moulder
Ferderick 16 b Ontario ditto
Louisa 21 ditto
Charles 13 ditto

1900 United States Federal Census
Name: Elizabeth King
Home in 1900: Detroit Ward 5, Wayne, Michigan
Age: 64
Birth Date: Aug 1835
Birthplace: England
Race: White
Ethnicity: American
Gender: Female
Immigration Year: 1892
Relationship to head-of-house: Head
Father's Birthplace: England
Mother's Birthplace: England

Mother: number of living children: 5
Mother: How many children: 6
Marital Status: Widowed
Residence : Detroit City, Wayne, Michigan
Household Members: Name Age
Elizabeth King 64
Louisa King 29
Fredrick King 25
Charles King 22 Mar 1878 imm 1892

Children of George King and Mary Harrison are:

+   31   i.   George[4] King, born 24 Feb 1844 in Puslinch Tp Wellington Co
                 Ontario; died 10 May 1903 in Keppel Tp Grey Co, Ontario.

     32   ii.   Francis King, born Abt. 1845 in Ontario; died Aft. 1870. He married
                 Mary Buntin 31 Jan 1870 in Wentworth Co. Ontario.

                 Notes for Francis King:
                 Ontario, Canada Marriages, 1857-1922
                 about Frank King
                 Name: Frank King
                 Birth Place: Canada
                 Age: 23
                 Father Name: George King
                 Mother Name: Mary Ann King
                 Estimated birth year: abt 1847
                 Spouse Name: Mary Buntin
                 Spouse's Age: 25
                 Spouse Birth Place: Ireland
                 Spouse Father Name: John Buntin
                 Spouse Mother Name : Mary Buntin
                 Marriage Date: 31 Jan 1870
                 Marriage Place: Wentworth
                 Marriage County: Wentworth
                 Source: Indexed by: Ancestry.com

     33   iii. Lewis King, born Abt. 1846 in Ontario.
     34   iv.   Elizabeth King, born Abt. 1849 in Arkell, Puslinch Tp Wellington
                 County Ontario. She married James Henry Hall 14 Mar 1881 in
                 Wellington Co. Ontario; born Abt. 1847.

                 Notes for Elizabeth King:

Name: James Henry Hall
Birth Place: Pilkington
Age: 34
Father Name: Joseph Hall
Mother Name: Maria Hall
Estimated Birth Year: abt 1847
Spouse Name: Elizabeth King
Spouse's Age: 30
Spouse Birth Place: Arkell
Spouse Father Name: George King
Spouse Mother Name : Ann L King
Marriage Date: 14 Mar 1881
Marriage Place: Wellington
Marriage County: Wellington
Source: Indexed by: Ancestry.com

1901 Census of Canada
about MRS Elizabeth Hall
Name: MRS Elizabeth Hall
Gender: Female
Marital Status: Widowed
Age: 53
Birth Date: 25 Sep 1847
Birthplace: Ontario
Relation to Head of House: Head
Racial or Tribal Origin: English
Nationality: Canadian
Religion: Methodist
Province: Ontario
District: Toronto (Centre) (City/Cité)
District Number: 116
Sub-District: Toronto (Centre) (City/Cité) Ward/Quartier No 3
Sub-District Number: A-32
Family Number: 14
Page: 2
Neighbors: View others on page
Household Members: Name Age
MRS Elizabeth Hall 53
Ethel Hall 16
Fred B Hall 25
May Hall 21
Thomas Hall 23
???

35   v.   Martha King, born Abt. 1853 in Puslinch Tp Wellington Co. Ontario;

died 28 Jan 1879 in Guelph, Wellington Co. Ontario. She married James Henry Hall 01 May 1872 in Wellington Co. Ontario; born Abt. 1847.

Notes for Martha King:
Either Elizabeth or Martha died in 1852 [Elizabeth!]

Name: James Henry Hall
Birth Place: Pilkington
Age: 24
Father Name: Jos Hall
Mother Name: Maria Hall
Estimated Birth Year: abt 1848
Spouse Name: Martha King
Spouse's Age: 19
Spouse Birth Place: Pushich
Spouse Father Name: George King
Spouse Mother Name : Ann King
Marriage Date: 1 May 1872
Marriage Place: Wellington
Marriage County: Wellington
Source: Indexed by: Ancestry.com

Name: Martha Hall
Titles:
Death date: 28 Jan 1879
Estimated death year:
Age at death: 26 years
Death place: Wellington, Guelph, Canada
Birth date: 1853
Estimated birth year: 1853
Birth place:
Gender: Female
Marital status:
Race or color (expanded):
Race:
Ethnicity:
Spouse name:
Spouse titles:
Father name:
Father titles:
Mother name:
Mother titles:
GSU film number: 1853228
Digital GS number: 4171353
Image number: 403
Reference number: p 156

Children of George King and Sarah Thompson are:

36   i.   Albert E.[4] King, born 04 Sep 1860 in Ontario; died 15 Jul 1932 in Fairbanks, York Co. Ontario. He married Mary Ann; born Abt. 1869 in England; died Aft. 15 Jul 1932.

Notes for Albert E. King:
1891 census city of Guelph Div 4
p 15
B 1/5, 75. King Albert, 30 b Ontaro father and mother b England, methodist, groom and labourer
Mary Ann 22 b England Father b England mother b Scotland, Church of England

1901 census Guelph, E-14 page 13
King, Albert E. b 4 Sept. 1860, 40, b Ontario , Eng, Meth, Gardener
Mary A. born 5 July 1868, 32 b. Eng, imm 1884, Eng. Meth

37   ii.   Emma King, born Abt. 1862.
38   iii. Thomas King, born Abt. 1864.

Children of George King and Elizabeth Parker are:

+ 39   i.   James Parker[4] King, born 19 Jul 1867 in Arkell, Puslinch Tp Wellington County Ontario; died Aft. 1916 in Possibly Red Deer Alberta.
40   ii.   Mary Louisa (Louisa) King, born Dec 1870 in Ontario; died Aft. 1900.

Notes for Mary Louisa (Louisa) King:
Detroit Border Crossings and Passenger and Crew Lists, 1905-1957
Name: Louise King
Birth Date: 27 Apr 1870
Birthplace: Wellington Ont
Birth Country: Canada
Gender: Female
Race/Nationality: English
Port of Departure: Detroit Michigan
Departure Contact: Cousin Clara Stevenson
Microfilm Roll Number: M1478_
Apr. 12, 1936. (probably not the right Louisa)

+ 41   iii. William H. King, born 06 Mar 1873 in Guelph, Wellington Co.

Ontario; died Aft. 1930 in probably Detroit, Wayne Co. Michigan.

+   42   iv.   Frederick Temple King, born 09 Aug 1874 in Ontario; died Aft. 1930 in probably Detroit, Wayne Co. Michigan.

+   43   v.   Charles Joseph King, born 17 Mar 1878 in Ontario; died Aft. 1920.

7. Louisa[3] King (Lewis[2], James[1]) was born 10 Apr 1825 in England?, and died 13 Oct 1917 in Guelph, Wellington Co Ontario. She married **Carter Whiting** Bef. 1851. He was born Bet. 1828 - 1831 in Ontario, and died 07 Jan 1902 in Guelph, Wellington Co Ontario.

Notes for Louisa King:
1881   Census Place: Oakville, Halton, Ontario, Canada
     Source: FHL Film 1375893 NAC C-13257 Dist 150 SubDist D Page 16 Family 80
     Sex Marr Age   Origin Birthplace
Carter WHITING   50   English   England   Occ: Carpenter
     Religion: Methodist Canada
Louisa WHITING   50   English   England   Religion: Methodist
Canada
Malvina WHITING 16   English   Australia   Religion:
     Methodist Canada

1901 Census of Canada Page Information
District: Ontario WELLINGTON (South/Sud) (#126)
Subdistrict: Guelph (City/Cité) E-14 Page 12
Details: Schedule 1 Microfilm T-6505
Whiting Louisa F   Head M Apr 10 1825 75

Notes for Carter Whiting:
1851 Census of Canada East, Canada West, New Brunswick, and Nova Scotia
about Carter Whiting
Name: Carter Whiting
Gender: Male
Age: 29
Estimated birth year: abt 1823
Birthplace: England
Province: Canada West (Ontario)
District: Hamilton City
District Number: 45
Sub-District: St Lawrence
Sub-District Number: 439
Page: 109
Line: 1
Roll: C_11767
Schedule: A
Carter Whiting, 29, carpenter born England
Louisa Whiting, 23 born England
Malvina Turnbul, 11 born England

Elizabeth Whiting 1 born Canada
Thomas King, 18, born Canada, residence Puslinch

Frame house, 1 1/2 storey, 5 family members, 1/5 of an acre

Children of Louisa King and Carter Whiting are:

    44   i.   Elizabeth[4] Whiting, born Abt. 1851 in Canada.

    45   ii.   Northrup Whiting, born 11 Dec 1852 in New York City, New York; died 16 Mar 1929 in St. Catharines, Lincoln Co. Ontario. He married Minnie Hawarth 24 May 1922 in Welland Co., Ontario.

                  Notes for Northrup Whiting:
                  Ontario, Canada Marriages, 1857-1922
                  about Northup Whiting
                  Name: Northup Whiting
                  Birth Place: New York City
                  Age: 69
                  Father Name: Carter Whiting
                  Mother Name: Louisa King
                  Estimated birth year: abt 1853
                  Spouse Name: Minnie Howarth
                  Spouse's Age: 53
                  Spouse Birth Place: England
                  Spouse Father Name: Roland Schofield
                  Spouse Mother Name : Ellen Jones
                  Marriage Date: 24 May 1922
                  Marriage Place: Welland
                  Marriage County: Welland
                  Source: Indexed by: Ancestry.com

    46   iii. Malvina Whiting, born Abt. 1856 in Melbourne Australia; died May 1903 in Carleton Co. Ontario. She married Charles Welch 05 Mar 1890 in York Co. Ontario.

                  Notes for Malvina Whiting:
                  Ontario, Canada Marriages, 1857-1922
                  about Charles Welch
                  Name: Charles Welch
                  Birth Place: England
                  Age: 21
                  Father Name: Charles Welch
                  Mother Name: Rebecca Welch
                  Estimated birth year: abt 1869
                  Spouse Name: Melvina Whiting
                  Spouse's Age: 25

Spouse Birth Place: Melbourne South Australia
Spouse Father Name: Carter Whiting
Spouse Mother Name : Louisa Whiting
Marriage Date: 5 Mar 1890
Marriage Place: York
Marriage County: York
Source: Indexed by: Ancestry.com

47   iv.   Lewis Whiting, born Abt. 1857 in USA or Borchavok, Victoria, Australia. He married Mary Fimpel 25 Oct 1880 in Lincoln Co. Ontario.

Notes for Lewis Whiting:
Ontario, Canada Marriages, 1857-1922
about Lewis Whiting
Name: Lewis Whiting
Birth Place: Borchavok Victoria Australia
Age: 29
Father Name: Carter Whiting
Mother Name: Susan Whiting
Estimated birth year: abt 1858
Spouse Name: Ellen Williemae
Spouse's Age: 19
Spouse Birth Place: Westmeath Ont
Marriage Date: 1887
Marriage Place: Renfrew
Marriage County: Renfrew
Source: Indexed by: Ancestry.com

Ontario, Canada Marriages, 1857-1922
about Lewis Whitinger
Name: Lewis Whitinger
Birth Place: America
Age: 23
Father Name: Carter Whiting
Mother Name: Louisa Whiting
Estimated birth year: abt 1857
Spouse Name: Mary Fimpel
Spouse's Age: 21
Spouse Birth Place: On
Spouse Father Name: G M Fimpel
Spouse Mother Name : Fimpel Fimpel
Marriage Date: 25 Oct 1880
Marriage Place: Lincoln
Marriage County: Lincoln

Source: Indexed by: Ancestry.com

Name Marital Status Gender Ethnic Origin Age Birthplace Occupation Religion
Lewis WHITING M Male English 23 Australia Laborer Weslyan Methodist
Mary WHITING M Female German 22 Ontario Weslyan Methodist
Source Information:
Census Place St Catherines, Lincoln, Ontario
Family History Library Film   1375890
NA Film Number   C-13254
District 145
Sub-district A
Division 3
Page Number 50
Household Number 258

48   v. Wesley Fletcher Whiting, born Abt. 1862 in Australia; died 19 Oct 1879 in Oakville, Halton Co. Ontario.

8. Thomas William³ King (Lewis², James¹) was born Apr 1834 in Ontario, and died Aft. 1910 in Possibly Huron Co. Michigan. He married **(1) Helen (Ellen) Daville** 09 Jan 1858 in Nelson Tp, Halton Co. Ontario, daughter of William Daville and Sarah. She was born Abt. 1835 in England, and died Bet. 1888 - 1900 in Huron Co. Michigan. He married **(2) Amelia Lighthall Lamb** 10 May 1900 in Port Austin, Huron Co. Michigan. She was born 1852 in Canada.

Notes for Thomas William King:
Name: Thomas William King
Birth Place: Canada
Residence: Nelson Township
Age: 23
Father Name: Louis
Mother Name: Elizabeth
Estimated Birth Year: 1835
Spouse Name: Helen Daville
Spouse's Age: 18
Spouse Birth Place: England
Spouse Residence: Nelson Township
Spouse Estimated Birth Year: 1840
Spouse Father Name: William
Spouse Mother Name : Sarah
Marriage Date: 9 Jan 1858
Marriage County: Halton

Family History Library Microfilm: 1030057

1880 United States Federal Census
Name: Thomas King
Home in 1880: Huron, Huron, Michigan
Age: 47
Estimated Birth Year: abt 1833
Birthplace: New York
Relation to Head of Household: Self (Head)
Spouse's Name: Ellen
Father's birthplace: New York
Mother's birthplace: New York
Neighbors: View others on page
Occupation: Farmer
Marital Status: Married
Race: White
Gender: Male
Household Members: Name Age
Thomas King 47 farmer b NY, parents b NY
Ellen King 40 b Ohio, parents b Ohio [sic]
James King 21 works out, b Ohio [sic]
William King 18 works out, b Ohio [sic]
Ellen King 16 b Michigan
Thomas King 12   b Michigan
Viola King 8   b Michigan
George King 10M Michigan
Note the incorrect locations of birth. It is possible however that Thomas was born in New York, as that is the likely port of arrival for his father Lewis.

Groom name: Thomas King
Groom race or color (on document):
Groom age: 65 years
Groom birth year: 1835
Groom birth place: Canada
Bride name: Amelia Lighthall Lamb
Bride race or color (on document):
Bride age: 48 years
Bride birth year: 1852
Bride birth place: Canada
Marriage type:
Marriage date: 10 May 1900
Marriage place: Port Austin, Huron, Michigan
Father of groom name: Louis
Mother of groom name: Elizabeth Smith
Father of bride name: Unknown
Mother of bride name: Unknown
Marital status:

Groom previous wife name:
Bride marital status:
Bride previous husband name:
Additional relatives:
Film number: 2342515
Frame number:
Digital GS number: 4208648
Image number: 373
Reference number: v 2 p 233 rn 83
Collection: Michigan Marriages 1868-1925

1900 United States Federal Census
Name: Thomas King
Home in 1900: Hume, Huron, Michigan
Age: 66
Birth Date: Apr 1834
Birthplace: Canada Eng
[Canada English]
Race: White
Ethnicity: American
Gender: Male
Immigration Year: 1876
[1879]
Relationship to head-of-house: Head
Father's Birthplace: England
Mother's Birthplace: England
Spouse's Name: Amelia
Marriage Year: 1900
Marital Status: Married
Years Married: 0
Residence : Huron & Gore Townships, Huron, Michigan
Occupation: View on Image
Neighbors: View others on page
Household Members: Name Age
Thomas King 66
Amelia King 47 hybe 1852 Can. Eng, immigrated 1880
Orville King 12 Jan 1888 Michigan, son
Winford Carey 17 hired man

1910 United States Federal Census
about Thomas W King
Name: Thomas W King
Age in 1910: 76
Estimated Birth Year: abt 1834
Birthplace: Canada English
Relation to Head of House: Head
Father's Birth Place: England

Mother's Birth Place: England
Spouse's Name: Amelia A
Home in 1910: Port Austin, Huron, Michigan
Marital Status: Married
Race: White
Gender: Male
Year of Immigration: 1875
Neighbors: View others on page
Household Members: Name Age
Thomas W King 76
Amelia A King 68

Notes for Helen (Ellen) Daville:
1851 Census Nelson Tp Halton Co. Pt 1
http://data2.collectionscanada.ca/1851_pdf/e095/e002352702.pdf
Daville, William b England 43 tanner
Sarah b England 34
Ellen b England 34 [numbers are messed up and crossed out - this probably should be 14]
Elizabeth b England 11
Francis J b Upper Canada 61 [sic] (male)
Sarah b Upper Canada 2

Children of Thomas King and Helen Daville are:
    49   i.   James[4] King, born Abt. 1859 in Ontario.

                    Notes for James King:
                    possibilities to be checked

                    1900 United States Federal Census
                    Name: James King
                    Home in 1900: Turner, Arenac, Michigan
                    Age: 41
                    Birth Date: Nov 1858
                    Birthplace: Canada Eng
                    [Canada English]
                    Race: White
                    Ethnicity: American
                    Gender: Male
                    Immigration Year: 1870
                    Relationship to head-of-house: Head

Father's Birthplace: Canada Eng
Mother's Birthplace: England
Spouse's Name: Nettie
Marriage Year: 1884
Marital Status: Married
Years Married: 16
Residence : Turner & Whitney Townships, Arenac, Michigan
Occupation: View on Image
Neighbors: View others on page
Household Members: Name Age
James King 41
Nettie King 38
Arther King 15
Hattie L King 13
Osro J King 11
Mildrid A King 9
Winnafred King 90
Nellie A King 3

50   ii.   Elizabeth King, born Abt. 1861 in Ontario.

51   iii. Louis King, born Feb 1861 in Puslinch Tp. Wellington Co. Ontario; died Oct 1871 in Nelson Tp. Halton Co. Ontario.

52   iv. William D. King, born Abt. 1863 in Ontario; died Aft. 1920 in Michigan. He married (1) Margaret Jarks 05 Jul 1904 in Delray, Wayne, Michigan; born Abt. 1868 in Germany. He married (2) Nellie Peel 08 Jun 1915 in L'Anse, Baraga, Michigan; born Abt. 1892 in Michigan.

Notes for William D. King:
Groom name: William D. King
Groom race or color (on document):
Groom age: 50 years
Groom birth year: 1865
Groom birth place: Canda
Bride name: Nellie Peel
Bride race or color (on document):
Bride age: 23 years
Bride birth year: 1892
Bride birth place: Michigan
Marriage type:
Marriage date: 08 Jun 1915
Marriage place: L'Anse, Baraga, Michigan
Father of groom name: Thomas K...

Mother of groom name: ...elen Devalle
Father of bride name: Alfred Pee...
Mother of bride name: Unknown
Marital status:
Groom previous wife name:
Bride marital status:
Bride previous husband name:
Additional relatives:
Film number: 2342709
Frame number:
Digital GS number: 4209290
Image number: 281
Reference number: v 1 p 76 rn 26
Collection: Michigan Marriages 1868-1925

Groom name: William D King
Groom race or color (on document):
Groom age: 38 years
Groom birth year: 1866
Groom birth place: Canada
Bride name: Margaret Jarks
Bride race or color (on document):
Bride age: 36 years
Bride birth year: 1868
Bride birth place: Germany
Marriage type:
Marriage date: 05 Jul 1904
Marriage place: Delray, Wayne, Michigan
Father of groom name: Thomas
Mother of groom name: Ellen King
Father of bride name: Unknown
Mother of bride name: Unknown
Marital status:
Groom previous wife name:
Bride marital status:
Bride previous husband name:
Additional relatives:
Film number: 2342669
Frame number:
Digital GS number: 4208698
Image number: 376
Reference number: vol 4 p 529 rn 43098
Collection: Michigan Marriages 1868-1925

1910 United States Federal Census
about William D King

Name: William D King
Age in 1910: 48
Estimated Birth Year: abt 1862
Birthplace: Canada English
Relation to Head of House: Head
Father's Birth Place: Canada English
Mother's Birth Place: England
Spouse's Name: Margaret E
Home in 1910: Negaunee Ward 3, Marquette, Michigan
Marital Status: Married
Race: White
Gender: Male
Year of Immigration: 1877
Neighbors: View others on page
Household Members: Name Age
William D King 48
Margaret E King 46
Note that the following are all boarders
Thomas Blendell 30
John Canary 24
Arthur Canary 18
Fabian Page 30
Duncan R A Fox 26
William Ditz 22
Clyde Defrance 19
Oscar Peterson 41
Hordan W Bloise 56
John Gertz 26
Morse Herman 20
Alfred Erickson 41
Dolph Lavamie 48
Alexander Turcott 39
Robert Fox 58
Nellie Peel 17
Leda Witlund 19
Marie Lumphrey 19
Lily Pazq 15

1920 United States Federal Census
Name: William King
Home in 1920: Detroit Ward 10, Wayne, Michigan
Age: 57 years
Estimated Birth Year: abt 1863
Birthplace: Canada
Relation to Head of House: Head
Spouse's Name: Ellen
Father's Birth Place: England

Mother's Birth Place: England
Marital Status: Married
Race: White
Sex: Male
Home owned: Own
Year of Immigration: 1890
Able to read: Yes
Able to Write: Yes
Image: 336
Household Members: Name Age
William King 57 naturalized in 1900
Ellen King 57

53	v.	Ellen or Helen King, born Abt. 1864 in Ontario.
54	vi.	Louise King, born Abt. 1866 in Ontario.
55	vii.	Thomas King, born Abt. 1868 in Ontario.
56	viii.	Lewis King, born 07 Jul 1869 in Halton Co. Ontario; died 05 Oct 1870 in Nelson Tp, Halton Co. Ontario.

Notes for Lewis King:
Birth Registration: Lewis King, 7 Jul 1869, Male, Halton, Thomas William King & Ellen Daville

+ 57	ix.	Viola King, born Abt. 1873 in Michigan; died Aft. 1930 in Michigan.
+ 58	x.	George Lewis King, born 06 Aug 1879 in Huron, Huron Co. Michigan; died 15 Feb 1966 in Bad Axe, Michigan.
59	xi.	Orville King, born Jan 1888 in Michigan.

10. Harriet Jane (Jane)[3] King (Lewis[2], James[1]) was born 31 May 1842 in Puslinch Tp. Wellington Co. Ontario, and died Aft. 1901 in Possibly London Ontario. She married **Thomas Parker** 1863 in Wellington Co. Ontario, son of Francis Parker and Rachel. He was born Abt. 1840 in England, and died Aft. 1901 in Possibly Sarnia, Lambton Co. Ontario.

Notes for Harriet Jane (Jane) King:
1891 Census of Canada
Province: Ontario
District Number: 90
District: Middlesex East
Subdistrict: London
Archive Roll #: T-6352
Household Members: Name Age

Harriet Parker 48 married born Ontario, Congregationalist

1901 Census of Canada
Province: Ontario District: Middlesex (East/est) District Number: 87
Sub-District: London Sub-District Number: C-7 Family Number: 11
Page: 6 Hospital for the Insane.
Harriet Jane Parker, Married Age: 58 Birthplace: Ontario, Patient, English origin,
Religion: Congregationalist Occupation: Housekeeper

Notes for Thomas Parker:
1871 Census   District: HALTON (038)   Sub-district: Nelson (A)   Division: 3
Page: 66   Microfilm reel: C-9955

Parker Thomas, 32, b Eng, English origin, sawyer Wesleyan Methodist
harriet Jane 28 B Ont
Elizabeth A. 7 b Ont
Mary Louise 5 b Ont
Fanny Jane 3 b Ont
Rachel b 1870 d Feb 1871
C 2 Lot 8 1/4 acre, tenants

1851 PARKER Thomas Francis Rachel b 1838 England Puslinch (1851) attending school
1871 farmer living in Puslinch Con 4 Lot 17

1891 Census of Canada
Province: Ontario
District Number: 82
District: Lambton West
Subdistrict: Sarnia Town
Archive Roll #: T-6348
Household Members: Name Age
Thomas Parker 50 b England, Congregationalist parents born England, married, Occ:
Wharfinger [sic]
William F Parker 14 b. Ontario, single mother born Ontario

1901 Census of Canada
Province: Ontario
District: Lambton (West/Ouest)
District Number: 79
Sub-District: Sarnia (Town/Ville)
Sub-District Number: F-4
Family Number: 15
Page: 1
Household Members: Name Age

Thomas Parker 60 b 29 Mar 1844 England, Occ: Warfinger. Methodist, Immigrated 1860. Married

Children of Harriet King and Thomas Parker are:

60   i.   Elizabeth[4] Parker, born Abt. 1864 in Ontario; died Aft. 1930 in probably Detroit, Wayne Co. Michigan. She married (1) Mr. Tyrell Abt. 1882. She married (2) Herbert L. Brydel 25 Aug 1925 in Mt Clemens, Macomb, Michigan; born 1875 in Cincinnati Ohio.

Notes for Elizabeth Parker:
Groom name: Herbert L. Brydel
Groom age: 50 years
Groom birth year: 1875
Groom birth place: Cincinnati, Ohio
Bride name: Elizabeth Parker Tyrrell
Bride race or color (on document):
Bride age: 58 years
Bride birth year: 1867
Bride birth place: Canada
Marriage date: 25 Aug 1925
Marriage place: Mt Clemens, Macomb, Michigan
Father of groom name: John Brydel
Mother of groom name: Margaret Lowson
Father of bride name: Thomas Parker
Mother of bride name: Harriet J. King
Film number: 2342769
Digital GS number: 4209971
Image number: 550
Reference number: v 6 rn 12167
Collection: Michigan Marriages 1868-1925

1930 United States Federal Census Detroit, Wayne, Michigan
Household Members: Name Age
Herbert L Bryden 54 b abt 1876 Ohio, head of house, parents born Scotland, bookkeeper, 49 at first marriage
Elizabeth Bryden 63 b Michigan, father b England, mother b Canada English. 18 at first marriage.

61   ii.   Mary Louise (Louise) Parker, born Abt. 1866 in Ontario. She married Lawrence Sella 16 Feb 1889 in Detroit, Wayne, Michigan; born Abt. 1867 in France.

Notes for Mary Louise (Louise) Parker:
Groom name: Lawrence Sella
Groom race or color (on document):
Groom age: 22 years
Groom birth year: 1867
Groom birth place: France
Bride name: Louise Parker
Bride race or color (on document):
Bride age: 22 years
Bride birth year: 1867
Bride birth place: Canada
Marriage type:
Marriage date: 16 Feb 1889
Marriage place: Detroit, Wayne, Michigan
Father of groom name: Lawrence Sella
Mother of groom name: Madeline Brelt
Father of bride name: Thomas Parker
Mother of bride name: Harriet King
Marital status:
Groom previous wife name:
Bride marital status:
Bride previous husband name:
Additional relatives:
Film number: 2342487
Frame number:
Digital GS number: 4207811
Image number: 491
Reference number: v 3 p 415 rn 3196
Collection: Michigan Marriages 1868-1925

62   iii.   Fanny (Anne?) Jane Parker, born 02 Nov 1868 in Puslinch Tp. Wellington Co. Ontario.

63   iv.   Rachel Parker, born Abt. 1869 in Arkell, Puslinch Tp. Wellington Co. Ontario; died Feb 1871 in Arkell, Puslinch Tp. Wellington Co. Ontario.

64   v.   William J. Parker, born 1878 in Sarnia, Lambton Co. Ontario. He married Margaret Buckeridge 16 Jul 1903 in Port Huron, St. Clair Michigan; born 1878 in Port Huron, St. Clair Michigan.

Notes for William J. Parker:
Groom name: Wm. J. Parker
Groom race or color (on document):
Groom age: 25 years
Groom birth year: 1878
Groom birth place: Sarnia, Ontario

Bride name: Margaret Buckeridge
Bride race or color (on document):
Bride age: 25 years
Bride birth year: 1878
Bride birth place: Port Huron
Marriage type:
Marriage date: 16 Jul 1903
Marriage place: Port Huron, St Clair, Michigan
Father of groom name: Thos. Parker
Mother of groom name: Harriet King
Father of bride name: Byron Buckeridge
Mother of bride name: Benaway
Marital status:
Groom previous wife name:
Bride marital status:
Bride previous husband name:
Additional relatives:
Film number: 2342665
Frame number:
Digital GS number: 4033089
Image number: 384
Reference number: v 4 p 201 rn 7799
Collection: Michigan Marriages 1868-1925

Notes for Margaret Buckeridge:
894 State of Michigan Census - City of Port Huron, Ward 3, St. Clair
County, Michigan
63 8 Broad 612 270 270 Buckeridge Byron 43 M W Husband M N ~ ~
Can Eng Can ~ N N ~ Teamster N N N N N N Y Y Y 40 40 N
63 9 Broad 612 270 270 Buckeridge Jennie 40 F W Wife M N 3 2 PA
NY NY ~ ~ ~ 3 Housewife N N N N N N Y Y Y 30 40 N
63 10 Broad 612 270 270 Buckeridge Maud A. 18 F W Daughter S N ~
~ MI Can PA ~ ~ ~ ~ At School N N N N Y 10 Y Y Y 18 18 N
63 11 Broad 612 270 270 Buckeridge Margret M. 16 F W Daughter S N
~ ~ MI Can PA ~ ~ ~ ~ At School N N N N Y 10 Y Y Y 16 16 N
http://www.rootsweb.ancestry.com/~mistcla2/t1894_Port_Huron_
Ward_3.htm

65   vi. Isabella Emma Parker, born 23 Mar 1881 in Sarnia, Lambton Co.
           Ontario; died 29 Apr 1888 in Lambton Co. Ontario.

           Notes for Isabella Emma Parker:
           Name: Isabella Parker
           Date of Birth: 23 Mar 1881
           Gender: Female
           Birth County: Lambton

Father's name: Thomas Parker
Mother's name: Harriet Jane King
Roll Number: MS929_49

Name: Isabella Emma Parker
Death Date: 29 Apr 1888
Death Location: Lambton
Gender: Female
Estimated birth year: abt 1882
Birth Location: Sarnia

11. David³ King (Thomas², James¹) was born 25 Dec 1817 in Frostenden, Suffolk Eng, and died 24 May 1907 in Johnson, Algoma District, Ontario. He married **Mary Bell** Bef. 1841 in Ontario, daughter of Peter Bell and Elizabeth Higginson. She was born 03 Oct 1819 in Lower Peover Cheshire England, and died 03 Dec 1885 in Arkell, Puslinch Tp. Wellington Co. Ontario.

Notes for David King:
"Suffolk, an English COUNTY 47 miles in length and 30 miles in breadth, bounded on the West by
    Cambridgeshire,on the North by Norfolk, on the South by Essex and on the East by the German Ocean. It contains 575 parishes, 28 market towns and sends 16 members to Parliament. The air is generally wholesome, but the soil is various, on the sea coast it is sandy and there are several small hills which yield hemp, pease and rye. The inland parts are clayey and more full of trees. The borders towards Essex are fit for pastures and the NW produces corn of all sorts. There are manufactures of several kinds, particularly all sorts of broad-cloth, stuffs and coarse linen. The principal rivers are Little Ouse, the Waveney, the Stour, The Breton, the Orwell or Gippe, the Ove and the Blyth. Ipswich and St. Edmundsberry are the principal towns". From "The Complete and Universal Dictionary" by Rev James Barclay - 1812

Transcription from the inGeneas Database
Location: Puslinch Township, part 2,   Wellington County
Source: Transcribed from the microfilm of original   documents held in the collection of the National   Archives of Canada [Ottawa]: Personal Census   Returns of Canada West [Ontario], 1851; RG 31;   Reel# C11743, Twp# 248, page 27.

Record ID: 569918
Occupant: David King
Occupation: farmer
Birthplace: England
Religion: Church of England [Anglican]
Age: 34
Status: married
Number of Families   in Household: 1

Names & Ages of other members in household:
King, Mary 32;
King, Thomas W 9;
King, David 7;
King, Mary Anne 5;
King, Harriett 4;
King, John 2;
King, Joseph 1;
King, Thos 18.

Misindexed as Name: David King
Gender: Male
Age: 34
Estimated Birth Year: abt 1818
Birthplace: England
Province: Canada West (Ontario)
District: Ontario County
District Number: 26
Sub-District: Brock
Sub-District Number: 248
Page: 27
Line: 1
Roll: C_11743
Schedule: A

1861 census Puslinch Tp Ward #1p. 1 Line 39
Thomas King, labourer 20, b CW WM
David King, labourer   45 b Eng WM
Mrs. King 45 b Eng
David King 16 b CW
John King 9 b CW
Joseph King 7 b CW
George King 6 b CW
Mary Ann King 15 b CW [also listed separately as a servant on line 50]
Harriett King 12 b CW

11 March 1863: David assigned front half Conc 10 Lot 6, Arkell, Puslinch Tp. Wellington
Co. Ontario ID 2.
01 C15 005 104

Directory of Wellington County, 1867
1867 Puslinch Tp. Residents
KING
David C 10 L 6 Free
George C 10 L5 Free
Thomas W. C 9 L 7 Householder
BELL

Joseph C 10 L7 Free
Richard C 8 L17 Free
HEWER
James C 9 L6 Free
William C 9 L 10 Householder

1871 Index
KING , DAVID

Sex: Male
Age: 53
Birthplace: ENGLAND
Religion: Wesleyan Methodist
Origin: ENGLISH
Occupation: FARMER
District: WELLINGTON SOUTH (033)
Sub-district: Puslinch (A)
Division: 4
Page: 26
Microfilm reel: C-9945

David King, 53, farmer, b Eng WM,
mary, 51, b Eng WM
Thomas, 29 farmer widower with 5 [?] kids
Richard, 27, butcher
harriet, 23
John, 21, farmer
Joseph 19 farmer
George 16 farmer
living Co 10 L 6 100 acres

1881
    Census Place: Puslinch, Wellington South, Ontario, Canada
    Source: FHL Film 1375894 NAC C-13258 Dist 151 SubDist A Div 1 Page 43
Family 187
    Sex Marr   Age   Origin Birthplace
David KING   M   M   63   English   England
    Occ: Gentleman   Religion: C. Methodist
Mary KING   F   M   61   English   England
        Religion: C. Methodist
Thomas H KING   M   M   39   English   Ontario
    Occ: Farmer Religion: C. Methodist
Maryann KING   F   M   39   Irish   Ontario
        Religion: C. Presbyterian
Marion KING F   2   English   Ontario
        Religion: C. Presbyterian

1891 Census of Canada
about David King
Name: David King
Gender: Male
Marital Status: Widowed
Age: 74
Birth Year: abt 1817
Birthplace: England
Relation to Head of House: F
Religion: Methodist
French Canadian: No
Father's Birth Place: England
Mother's Birth Place: England
Province: Ontario
District Number: 46
District: Algoma
Subdistrict: Port Findlay
Archive Roll #: T-6323
Neighbors: View others on page
Household Members: Name Age
Thomas King 49
Maryann King 49
Marion King 12
Stella King 8
David King 74 widower

Notes for Mary Bell:
From County of Wellington, Township of Puslinch by W. MacKenzie, published in the Guelph Weekly Mercury and Advertiser 7 March 1907: Early Settlers of Puslinch

"Peter Bell, a native of Chesshire Eng, left his native land in 1832 and after spending 6 years in New York State, came to Puslinch in 1838 with two sons, Peter and Joseph and one daughter, Mary. He settled on parts of lots 7,8 and 9, next to the Petty farm. This afterwards became the property of his son Joseph Bell, who sold it a few years ago to his son in law, Peter Laing, and now lives with Mrs. Bell who was a daughter of Joseph Dory's, retired in the village"

Bell, Mary Gender : Female
 Age : 12
 Country of Origin : England
 Country of Destination : United States of America
 Ship Name : Brig Charles Joseph
 Port of Arrival : New York1

Arrival Date : Dec 3, 1831
Nat'l Archive Series No. : M237
Microfilm Number : 15
List Number : 434
child of Elizabeth

Children of David King and Mary Bell are:

+ 66   i.   Thomas William[4] King, born 15 Aug 1841 in Puslinch Tp. Wellington Co. Ontario; died 24 Apr 1906 in Algoma District.

+ 67   ii.   David King, born 28 Feb 1843 in Arkell, Puslinch Tp. Wellington Co. Ontario; died 06 Jan 1921 in Waterdown, Wentworth Co. Ontario.

    68   iii.   Mary Ann King, born 16 Feb 1844 in Arkell, Puslinch Tp. Wellington Co. Ontario; died Aug 1903 in Guelph Wellington Co. Ontario. She married John Daniels 15 Nov 1864 in Nelson Tp, Halton Co. Ontario; born 08 May 1836 in Nassagaweya Tp Halton Co. Ontario; died 07 Nov 1927 in Nassagaweya Tp Halton Co. Ontario.

Notes for Mary Ann King:
1891 Census of Canada
Name: John Daniels
Gender: Male
Marital Status: Married
Age: 55
Birth Year: abt 1836
Birthplace: Ontario
Relation to Head of House: Head
Religion: Methodist
French Canadian: No
Father's Birth Place: United States
Mother's Birth Place: United States
Province: Ontario
District Number: 71
District: Halton
Subdistrict: Nassagaweya
Archive Roll #: T-6341
Household Members: Name Age
John Daniels 55
Mary A Daniels 46 b. Ontario, parents b. England

Notes for John Daniels:
Index to the 1871 Census of Ontario

DANIELS , JOHN	Sex:	Male	Age:	34
Birthplace:	ONT	Religion:		Wesleyan Methodist
Origin:	SCOTCH	Occupation:		FARMER

District: WELLINGTON SOUTH (033)   Sub-district:
Puslinch (A)   Division: 4   Page: 25
Microfilm reel: C-9945

1881   Census Place: Nassagaweya, Halton, Ontario, Canada
    Source:FHL Film 1375894 NAC C-13258 Dist 150 SubDist F Div
2 Page 29 Family 122
    Sex   Marr   Age   Origin Birthplace
John DANIELS   M   M   44   English   Ontario
    Occ: FarmerReligion: C. Methodist
Mary A. DANIELS   F   M   35   English
Ontario
                Religion: C. Methodist
1891 Census of Canada
Name: John Daniels
Gender: Male
Marital Status: Married
Age: 55
Birth Year: abt 1836
Birthplace: Ontario
Relation to Head of House: Head
Religion: Methodist
French Canadian: No
Father's Birth Place: United States
Mother's Birth Place: United States
Province: Ontario
District Number: 71
District: Halton
Subdistrict: Nassagaweya
Archive Roll #: T-6341
Neighbors: View others on page
Household Members: Name Age
John Daniels 55
Mary A Daniels 46

Source Information: 1901 Census of Canada
Subdistrict: Puslinch, WELLINGTON (South/Sud), ONTARIO
District Number: 126 Subdistrict Number: f-1 Archives Microfilm: T-
6505
 24 96 Daniels John M   Head M May 8 1836 64
 25 96 Daniels Mary A F   Wife M Feb 16 1844 57

+   69   iv.   Harriet King, born 19 Aug 1847 in Arkell, Puslinch Tp. Wellington
                Co. Ontario; died 19 Jan 1928 in Guelph, Wellington Co. Ontario.
+   70   v.   John (David John?) King, born Abt. 1852 in Puslinch Tp Wellington
                Co. Ontario; died Bet. 1897 - 1930.
+   71   vi.   Joseph King, born 15 Nov 1851 in Ontario; died 09 Mar 1922 in

Johnson, Algoma District.

+ 72   vii. George King, born 31 Aug 1855 in Ontario; died Aft. 05 Nov 1913 in
                   Blind River, Algoma?.

Generation No. 4

21. William J. L.[4] Hewer (Sarah Catherine[3] King, Lewis[2], James[1]) was born 07 Mar
1845 in England, and died 17 May 1917 in Guelph Twp., Wellington, Ontario. He
married **Mary Jane Gibson** Bef. 1869, daughter of Johnston Gibson and J. Sinclair. She
was born 03 Nov 1847 in Ontario, and died 14 May 1919 in Guelph, Wellington, Ontario.

Notes for William J. L. Hewer:
1881 Census Place: Guelph, Wellington South, Ontario, Canada
    Source: FHL Film 1375894 NAC C-13258 Dist 151 SubDist B Div 3 Page 15
Family 58

Sex	Marr	Age	Origin	Birthplace
Willm. J. L. HEWER	M	M	36	English	England

    Occ: Butcher   Religion: Church of England

| Mary Jane HEWER | F | M | 34 | Scottish | O. <Ontario> |

            Religion: Church of England

| Sarah S. HEWER | F | | 12 | English | O. <Ontario> |

            Religion: Church of England

| Frederick HEWER | M | | 11 | English | O. <Ontario> |

            Religion: Church of England

| Sinclair HEWER | M | | 10 | English | O. <Ontario> |

            Religion: Church of England

| Ethel A. HEWER | F | | 9 | English | O. <Ontario> |

            Religion: Church of England

| Fanny HEWER | F | | 7 | English | O. <Ontario> |

            Religion: Church of England

| Leona HEWER | F | | 5 | English | O. <Ontario> |

            Religion: Church of England

| Irvine HEWER | M | | 1 | English | O. <Ontario> |

            Religion: Church of England

| Beredal HEWER | M | | <1 | English | O. <Ontario> |

            Religion: Church of England
    Born: Feb; 1/12

1901 census Guelph Wellington South Dist. 126 Subdistrict d-4 p 4
William Hewer
Mary
Irvine, son
Leona, dau
Zindue, male, grandchild, 7 Jan 1896, 5 yrs old

Name: William J.S. Hewer

Titles:
Death date: 17 May 1917
Estimated death year:
Age at death: 72 years 2 months
Death place: Guelph Twp., Wellington, Ontario
Birth date: 1845
Estimated birth year: 1845
Birth place: England
Gender: Male
Marital status: Married
Father name: Wm. Hewer
Mother name: Sara Smith [sic]
GSU film number: 1862690
Digital GS number: 4170678
Image number: 69
Reference number: yr 1917 cn 33811
Collection: Ontario Deaths 1869-1947

Notes for Mary Jane Gibson:
Name: Mary Jane Gibson Hewer
Titles:
Death date: 14 May 1919
Estimated death year:
Age at death: 71 years 6 months
Death place: Guelph, Wellington, Ontario
Birth date: 1848
Estimated birth year: 1848
Birth place: Canada
Gender: Female
Marital status: Widowed
Race or color (expanded):
Race:
Ethnicity:
Spouse name:
Spouse titles:
Father name: Johnston Gibson
Father titles:
Mother name: J. Mary Sinclair
Mother titles:
GSU film number: 1862969
Digital GS number: 4170965
Image number: 317
Reference number: yr 1919 cn 34472
Collection: Ontario Deaths 1869-1947

Children of William Hewer and Mary Gibson are:

73	i.	Sarah S.⁵ Hewer, born Abt. 1869.
74	ii.	Frederick Hewer, born Abt. 1870.
75	iii.	Ethel Adelaide Hewer, born 08 Mar 1873 in Guelph Ontario; died 22 Mar 1928 in Wellington, Ontario. She married x Brown.

Notes for Ethel Adelaide Hewer:
Name: Ethel Adelaide Hewer Brown
Titles:
Death date: 22 Mar 1928
Estimated death year:
Age at death: 55 years 12 days
Death place: Wellington, Ontario, Canada
Birth date: 08 Mar 1873
Estimated birth year:
Birth place: Guelph Ontario
Gender: Female
Marital status: Married
Race or color (expanded): English
Race: White
Ethnicity: English
Spouse name:
Spouse titles:
Father name: William Hewer
Father titles:
Mother name: Mary Jane Gibson
Mother titles:
GSU film number: 2184485
Digital GS number: 4000413
Image number: 01512
Reference number: 36647
Collection: Ontario Deaths 1869-1947

76	iv.	Sinclair Hewer, born Abt. 1871.
77	v.	Fanny Hewer, born Abt. 1873.
78	vi.	Leona Hewer, born 03 Jun 1878.
79	vii.	Beredal Hewer, born 07 May 1880.
80	viii.	Irvine Hewer, born 07 May 1880.

22. Elizabeth⁴ Hewer (Sarah Catherine³ King, Lewis², James¹) was born 22 Nov 1847, and died Aft. 1901. She married **John Marriott**. He was born 14 Aug 1834 in England.

Notes for Elizabeth Hewer:
123 Paisley Rd

John Mariott

Elizabeth Hewer Marriott (Sarah and Wm.'s daughter) b Nov 22, 1847, 53, Ont There were 2 children from this marriage called the MARRIOTT TWINS who were world famous trapeze artists....They were in the Andrew Downie Company of Vancouver fame....the owner, Andrew Downie was married to Tina Hewer, another cousin.

Notes for John Marriott:
1891 Census Guelph, Wellington Co. Ontario

Name: John Marriott
Gender: Male
Marital Status: Married
Age: 54
Birth Year: abt 1837
Birthplace: England
Relation to Head of House: Head
Religion: Methodist
French Canadian: No
Father's Birth Place: England
Mother's Birth Place: England
Province: Ontario
District Number: 127
District: Wellington South
Subdistrict: Guelph City
Archive Roll #: T-6377
Neighbors: View others on page
Household Members: Name Age
John Marriott 54
Elizabeth Marriott 44
William Marriott 23
Fredrick Marriott 17
Ada Marriott 15
Bertha Marriott 12
Minard Marriott 8
Albert Marriott 8
Kate W Marriott 6

Children of Elizabeth Hewer and John Marriott are:
   81   i.   William[5] Marriott, born Abt. 1868.
   82   ii. Elizabeth Ann Marriott, born 01 Mar 1870 in Guelph Ontario.

        Notes for Elizabeth Ann Marriott:

83	iii.	Frederick Marriott, born Abt. 1874.
84	iv.	Ada S. Marriott, born 13 Sep 1876.
85	v.	Bertha Marriott, born Abt. 1879.
86	vi.	Albert George Marriott, born 22 Jun 1882 in Guelph Ontario. He married Maud Morrill 14 Mar 1907 in Wellington Co. Ontario; born 1884 in Midland, Simcoe County Ontario.

Notes for Albert George Marriott:
Albert Marriott 22 Jun 1882 Male Wellington John Maniott Elizabeth Hewer

1901 Census Guelph Ontario

12 36   123 Marriott John M   Head M Aug 14 1834 66
12 37   123 Marriott Elizabeth F   Wife M Nov 22 1847 53
12 38   123 Marriott Ada S. F   Daughter S Sep 13 1876 24
12 39   123 Marriott Albert G. M   Son S Jun 22 1882 18
12 40   123 Marriott Mes?? J. M   Son S Jun 22 1882 18
12 41   123 Marriott Kate W. F   Daughter S Nov 4 1885 15

Source Information: 1901 Census of Canada
Subdistrict: Guelph (City/Cité), WELLINGTON (South/Sud), ONTARIO
District Number: 126
Subdistrict Number: e-14
Archives Microfilm: T-6505

U.S. Naturalization Records Indexes, 1794-1995
Name: Albert George Marriott
Birth Date: 2 Jul 1885
State: Michigan
Locality, Court: Detroit, District Court
Title: Index Cards to Naturalization Petitions for the U.S. District Court for the Eastern District of Michigan, Southern Division, Detroit, 1907-1995
Description: M-625 Marchinkowski, Antony-M-632 Murdock, Olive
Series: M1917

Ontario, Canada Marriages, 1857-1924
about Albert Geo Marriott

Name: Albert Geo Marriott
Birth Place: Guelph
Age: 23
Estimated Birth Year: abt 1884
Father Name: John Marriott Marriott
Mother Name: Elizabeth Marriott
Spouse Name: Maud Morrill
Spouse's Age: 23
Spouse Estimated Birth Year: abt 1884
Spouse Birth Place: Midland
Spouse Father Name: Thomas Morrill
Spouse Mother Name: Phoebe Merrett
Marriage Date: 14 Mar 1907
Marriage Place: Wellington
Marriage County: Wellington
Family History Library Microfilm: MS932_131

3 Dec. 1907 sailing from Havana Cuba to New York on board the
Havana
Albert G. Marriot, 24 juggler, artist, father John, non immigrant alien
Manet Marriot, 24 juggler

New York Passenger Lists, 1820-1957
Name: Manet Marriott
Arrival Date: 3 Dec 1907
Estimated Birth Year: abt 1883
Age: 24
Gender: Male
Port of Departure: Havana, Cuba
Ship Name: Havana
Port of Arrival: New York, New York
Nativity: Ontario
Line: 11
Microfilm Serial: T715
Microfilm Roll: T715_1053
Birth Location: Ontario
Birth Location Other: guelph
Page Number: 170

1891 Census Guelph Wellington Co. Ontario with his parents and
siblings

1930 United States Federal Census
Name: Albert G Marriott

Home in 1930: Pine Grove, Van Buren, Michigan
Age: 45
Estimated Birth Year: abt 1885
Birthplace: Canada
Relation to Head of House: Head
Spouse's Name: Maude
Race: White
Household Members: Name Age
Albert G Marriott 45 born Canada immigrated 1902, naturalized, vaudeville performer
Maude Marriott 44 born Canada, immigrated 1886, vaudeville performer

1937 sailed from Japan to New York on Kongo Maru
Albert George, 54, Aerial Act, American, Naturalized Circut Court
Van Buren Co. Paw Paw Michigan Jan 21, 1933. born Guelph Ontario,
Visa permit issued Tokyo June 8, 1937, Residence Allegan Michigan
Maude Morrill, 53, housewife, born Barrie Ontario, US Passport
359567 issued Washington DC June 4, 1937

New York Passenger Lists, 1820-1957
about Albert George Marriott
Name: Albert George Marriott
Arrival Date: 8 Jul 1937
Estimated Birth Year: abt 1883
Age: 54
Gender: Male
Port of Departure: Yokohama, Japan
Place of Origin: United States of America
Ethnicity/Race-/Nationality: American;English (American)
Ship Name: Kongo Maru
Port of Arrival: New York, New York
Nativity: Canada
Line: 2
Microfilm Serial: T715
Microfilm Roll: T715_6006
Birth Location: Canada
Birth Location Other: Guelph,On
Page Number: 154A
Port Arrival State: New York
Port Arrival Country: United States

New York Passenger Lists, 1820-1957
Name: Maude Morrill Marriott
Arrival Date: 8 Jul 1937
Estimated Birth Year: abt 1884
Age: 53

Gender: Female
Port of Departure: Yokohama, Japan
Place of Origin: United States of America
Ethnicity/Race-/Nationality: American;Canadian (American)
Ship Name: Kongo Maru
Port of Arrival: New York, New York
Nativity: Canada
Line: 1
Microfilm Serial: T715
Microfilm Roll: T715_6006
Birth Location: Canada
Birth Location Other: Barrie,On
Page Number: 154A
Port Arrival State: New York
Port Arrival Country: United States

"The Marriott Twins Scored World Fame"

...Guelph's famous Marriott Twins. The winning of a baton contest in the old Guelph skatin grink gave the Marriotts their start for 60 years in the show business, gaining them international fame.

In 1896 they joined the Harry Lindely Dramatic Company, playing in Canada up to tDawson City in the Yukon. Engagements with other companies included the Andrew Downie Company of Vancouver, Mrs. Downie was a former Guelph girl, Tena Hewer. The Downies built up a creditble circus later sold to Charles Sparks, becomign quite noted.

It was with the DOwnie circus that the Marriotts orignated their bicycle juggling act which they repeated at the opening of Tony Pastor's Theatre in New York.

[letter from Al Marriott] ..."We played with the Orrin Circus in Mexico for three years then going to the Million Dollar Theatre [note from Lorine - this was built in 1918 so we have a vague timeline] in Buenos Aires, Argentina for six months. Next came several months at theatres in Havana Cuba. On five occasions we played return engagement sin front of the grandstand at Toronto Exhibition and making appearnaces before the Prince of Wales"

The Marriott Twins were booked for a world tour and played the large cities of Europe and other continents. Following this was a booking to represent the USA at th ePan-Pacific Peace Exposition at Nagoya Japan for six months.

Among the engagements was one with President Truman at a county fair in Missouri and the following week at Washington DC. There followed references in Al Marriott's letter to numreous other engagements including seven years at the Hippodrome in New York.

In later years with the coming of the aeroplane their act took the form of a large plane mounted on a high tower. The players performed on a trapeze hanging from the plane, as well as being fastened to the propeller. The home of Mr. and Mrs. Al Marriott is now Georgia [Guelph Mercury Sept 21, 1939]

Andrew Downie had already been in show business for over 30 years when he took out the LaTena Circus in 1914. This ad was found in the Billboard on November 15, 1913 on page 23.

1886 - Downie & Austin's Parlor Circus
1890 - Rich & Downie Circus
1891 - 1892 - Downie & Gallagher Circus
1905 - Downie's Dog & Pony Show
1905 - McPhee's Big Company
1909 - 1910 - Andrew Downie's Circus
1911 -1913 - Downie & Wheeler's Circus
1914 - 1917 - LaTena's Circus
1918 - 1923 - Walter L. Main Circus
1924 - Andrew Downie's Circus
1926 - 1929 - Downie Bros. Circus (sold it to Charles Sparks)

Andrew Downie
By John Van Matre, CHS. Bandwagon, Vol. 3, No. 4 (Aug), 1944, pp. 1-2.
This well known circus owner was born Andrew Downie McPhee, August 13th, 1863 at Stephens Township, Ontario, Canada. Died December 7th, 1930 at Medina, N.Y.

At an early age he moved with his family to nearby Stratford, Ont., Canada, and at the age of 21 went into partnership with Clarence Austin and they put out a one-ring circus entitled "Downie & Austin Parlor Circus."

Two years later he went with the Ryan & Robinson Show as a performer. Some of the many things he could do were tumbling, spade dancing, break-away ladder, acrobat, wire walker, juggler and also work some animals.

In 1889 he and a man named Rich organized the Rich & Downie Circus which they took out the following Spring. In 1890 at Guelph, Ont., Canada, he met and married Christena Hewer. She was better known as Millie La Tena. Many years later he put out a wild animal circus and named it after his wife. In fact it was 1914 that he put out the LaTena Wild Animal Circus and it was a ten car railroad show.

At one time he owned the famous Diamond Minstrel Show. After this he bought out Rich and took the show out under the title Andrew Downie Dog & Pony Circus.

His next venture was as a partner in the Downie & Gallagher Wagon Show. Following this he went with the Great Wallace Show. In 1911 he and Al. F. Wheeler took out the Downie & Wheeler Show. This show started out from Oxford, Penna., and they remained partners till the end of the season of 1913.

It was in 1914, as stated above, that he took out his own show (LaTena) and in two years enlarged it from a 10 car show to a 15 car show and made a tour of Canada. The show folded in 1917 at Havre de Grace, Md.

He next leased the title of the Main Circus from Walter L. Main and rolled up a fortune. Then in 1924 he sold out to Miller Bros., famous for their 101 Ranch Wild West Show.

In 1926 he was back and out with Downie Bros. Circus, and it was motorized. This show stayed on the road till 1930 when Downie retired and Charles Sparks took over the title.

Downie was a very loveable person, and certainly made a name for himself in the show business, and remained very active, even up to the time of his death, at the age of 67 years.
[http://www.circushistory.org/Bandwagon/bw-1944Aug.htm]

Harry Lindley was a prominent theatrical figure in Canada around the turn of the 20th century, and has been called Vancouver's first resident professional. His company performed plays in the 1890s with titles like In the Cariboo and A Scene on Hastings. Lindley and his company made annual tours of Canada, performing at various cities. One of his company's hits was a play titled The Duplicate Man, in turn written by the Prairie playwright and journalist Kate Simpson Hayes. So there was lots of Canadian content, even more than a hundred years ago. (They spread it around, too: Lindley's company ventured into the U.S. with some success.)

The circus, started by Andrew Downie, but by the 1930s owned by famed showman Charles Sparks,

n 1906 the famous clown Richard Bell, patriarch of the family, bought the Orrin circus in Mexico. The clown turned entrepreneur opened the Gran Circo Ricardo Bell, which featured him and his thirteen children. The family circus lasted until 1910, with varying degrees of success. Rumors of an imminent revolution in Mexico, as well as the need to buy new equipment, pushed Richard and his family to travel to the United States. The popular clown died in New York in 1911, never having seen Mexico again.

"ANDREW DOWNIE'S CIRCUS" made several successful visits around the turn of the century. For a one-ring show hauled overland by wagons, Downie achieved maximum results from 50 performers and a profusion of animals

Having come from a Rep Show background, Andrew (McPhee) Downie's first circus was formed by a partnership with veteran showman Al F. Wheeler (Downie & Wheeler Circus 1911-13).
After this partnership was dissolved, Downie framed his own show named after his wife (LaTena Circus 1914-17.)
Starting in 1918 he leased the name Walte L. Main from that well know retired circus owner (Walter L. Main Circus 1918-24.)
After a brief retirement, Mr. Downie became one of the first owners of a successful motorized circus (Downie Bros. Circus 1926-30) which he sold to Charles Sparks in 1931 and who continued on with it thru 1938.

87 vii. Murray (Minard aka Manet) John Marriott, born 22 Jun 1882 in Guelph Ontario; died 06 Sep 1926 in Wellington Co. Ontario.

Notes for Murray (Minard aka Manet) John Marriott:
Name: Mermaid John Marriott
Titles:
Death date: 06 Sep 1926
Estimated death year:
Age at death: 44 years
Death place: Wellington, Ontario
Birth date: 1882
Estimated birth year: 1882

Birth place:
Gender: Male
Marital status:
Race or color (expanded):
Race:
Ethnicity:
Spouse name:
Spouse titles:
Father name: John Marriott
Father titles:
Mother name: Elizabeth Hewer
Mother titles:
GSU film number: 2079859
Digital GS number: 4171426
Image number: 993
Reference number: 035975
Collection: Ontario Deaths 1869-1947

88   viii.   Kate W. Marriott, born 04 Nov 1884.

Notes for Kate W. Marriott:
Kate Marriott 4 Nov 1884 Female Wellington John Marriott
Elizabeth Hewer

31. George[4] King (George A.[3], Lewis[2], James[1]) was born 24 Feb 1844 in Puslinch Tp Wellington Co Ontario, and died 10 May 1903 in Keppel Tp Grey Co, Ontario. He married **Jane Scott** 25 Nov 1868 in Guelph, Wellington Co. Ontario, daughter of James Scott and Margaret Anderson. She was born 18 Mar 1848 in Puslinch Tp Wellington Co Ontario, and died 29 Feb 1920 in Owen Sound, Grey Co., Ontario.

Notes for George King:
KING George William George Ann Guelph b 1844-02-24 1844-10-09 Guelph
Byers, Rev. Henry, 1871 farmer living in Puslinch Con 10 Lot 5, buried Arkell Church cemetery, Husband of Sarah King

1871 census for Arkell: Lewis and Elizabeth King are living with their grandson George, age 27 and his wife Jane, on Lot 5, Conc 10, Arkell.

1871 Census Wellington South, Puslinch Division: 4 Page: 24 Microfilm reel: C-9945
Lewis King, 75 b England WM
Elizabeth 71 b Eng
George 27 b Canada, C. Presbyterian, farmer
Jane 24, b Canada, C. Presbyterian

1901 Census of Canada District: Grey (North/Nord) District Number: 65

Sub-District: Keppel Sub-District Number: C-7 Family Number: 10 Page: 2
Geo King 56   24 Feb 1844 Ontario, farmer Presbyterian
Jean King 53 Mar 1847 ontario Scotch
James King 31 14 Sep 1869 single
Mary King 25 11 Oct 1875 single

 Name : George King
Death date : 10 May 1903
Age at death : 59 years
Death place : Keppel, Grey, Ontario
Birth date : 1844
Estimated birth year : 1844
Birth place : Ontario
Gender : Male
Marital status : Married
GSU film number : 1854188
Digital GS number : 4175424
Image number : 741
Certificate number : yr 1903 cn 10786
Collection : Ontario Deaths 1869-1947

Notes for Jane Scott:
Name: Jean Scott King
Death date: 29 Feb 1920
Age at death: 71 years 11 months
Death place: Owen Sound, Grey Co., Ontario
Birth date: 18 Mar 1848
Birth place: Wellington County
Gender: Female
Marital status: Widowed
Race or color (expanded):
Father name: James Scott
Mother name: Margaret Anderson
GSU film number: 1863285
Digital GS number: 4170968
Image number: 582
Reference number: yr 1920 cn 16975
Collection: Ontario Deaths 1869-1947

Children of George King and Jane Scott are:
     89   i.   James[5] King, born 14 Oct 1869 in Wellington Co. Ontario; died 22 Apr 1919 in Grey Co. Ontario.

| 90 | ii. | Ann King, born May 1871; died 24 Aug 1873 in Arkell, Wellington Co. Ontario. |
| 91 | iii. | Mary King, born 11 Oct 1875 in Wellington Co. Ontario; died Aft. 1901. |

39. James Parker[4] King (George A.[3], Lewis[2], James[1]) was born 19 Jul 1867 in Arkell, Puslinch Tp Wellington County Ontario, and died Aft. 1916 in Possibly Red Deer Alberta. He married **Clara Gertrude Partridge** 27 Apr 1887 in Wellington Co. Ontario, daughter of William Partridge and Martha Sealey. She was born 22 Aug 1869 in Ashbury, Berkshire England, and died Aft. 1916 in Possibly Red Deer Alberta.

Notes for James Parker King:
Name: James Parker King
Birth Place: Arkell
Age: 21
Father Name: George King
Mother Name: Elizabeth King
Estimated Birth Year: abt 1866
Spouse Name: Clara Gertrude Partridge
Spouse's Age: 18
Spouse Birth Place: Ashby England
Spouse Father Name: Wm H Partridge
Spouse Mother Name : Martha Partridge
Marriage Date: 27 Apr 1887
Marriage Place: Wellington
Marriage County: Wellington
Source: Indexed by: Ancestry.com

KING, James Parker
Section 7 Township 35 Range 12 Meridian 4
Film # 2882 in Accession # 1970.313 at Provincial Archives of Alberta
File # 1829084
Alberta Homestead Records 1870-1930

1900 his wife and daughters are in Detroit Michigan

1901 Census of Canada
Name: James P King
Gender: Male
Marital Status: Married
Age: 33
Birth Date: 19 Jul 1867
Birthplace: Ontario
Relation to Head of House: Head
Spouse's Name: Clara G
Immigration Year: 1900

Racial or Tribal Origin: English
Nationality: Canadian
Religion: Methodist
Occupation: Farmer
Province: The Territories
District: Alberta
District Number: 202
Sub-District: Ponoka
Sub-District Number: Q3-1
Family Number: 200
Page: 18
Neighbors: View others on page
Household Members: Name Age
James P King 33
Clara G King 31
Henry G King 13
Flossie M King 11
Agnes G King 8

1911 Census of Canada
about James P King
Name: James P King
Gender: Male
Marital Status: Married
Age: 45
Birth Date: Oct 1866
Birthplace: Ontario
Family Number: 139
Relation to Head of House: Head
Spouse's Name: Clara
Tribal: English
Province: Alberta
District: Red Deer
District Number: 5
Sub-District Number: 63
Census Year: 1911
Page: 8
Neighbors: View others on page
Household Members: Name Age
James P King 45
Clara King 43 Mar 1868 Ontario

1916 Canada Census of Manitoba, Saskatchewan, and Alberta
about James P King
Name: James P King
Gender: Male
Marital Status: Married

Age: 51
Est. Birth Year: 1865
Birthplace: Ontario
Home in 1916: Alberta, Red Deer, 01
Address: 35, 12, 4, Whiteside
Racial or Tribal Origin: English
Relation to Head of Household: Father
Household Members: Name Age
Harry King 28 md b 1881 Ontario
Thelma King 23 md b Ontario
Thelma King 4 b BC
James P King 51
Clara King 48

Notes for Clara Gertrude Partridge:
see 1900 census William King, her brother in law
Clara King 28 Jul 1871 can. imm 1891 sis in law b Eng (hubby b Can)
Florence King 9 aug 1890 Ontario clara's dau
Agnes King 7 june 1892 michigan

Children of James King and Clara Partridge are:

+	92	i.	Henry George (Harry)[5] King, born 10 Feb 1888 in Wellington Co. Ontario; died Aft. 1916.
	93	ii.	Florence (Flossie) May Martha King, born 17 Dec 1889 in Wellington Co. Ontario.
	94	iii.	Agnes G. King, born Bet. Jun - 17 Jul 1892 in Michigan.

41. William H.[4] King (George A.[3], Lewis[2], James[1]) was born 06 Mar 1873 in Guelph, Wellington Co. Ontario, and died Aft. 1930 in probably Detroit, Wayne Co. Michigan. He married **Margaret House** Abt. 1895. She was born 05 Aug 1873 in Guelph Ontario, and died Aft. 1930 in probably Detroit, Wayne Co. Michigan.

Notes for William H. King:
1900 United States Federal Census
about William King
Name: William King
Home in 1900: Detroit Ward 7, Wayne, Michigan
Age: 27
Birth Date: Mar 1873
Birthplace: Canada Eng
[Canada English]

Race: White
Ethnicity: American
Gender: Male
Immigration Year: 1892
Relationship to head-of-house: Head
Father's Birthplace: England
Mother's Birthplace: England
Spouse's Name: Margaret
Marriage Year: 1895
Marital Status: Married
Years Married: 5
Residence : Detroit City, Wayne, Michigan
Household Members: Name Age
William King 27
Margaret King 26 aug 1872 par b Can
Clarence J King 4
Olive M King 1
Henry G King 3/12
Clara King 28 Jul 1871 can. imm 1891 sis in law b Eng (hubby b Can)
Florence King 9 aug 1890 Ontario clara's dau
Agnes King 7 june 1892 michigan

1901 Census of Canada
about William H King
Name: William H King
Gender: Male
Marital Status: Married
Age: 28
Birth Date: 9 Mar 1873
Birthplace: Ontario
Relation to Head of House: Head
Spouse's Name: Margaret M
Immigration Year: 1900
Racial or Tribal Origin: English
Nationality: Canadian
Occupation: Farmer
Province: The Territories
District: Alberta
District Number: 202
Sub-District: Ponoka
Sub-District Number: Q3-1
Family Number: 199
Page: 18
Neighbors: View others on page
Household Members: Name Age
William H King 28
Margaret M King 27 5 Aug 1873, R.C. German origin

Clarence J King 4 14 Apr 1896 USA
Olive M King 2 14 Aug 1898 USA
Henry G King 1 6 Feb 1899 USA

Detroit Border Crossings and Passenger and Crew Lists, 1905-1957
Name: Margaret King
Arrival Date: 29 Oct 1908
Age: 36
Birth Date: abt 1872
Birthplace: Guelph Ont
Birth Country: Canada
Gender: Female
Race/Nationality: German
Port of Arrival: Detroit, Michigan
Accompanied by: Husband William H and 6 children; Son Clarence; Son George; Son
Albert; Son Spencer; Daughter Olive; Daughter Myrtle
last residence Ponoka Alberta
Departure Contact: Brother Joseph House, Yorktown, Sask
Arrival Contact: Brother-in-law Fred King 340 Gratiot Ave   Detroit MI farmer
1896-Oct 1900 lived Laconia NH and Detroit MI 5"7" fair, lt brown hair, blue eyes
Microfilm Roll Number: M1478_38

1910 United States Federal Census
about William H King
Name: William H King
Age in 1910: 38
Estimated Birth Year: abt 1872
Birthplace: Canada English
Relation to Head of House: Head
Father's Birth Place: Canada English
Mother's Birth Place: Canada English
Spouse's Name: Margaret
Home in 1910: Redford, Wayne, Michigan
Marital Status: Married
Race: White
Gender: Male
Year of Immigration: 1892
Household Members: Name Age
William H King 38
Margaret King 38
Clarence King 14
Olive King 10
George King 10
Albert King 6
Spencer King 3
Francis King 1 8/12 abt 1908 daughter

1920 United States Federal Census
Name: William H King
Home in 1920: Redford, Wayne, Michigan
Age: 46 years
Estimated Birth Year: abt 1874
Birthplace: Canada
Relation to Head of House: Head
Spouse's Name: Margret
Father's Birth Place: England
Mother's Birth Place: England
Marital Status: Married
Race: White
Sex: Male
Home owned: Own
Year of Immigration: 1909
Able to read: Yes
Able to Write: Yes
Image: 562
Household Members: Name Age
William H King 46
Margret King 46
Clarence King 23
Olive King 21
George King 19
Albert King 16
Spencer King 13
Frances King 11
Harold King 8 6/12
Elmer Lefevre 21

1930 United States Federal Census
about William H King
Name: William H King
Home in 1930: Detroit, Wayne, Michigan
Age: 59
Estimated Birth Year: abt 1871
Birthplace: Canada
Relation to Head of House: Head
Spouse's Name: Margaret
Race: White
Household Members: Name Age
William H King 59 imm 1894 PA (first papers) gardener at private house
Margaret King 59
Clarence J King 32
Albert J King 26
Frances King 21

Harold King 18
Spencer King 23

Detroit Border Crossings and Passenger and Crew Lists, 1905-1957
about Margaret M King
Name: Margaret M King
Arrival Date: 7 Sep 1950
Age: 78
Birth Date: 5 Aug 1872
Birthplace: Guelph Ont
Birth Country: Canada
Gender: Female
Race/Nationality: Canadian
Port of Arrival: Detroit, Michigan
Microfilm Roll Number: M1478_38

Children of William King and Margaret House are:
    95   i.   Clarence J.[5] King, born Bet. Mar - 14 Apr 1896 in Michigan.

                    Notes for Clarence J. King:
                    Name: Clarence J King
                    Titles:
                    Residence: Detroit city, Wayne, Michigan
                    Birth date: Mar 1896
                    Birth place: Michigan
                    Relationship to head-of-household: Son
                    Spouse name:
                    Spouse titles:
                    Spouse birth place:
                    Father name: William King
                    Father titles:
                    Father birth place: Canada Eng
                    Mother name: Margaret King
                    Mother titles:
                    Mother birth place: Canada Eng
                    Race or color (expanded): White
                    Head-of-household name: William King
                    Gender: Male
                    Marital status: Single
                    Years married:
                    Estimated marriage year:

Mother how many children:
Number living children:
Immigration year:
Enumeration district: 0077
Sheet number and letter: 4A
Household id: 68
Reference number: 11
GSU film number: 1240749
Image number: 00831
Collection: 1900 United States Census

96 ii. Olive M. King, born 14 Aug 1898 in Michigan.

Notes for Olive M. King:
Name: Olive M King
Titles:
Residence: Detroit city, Wayne, Michigan
Birth date: Aug 1898
Birth place: Michigan
Relationship to head-of-household: Daughter
Spouse name:
Spouse titles:
Spouse birth place:
Father name: William King
Father titles:
Father birth place: Canada Eng
Mother name: Margaret King
Mother titles:
Mother birth place: Canada Eng
Race or color (expanded): White
Head-of-household name: William King
Gender: Female
Marital status: Single
Years married:
Estimated marriage year:
Mother how many children:
Number living children:
Immigration year:
Enumeration district: 0077
Sheet number and letter: 4A
Household id: 68
Reference number: 12
GSU film number: 1240749
Image number: 00831
Collection: 1900 United States Census

97 iii. Henry G. (George?) King, born Bet. 06 Feb 1899 - Feb 1900 in Michigan.

     Notes for Henry G. (George?) King:
     Name: Henry G King
     Titles:
     Residence: Detroit city, Wayne, Michigan
     Birth date: Feb 1900
     Birth place: Michigan
     Relationship to head-of-household: Son
     Spouse name:
     Spouse titles:
     Spouse birth place:
     Father name: William King
     Father titles:
     Father birth place: Canada Eng
     Mother name: Margaret King
     Mother titles:
     Mother birth place: Canada Eng
     Race or color (expanded): White
     Head-of-household name: William King
     Gender: Male
     Marital status: Single
     Years married:
     Estimated marriage year:
     Mother how many children:
     Number living children:
     Immigration year:
     Enumeration district: 0077
     Sheet number and letter: 4A
     Household id: 68
     Reference number: 13
     GSU film number: 1240749
     Image number: 00831
     Collection: 1900 United States Census

98 iv. Albert J. King, born Abt. 1904 in Ponoka, Alberta.
99 v. Myrtle King, born Abt. 1906 in Ponoka, Alberta.
100 vi. Spencer King, born Abt. 1907 in Ponoka, Alberta.
101 vii. Frances King, born Abt. 1908 in Michigan.
102 viii. Harold King, born Abt. 1911 in Michigan.

     Notes for Harold King:
     Social Security Death Index
     about Harold King

Name: Harold King
SSN: 381-20-5598
Last Residence: 48223 Detroit, Wayne, Michigan, United States of America
Born: 27 Jun 1911
Died: 21 Mar 1991
State (Year) SSN issued: Michigan (Before 1951)

42. Frederick Temple[4] King (George A.[3], Lewis[2], James[1]) was born 09 Aug 1874 in Ontario, and died Aft. 1930 in probably Detroit, Wayne Co. Michigan. He married **Alice Maude Moynes** 18 Feb 1902 in Detroit Wayne Co. Michigan. She was born Abt. 1879 in Ontario, and died Aft. 1930.

Notes for Frederick Temple King:
Groom name: Frederick T. King
Groom race or color (on document):
Groom age: 27 years
Groom birth year: 1875
Groom birth place: Canada
Bride name: Alice N. Moynes
Bride race or color (on document):
Bride age: 23 years
Bride birth year: 1879
Bride birth place: Canada
Marriage type:
Marriage date: 18 Feb 1902
Marriage place: Detroit, Wayne, Michigan
Father of groom name: George
Mother of groom name: Elizabeth Parker
Father of bride name:
Mother of bride name:
Marital status:
Groom previous wife name:
Bride marital status:
Bride previous husband name:
Additional relatives:
Film number: 2342523
Frame number:
Digital GS number: 4001634
Image number: 250
Reference number: v 4 p 451 rn 35605
Collection: Michigan Marriages 1868-1925

1910 United States Federal Census

about Fred King
Name: Fred King
Age in 1910: 35
Estimated Birth Year: abt 1875
Birthplace: Canada English
Relation to Head of House: Head
Father's Birth Place: England
Mother's Birth Place: England
Spouse's Name: Alice
Home in 1910: Detroit Ward 5, Wayne, Michigan
Marital Status: Married
Race: White
Gender: Male
Year of Immigration: 1892
Household Members: Name Age
Fred King 35
Alice King 32
Clarence King 5
Gladis King 7

World War I Draft Registration Cards, 1917-1918
Name: Fredrick Temple King
City: Detroit
County: Wayne
State: Michigan
Birth Date: 9 Aug 1874
Race: White
Roll: 2032764
DraftBoard: 26
 Naturalized. Relative Alice Maude King, 450 Mamotique, Detroit Michigan. Retail Shoe
Merchant, self employed at 316 Gratiot Ave, Detroit Michigan. Medium height, blue
eyes, brown hair, Sept 12, 1918

 1920 United States Federal Census
about Fred T King
Name: Fred T King
Home in 1920: Detroit Ward 21, Wayne, Michigan
Age: 42 years
Estimated Birth Year: abt 1878
Birthplace: Canada
Relation to Head of House: Head
Spouse's Name: Alice
Father's Birth Place: England
Mother's Birth Place: England
Marital Status: Married
Race: White
Sex: Male

Home owned: Rent
Year of Immigration: 1890
Able to read: Yes
Able to Write: Yes
Image: 914
Household Members: Name Age
Fred T King 42
Alice King 40
Clerance King 15
Gladys King 17

1930 United States Federal Census
Name: Frederick T King
Home in 1930: Detroit, Wayne, Michigan
Age: 53
Estimated Birth Year: abt 1877
Birthplace: Canada
Relation to Head of House: Head
Spouse's Name: Alice
Race: White
Occupation:
Education:
Military service:
Rent/home value:
Age at first marriage:
Parents' birthplace:
Household Members: Name Age
Frederick T King 53 imm 1895, naturalized, merchant, shoe store
Alice King 52 unn 1883, naturalized
Clarence King 25 sales clerk, shoe store
James Powell 26 roomer

Children of Frederick King and Alice Moynes are:
- 103   i.   Gladys[5] King, born Abt. 1903 in Michigan.
- 104   ii.   Clarence King, born Abt. 1905 in Michigan; died Aft. 1930.

43. Charles Joseph[4] King (George A.[3], Lewis[2], James[1]) was born 17 Mar 1878 in Ontario, and died Aft. 1920. He married **Etta E..** She was born Abt. 1880.

Notes for Charles Joseph King:
1910 United States Federal Census
Name: Charles J King

Age in 1910: 35
Estimated Birth Year: abt 1875
Birthplace: Canada English
Relation to Head of House: Head
Father's Birth Place: England
Mother's Birth Place: England
Spouse's Name: Etta E
Home in 1910: Farmington, Oakland, Michigan
Marital Status: Married
Race: White
Gender: Male
Year of Immigration: 1887
Neighbors: View others on page
Household Members: Name Age
Charles J King 35
Etta E King 33
Dora J King 9
Shiney R King 7
Francis F King 5
Maude E King 4
Alfred C King 2

World War I Draft Registration Cards, 1917-1918
about Charles Joseph King
Name: Charles Joseph King
City: Detroit
County: Wayne
State: Michigan
Birth Date: 17 Mar 1878
Race: White
Roll: 2032418
DraftBoard: 15
Sept 1918. Shoe Business, self employed 1175 Gratiot Ave (also his residence). Nearest relative Mrs Elizabeth King, Redford Michigan

1920 United States Federal Census
Name: Charles J King
Home in 1920: Detroit Ward 13, Wayne, Michigan
Age: 43 years
Estimated Birth Year: abt 1877
Birthplace: Canada
Relation to Head of House: Head
Spouse's Name: Etta
Father's Birth Place: England
Mother's Birth Place: England
Marital Status: Married
Race: White

Sex: Male
Home owned: Rent
Year of Immigration: 1889
Able to read: Yes
Able to Write: Yes
Image: 934
Neighbors: View others on page
Household Members: Name Age
Charles J King 43
Etta King 43
Dora King 18
Shirley King 17
Francis King 15
Maud King 13
Alfred King 11
Esther King 5

Children of Charles King and Etta are:

105   i.   Dora J.[5] King, born 01 Apr 1901 in Detroit, Wayne Co. Michigan.

Notes for Dora J. King:
Name: Dora J. King
Birth date:Name: Dora J. King
Birth date: 01 Apr 1901
Birth place: Detroit, Wayne, Michigan
Gender: Female
Race or color (on document):
Father name: Charles King
Father birth place: Canada
Age of father:
Mother name: Etta King
Mother birth place: Canada
Mother age:
Christening date:
Christening place:
Additional relatives:
Death date:
Age at death:
Film number: 2363036
Digital GS number: 4208778
Image number: 447
Frame number:
Reference number: item 2 p 204 rn 3058
Collection: Michigan Births 1867-1902

Birth place: Detroit, Wayne, Michigan
Gender: Female
Race or color (on document):
Father name: Charles King
Father birth place: Canada
Age of father:
Mother name: Etta King
Mother birth place: Canada
Mother age:
Christening date:
Christening place:
Additional relatives:
Death date:
Age at death:
Film number: 2363036
Digital GS number: 4208778
Image number: 447
Frame number:
Reference number: item 2 p 204 rn 3058
Collection: Michigan Births 1867-1902

106   ii.   Shirley R. King, born 1902 in Detroit, Wayne Co. Michigan.

Notes for Shirley R. King:
Name: Spirley King
Birth date: 1902
Birth place: Detroit, Wayne, Michigan
Gender: Female
Race or color (on document):
Father name: Charles King
Father birth place: Canada
Age of father:
Mother name: Etta King
Mother birth place: Canada
Mother age:
Christening date:
Christening place:
Additional relatives:
Death date:
Age at death:
Film number: 2363099
Digital GS number: 4208780
Image number: 313
Frame number:
Reference number: item 1 p 590 rn 8851

107	iii.	Francis F. King, born 1905 in Michigan.
108	iv.	Maude E. King, born 1906 in Michigan.
109	v.	Alfred C. King, born 1908 in Michigan.
110	vi.	Esther King, born 1915 in Michigan.

57. Viola[4] King (Thomas William[3], Lewis[2], James[1]) was born Abt. 1873 in Michigan, and died Aft. 1930 in Michigan. She married **(1) John Sturck** 19 Dec 1898 in Port Austin, Huron, Michigan, son of Jonathan Stuck and Betsy Hauspiller. He was born Abt. 1837 in Canada, and died Bet. 1913 - 1920 in Michigan. She married **(2) Henry Manning Shepherd** 15 Jul 1920 in Corunna, Shiawassee, Michigan. He was born 1880 in Canada. She married **(3) James McNeal** 30 Oct 1923 in Corunna, Shiawassee, Michigan. He was born Abt. 1872 in Canada.

Notes for Viola King:
Groom name: John Stuck
Groom race or color (on document):
Groom age: 61 years
Groom birth year: 1837
Groom birth place: Canada
Bride name: Viola King
Bride race or color (on document):
Bride age: 26 years
Bride birth year: 1872
Bride birth place: Michigan
Marriage type:
Marriage date: 19 Dec 1898
Marriage place: Port Austin, Huron, Michigan
Father of groom name: Jno. Stuck
Mother of groom name: Betsy Hauspiller
Father of bride name: Thos. King
Mother of bride name: Helen Davill
Marital status:
Groom previous wife name:
Bride marital status:
Bride previous husband name:
Additional relatives:
Film number: 2342509
Frame number:
Digital GS number: 4208258
Image number: 417
Reference number: p 213 rn 238
Collection: Michigan Marriages 1868-1925

1900 United States Federal Census
about John Sturk
Name: John Sturk
[John J Sturk]
Home in 1900: Dwight, Huron, Michigan
Age: 62
Birth Date: Sep 1837
Birthplace: Canada Eng
[Canada English]
Race: White
Ethnicity: American
Gender: Male
Immigration Year: 1880
Relationship to head-of-house: Head
Father's Birthplace: Canada
Mother's Birthplace: Canada
Spouse's Name: Viola
Marriage Year: 1898
Marital Status: Married
Years Married: 2
Residence : Dwight Township, Huron, Michigan
Occupation: View on Image
Neighbors: View others on page
Household Members: Name Age
John Sturk 62
Viola Sturk 28 b Can. Eng. Jul 1871 imm 1890 father b Can, mother b Eng mother of 1
living child, md 1898
Verney Sturk 3 b Apr 1897 Michigan
Ellen Sturk 1 b Oct 1899 MIchigan
Lottie Sturk 11 b Apr 1889 location unknown, adopted daughter

1910 United States Federal Census
about John Stank
Name: John Stank
[John Sturk]
Age in 1910: 72
Estimated Birth Year: abt 1838
Birthplace: Canada English
Relation to Head of House: Head
Father's Birth Place: Canada English
Mother's Birth Place: Canada English
Spouse's Name: Viola
Home in 1910: Dwight, Huron, Michigan
Marital Status: Married
Race: White
Gender: Male

Year of Immigration: 1889
Neighbors: View others on page
Household Members: Name Age
John Stank 72
Viola Stank 38
Vernon Stank 13
Helen Stank 10

Groom name: Henry Manning Shepherd
Groom race or color (on document):
Groom age: 37 years
Groom birth year: 1883
Groom birth place: Michigan
Bride name: Viola Sturk
Bride race or color (on document):
Bride age: 40 years
Bride birth year: 1880
Bride birth place: Canada
Marriage type:
Marriage date: 15 Jul 1920
Marriage place: Corunna, Shiawassee, Michigan
Father of groom name: John Shepherd
Mother of groom name: Anna Bersett
Father of bride name: Thomas King
Mother of bride name: Helen Deville
Marital status:
Groom previous wife name:
Bride marital status:
Bride previous husband name:
Additional relatives:
Film number: 2342739
Frame number:
Digital GS number: 4032439
Image number: 536
Reference number: v 7 p 226 rn 11027
Collection: Michigan Marriages 1868-1925

Groom name: James Mcneal
Groom race or color (on document):
Groom age: 47 years
Groom birth year: 1876
Groom birth place: Michigan
Bride name: Viola King Sturk
Bride race or color (on document):
Bride age: 51 years

Bride birth year: 1872
Bride birth place: Canada
Marriage type:
Marriage date: 30 Oct 1923
Marriage place: Corunna, Shiawassee, Michigan
Father of groom name:
Mother of groom name: ...ary Stringham
Father of bride name: T. King
Mother of bride name:
Marital status:
Groom previous wife name:
Bride marital status:
Bride previous husband name:
Additional relatives:
Film number: 2342757
Frame number:
Digital GS number: 4210120
Image number: 507
Reference number: v 9 rn 272
Collection: Michigan Marriages 1868-1925

You have saved this record to My Ancestry (Shoebox).
You have saved this record to My Ancestry (People I'm Looking For).
This record has been added to your shoebox.
1930 United States Federal Census
about James McNail
Name: James McNail
Home in 1930: Rush, Shiawassee, Michigan
Age: 54
Estimated Birth Year: abt 1876
Birthplace: Michigan
Relation to Head of House: Head
Spouse's Name: Viola
Race: White
Household Members: Name Age
James McNail 54
Viola McNail 57
Russell G McNail 16
Dora V McNail 1 3/12 dau
Howard D Sturk 17 stepson b ca 1913 MI

Children of Viola King and John Sturck are:

111   i.   Vernon A.[5] Sturck, born 03 Apr 1897 in Grindstone City, Huron Co. Michigan; died Aft. 1918. He married Joy E. Temple 29 Dec 1917 in Owosso, Shiawassee, Michigan.

Notes for Vernon A. Sturck:
Groom name: Vernon A. Sturk
Groom race or color (on document):
Groom age: 21 years
Groom birth year: 1896
Groom birth place: Grindstone City, Michigan
Bride name: Joy E. Temple
Bride race or color (on document):
Bride age: 21 years
Bride birth year: 1896
Bride birth place: Grindstone City, Michigan
Marriage type:
Marriage date: 29 Dec 1917
Marriage place: Owosso, Shiawassee, Michigan
Father of groom name: John Sturk
Mother of groom name: Lola King
Father of bride name: Richard Temple
Mother of bride name: Eliza Barry
Marital status:
Groom previous wife name:
Bride marital status:
Bride previous husband name:
Additional relatives:
Film number: 2342723
Frame number:
Digital GS number: 4209966
Image number: 129
Reference number: v 5 p 192 rn 10212
Collection: Michigan Marriages 1868-1925

World War I Draft Registration Cards, 1917-1918
Name: Vernon Sturk
City: Not Stated
County: Shiawassee
State: Michigan
Birthplace: Michigan;United States of America
Birth Date: 3 Apr 1897
Roll: 1682900
DraftBoard: 0
Stetson No. 2, Owosso, Michigan
Born Huron Co. MI
Relative Joy Sturck
gray eyes, lt brown hair

June 5, 1918

112   ii.   Ellen Sturck, born Oct 1899 in Michigan.

Notes for Ellen Sturck:
Name: Ellen Sturk
Titles:
Residence: Dwight township, Huron, Michigan
Birth date: Oct 1899
Birth place: Michigan
Relationship to head-of-household: Daughter
Spouse name:
Spouse titles:
Spouse birth place:
Father name: John Sturk
Father titles:
Father birth place: Canada Eng
Mother name: Viola Sturk
Mother titles:
Mother birth place: Canada Eng
Race or color (expanded): White
Head-of-household name: John Sturk
Gender: Female
Marital status: Single
Years married:
Estimated marriage year:
Mother how many children:
Number living children:
Immigration year:
Enumeration district: 0007
Sheet number and letter: 12B
Household id: 210
Reference number: 92
GSU film number: 1240715
Image number: 00634
Collection: 1900 United States Census

113   iii.   Howard Sturck, born 1913 in Michigan.

Children of Viola King and James McNeal are:
114   i.   Dora V.[5] McNeal, born Abt. 1929 in Michigan.
115   ii.   Russell G. McNeal, born 1914 in Michigan.

58. George Lewis[4] King (Thomas William[3], Lewis[2], James[1]) was born 06 Aug 1879 in Huron, Huron Co. Michigan, and died 15 Feb 1966 in Bad Axe, Michigan. He married **Hattie Kirkpatrick** 23 Apr 1898 in Bad Axe, Huron Co. Michigan. She was born Nov 1879 in Michigan, and died 04 Feb 1937 in Michigan.

Notes for George Lewis King:
Name: George S. King
Birth date: 06 Aug 1879
Birth place: Huron, Huron, Michigan
Gender: Male
Race or color (on document):
Father name: Thomas King
Father birth place: Ontario
Age of father:
Mother name: Ellen King
Mother birth place: Ontario
Film number: 2320569
Digital GS number: 4206545
Image number: 367
Frame number:
Reference number: item 1 p 362 rn 7
Collection: Michigan Births 1867-1902

Groom name: George L King
Groom race or color (on document):
Groom age: 22 years
Groom birth year: 1876
Groom birth place: Michigan
Bride name: Hattie Kirkpatrick
Bride race or color (on document):
Bride age: 18 years
Bride birth year: 1880
Bride birth place: Michigan
Marriage type:
Marriage date: 23 Apr 1898
Marriage place: Bad Axe, Huron, Michigan
Father of groom name: Thos. King
Mother of groom name: Ellen Devill
Father of bride name: Jos. Kirkpatrick
Mother of bride name: Unknown
Marital status:
Groom previous wife name:
Bride marital status:
Bride previous husband name:
Additional relatives:
Film number: 2342509
Frame number:

Digital GS number: 4208258
Image number: 431
Reference number: p 196 rn 68
Collection: Michigan Marriages 1868-1925

Name: Not Named King
Birth date: 29 Nov 1890
Birth place: Carrollton, Saginaw, Michigan
Gender: Female
Race or color (on document):
Father name: George King
Father birth place: Canada
Age of father:
Mother name: Hattie King
Mother birth place: Canada
Mother age:
Christening date:
Christening place:
Additional relatives:
Death date:
Age at death:
Film number: 2321266
Digital GS number: 4207583
Image number: 1257
Frame number:
Reference number: item 3 p 50 rn 748
Collection: Michigan Births 1867-1902

1900 United States Federal Census
Name: George King
Home in 1900: Egleston, Emmet, Michigan
Age: 24
Birth Date: Aug 1879
Birthplace: Michigan
Race: White
Ethnicity: American
Gender: Male
Relationship to head-of-house: Head
Father's Birthplace: Canada Eng
Mother's Birthplace: Canada Eng
Spouse's Name: Hattie
Marriage Year: 1897
Marital Status: Married
Years Married: 3
Residence : Egleston & Center Townships, Emmet, Michigan
Occupation: View on Image
Neighbors: View others on page

Household Members: Name Age
George King 24
Hattie King 20 b Nov 1879 MI parents b Canada
Herbert King 1 son
Dale B Van Every 3   boarder b July 1896 MI

1910 United States Federal Census
Name: George L King
Age in 1910: 31
Estimated Birth Year: abt 1879
Birthplace: Michigan
Relation to Head of House: Head
Father's Birth Place: Canada English
Mother's Birth Place: Canada English
Spouse's Name: Hattie
Home in 1910: Colfax, Huron, Michigan
Marital Status: Married
Race: White
Gender: Male
Neighbors: View others on page
Household Members: Name Age
George L King 31
Hattie King 31
Herbert King 11 son
Nellie King 9 b 1901 MI daughter
Helen King 7 b 1903 MI daughter
Rusel King 5 b 1905 MI son
Velma King 3 b 1908 MI daughter
Dora King 1 b 1909 MI daughter

World War I Draft Registration Cards, 1917-1918
Name: George Lewis King
City: Not Stated [Bad Axe]
County: Huron
State: Michigan
Birth Date: 6 Aug 1879
Race: White
Roll: 1675754
DraftBoard: 0
Res: 3 Bad Axe, Huron MI
 Occ: farming, self employed. Relative Hattie King
Medium height and build, blue eyes brown hair
Sept 11, 1918

1920 United States Federal Census
Name: George L King
Home in 1920: Bingham, Huron, Michigan

Age: 40 years
Estimated Birth Year: abt 1880
Birthplace: Michigan
Relation to Head of House: Head
Spouse's Name: Hattie
Father's Birth Place: Canada
Mother's Birth Place: Canada
Marital Status: Married
Race: White
Sex: Male
Home owned: Rent
Able to read: Yes
Able to Write: Yes
Image: 70
Neighbors: View others on page
Household Members: Name Age
George L King 40
Hattie King 40
Helen King 17
Russell King 14
Velma King 12
Dora King 11
Bertha King 9
George King 7
Vera King 5
Hattie King 2 7/12
James King 4/12

1930 United States Federal Census
about George L King
Name: George L King
Home in 1930: Sheridan, Huron, Michigan
Age: 50
Estimated Birth Year: abt 1880
Birthplace: Michigan
Relation to Head of House: Head
Spouse's Name: Hattie
Race: White
Household Members: Name Age
George L King 50
Hattie King 50
Bertha King 19
George King 17
Vera King 15
Hattie King 12
James King 10
William King 4

Russel King 26

Cass City Chronicle, Feb. 24, 1966
[Funeral] Services Saturday for George King, 87
Funeral services for George L. King, 87, lifelong resident of the Thumb, were held
Saturday in Bad Axe funeral home. Rev. J. Arthur Murfin, pastor of the Baptist Church
m Port Huron,officiated and burial was in Colfax Cemetery.
Mr. King died Tuesday night, Feb. 15, in Huron Community Health Center after a long
illness.
Born Aug. 6, 1878, near Huron City, Mr. King was a farmer for many years. He also
operated a
service station at M-53 and M-81, Cass City. He and Miss Hattie Kirkpatrick were
married April 23, 1898, at
Bad Axe. Mrs. King died Feb. 4, 1937. Two daughters also preceded him in death.
He, is survived by five sons,Herbert King of Lapeer, Russell King of Trenton, George
King Jr.
and James King, both of Cass City,and William King of Port Huron;five daughters, Mrs.
Robert Smithers
of Toledo, Mrs. Stanley Wills of Cass City, Mrs. Robert Etzler of Port Austin, Mrs.
Wilford Wills
of Ubly and Mrs. William Paison of Lapeer, and four generations of grandchildren.

Children of George King and Hattie Kirkpatrick are:
116   i.   Herbert George[5] King, born 24 Jul 1898 in Huron, Huron Co.
                  Michigan; died Bet. 15 Feb 1966 - 31 Dec 1999.

                  Notes for Herbert George King:
                  Name: Herbert King
                  Birth date: 24 Jul 1898
                  Birth place: Huron, Huron, Michigan
                  Gender: Male
                  Race or color (on document):
                  Father name: George King
                  Father birth place: Michigan
                  Age of father:
                  Mother name: Hattie King
                  Mother birth place: Michigan
                  Mother age:
                  Christening date:
                  Christening place:
                  Additional relatives:
                  Death date:
                  Age at death:
                  Film number: 2322864
                  Digital GS number: 4207538

Image number: 1142
Frame number:
Reference number: item 1 rn 432
Collection: Michigan Births 1867-1902

World War I Draft Registration Cards, 1917-1918
about Herbert George King
Name: Herbert George King
City: Not Stated
County: Huron
State: Michigan
Birth Date: 24 Jul 1898
Race: White
Roll: 1675754
DraftBoard: 0
RFD 3, Bad Aze
age 20,clerk at E H Ormby & Co, grey eyes, brown hair, medium
height and build
Father George L. King, same address

117 ii. Nellie King, born 1901 in Michigan; died Bef. 15 Feb 1966. She married unknown Apley.

118 iii. Helen King, born 1903 in Michigan; died Bet. 15 Feb 1966 - 31 Dec 1999. She married Robert Smithers.

119 iv. Rusell King, born 1905 in Michigan; died Bet. 15 Feb 1966 - 01 Dec 1999.

120 v. Velma King, born 1907 in Michigan; died Bet. 15 Feb 1966 - 31 Dec 1999. She married Stanley or Wilford Wills.

121 vi. Dora King, born 1909 in Michigan; died Bet. 15 Feb 1966 - 31 Dec 1999. She married Robert Etzler.

122 vii. Bertha King, born Abt. 1911 in Michigan; died Bet. 15 Feb 1966 - 31 Dec 1999. She married (1) Stanley or Wilford Wills. She married (2) unknown Campbell.

+ 123 viii. George W. King, born 28 Dec 1912 in Huron Co. Michigan; died 31 Dec 1999 in Cass City, Michigan.

124 ix. Vera King, born 1915 in Michigan; died Bet. 15 Feb 1966 - 31 Dec 1999. She married William Paison.

125 x. Hattie King, born 1917 in Michigan; died Bef. 15 Feb 1966. She married unknown Wellock.

126 xi. James King, born 1920 in Michigan; died Bet. 15 Feb 1966 - 01 Dec 1999.

127 xii. William King, born 1926 in Michigan; died Aft. 31 Dec 1999.

66. Thomas William[4] King (David[3], Thomas[2], James[1]) was born 15 Aug 1841 in

Puslinch Tp. Wellington Co. Ontario, and died 24 Apr 1906 in Algoma District. He married **(1) Mary Ann Kemble** 06 Jul 1864 in Guelph, Wellington Co. Ontario, daughter of Jeremiah Kemble and Catherine. She was born Abt. 1844 in England, and died 1869 in Arkell, Puslinch Tp. Wellington Co. Ontario. He married **(2) Mary Ann Ramsey** 07 Dec 1871 in Rockwood, Eramosa Tp, Wellington Co Ontario, daughter of Henry Ramsey and Mary. She was born Abt. 1842 in Ontario, and died Bet. 1882 - 1901. He married **(3) Margaret Burgess** 26 Oct 1904 in Algoma, Ontario, daughter of Samuel Burgess and Nichola Murphy. She was born Abt. 1868 in Huron Co. Ontario.

Notes for Thomas William King:
Name: Mary Kimble
Birth Place: England
Residence: Puslinch Township
Age: 20
Father Name: Jeremiah Kimble
Mother Name: Catherine Kimble
Estimated Birth Year: 1844
Spouse Name: Thomas W. King
Spouse's Age: 22
Spouse Birth Place: Canada
Spouse Residence: Puslinch Township
Spouse Estimated Birth Year: 1842
Spouse Father Name: David King
Spouse Mother Name : Mary King
Marriage Date: 6 Jul 1864
Marriage County: Wellington
Family History Library Microfilm: 1030067
Source: Indexed by: Genealogical Research Library

Thomas King's first wife, Mary Ann Kemble, died in 1869, quite likely in childbirth. Her daughter Mary Ann was born 11 Oct. 1869.

Directory of Wellington County, 1867
1867 Puslinch Tp. Residents
KING
David C 10 L 56 Free
George C 10 L5 Free
Thomas W. C 9 L 7 Householder
BELL
Joseph C 10 L7 Free
Richard C 8 L17 Free

1881   Census Place: Puslinch, Wellington South, Ontario, Canada
    Source: FHL Film 1375894 NAC C-13258 Dist 151 SubDist A Div 1 Page 43
Family 187
    Sex Marr   Age   Origin Birthplace
David KING   M   M   63   English   England

Occ: Gentleman   Religion: C. Methodist
Mary KING   F   M   61   English   England
            Religion: C. Methodist
Thomas H KING   M   M   39   English   Ontario
  Occ: Farmer Religion: C. Methodist
Maryann KING   F   M   39   Irish   Ontario
            Religion: C. Presbyterian
Marion KING F   2   English   Ontario   Religion: C.
Presbyterian

1891 Census of Canada
Name: Thomas King
Gender: Male
Marital Status: Married
Age: 49
Birth Year: abt 1842
Birthplace: Ontario
Relation to Head of House: Head
Religion: Free Church
French Canadian: No
Father's Birth Place: England
Mother's Birth Place: England
Province: Ontario
District Number: 46
District: Algoma
Subdistrict: Port Findlay
Archive Roll #: T-6323
Neighbors: View others on page
Household Members: Name Age
Thomas King 49
Maryann King 49
Marion King 12
Stella King 8
David King 74

Source Information: 1901 Census of Canada
4 23   36 King Thomas M   Head W Sep 15 1841 59
4 24   36 King Estella F   Daughter S Sep 17 1882 18
Subdistrict: Tarbutt, ALGOMA, ONTARIO
District Number: 44
Subdistrict Number: c-1
Archives Microfilm: T-6458

Name: Margaret Burgess
Birth Place: Huron Co
Age: 36
Father Name: Samuel Burgess

Mother Name: Nicholas Murphy
Estimated Birth Year: abt 1868
Spouse Name: Thomas W King
Spouse's Age: 62
Spouse Birth Place: Wellington Co
Spouse Father Name: David King
Spouse Mother Name : Mary Bell
Marriage Date: 26 Oct 1904
Marriage Place: Algoma District
Marriage County: Algoma
Source: Indexed by: Ancestry.com

Children of Thomas King and Mary Kemble are:

128   i.   Catherine[5] King, born 23 Apr 1865 in Arkell, Puslinch Tp. Wellington
             Co. Ontario; died 09 Dec 1870 in Arkell, Puslinch Tp. Wellington Co.
             Ontario.

             Notes for Catherine King:
             Catherine is buried in a double grave with her sister Mary Ann, who
             died just 4 days after Catherine. Both died of diptheria. Their mother,
             Mary Ann, had died in 1869, possibly at the birth of Mary Ann. A
             double headstone marks their graves in the Pioneer Cemetery in
             Arkell, Ontario:

             "Mary Ann d. Dec 13, 1870 age 1 yr, 2 mos, 2 days
             Catherine d. Dec. 9 1870 age 5 yrs, 7 mos, 16 days
             Children of Thomas W. & Mary A. King"

             Deaths shown on 1871 census
             King, Catherine, 5, Wesleyan Methodist d Dec. 9 1870 of diptheria
             King, Mary Ann, 1, Wesleyan Methodist d Dec 13 1870 of diptheria

129   ii.   Mary Ann King, born 11 Oct 1869 in Arkell, Puslinch Tp. Wellington
             Co. Ontario; died 13 Dec 1870 in Arkell, Puslinch Tp. Wellington Co.
             Ontario.

             Notes for Mary Ann King:
             According to Methodist records, Marry Ann was born 13 Oct. 1869
             and baptised 15 Oct. 1869

             Deaths shown on 1871 census
             King, Catherine, 5, Wesleyan Methodist d Dec. 9 1870 of diptheria
             King, Mary Ann, 1, Wesleyan Methodist d Dec 13 1870 of diptheria

Children of Thomas King and Mary Ramsey are:

130   i.   Joseph[5] King, born 24 Dec 1872 in Arkell, Puslinch Tp. Wellington Co. Ontario; died 02 Oct 1873 in Arkell, Puslinch Tp. Wellington Co. Ontario.

               Notes for Joseph King:
               Pioneer Cemetery, Arkell Ontario: "Joseph, son of Thomas W. and Mary A. King, d. Oct 2, 173 aged 11 mos 9 days"

131   ii.   Mary King, born 02 Mar 1876 in Arkell, Puslinch Tp. Wellington Co. Ontario; died 12 Oct 1876 in Arkell, Puslinch Tp. Wellington Co. Ontario.

               Notes for Mary King:
               Pioneer Cemetery, Arkell Ontario:
               "Our darling Mary d. Oct. 12, 1876 age 7 mos, daughter of Thomas W. and Mary A. King. Sleep on my Mary in calm repose, though parted for awhile, To _ _ _ _ _ on _ _ _ will join praise And grace your happy smile"

132   iii.   May King, born 24 Dec 1878 in Plummor Tp. Algoma District.
+ 133   iv.   Marion King, born Abt. 1879.
134   v.   Estella (Stella) King, born 17 Sep 1882 in Algoma District; died 24 Sep 1906 in Algoma District. She married David Henry Quinn 31 Aug 1904 in Algoma District, Ontario; born Abt. 1881 in Kincardine Ontario.

               Notes for Estella (Stella) King:
               Ontario, Canada Marriages, 1857-1924
               about Estella King
               Name: Estella King
               Birth Place: Farbutt
               Age: 21
               Estimated Birth Year: abt 1883
               Father Name: Thomas King
               Mother Name: Mary A Ramsay King
               Spouse Name: David Henry Quinn
               Spouse's Age: 23
               Spouse Estimated Birth Year: abt 1881
               Spouse Birth Place: Kincardine
               Spouse Father Name: John P Quinn
               Spouse Mother Name: Margaret Siddon Quinn
               Marriage Date: 31 Aug 1904
               Marriage Place: Algoma District
               Marriage County: Algoma

Family History Library Microfilm: MS932_113
Source: Indexed by: Ancestry.com

Ontario, Canada Deaths, 1869-1934
Name: Estella Quinn
Death Date: 24 Sep 1906
Death Location: Algoma District
Gender: Female
Estimated Birth Year: abt 1883
Birth Location: On

Notes for David Henry Quinn:
He married again on 15 Dec 1909 in Nipissing District to Alina Mary Hobin

67. David⁴ King (David³, Thomas², James¹) was born 28 Feb 1843 in Arkell, Puslinch Tp. Wellington Co. Ontario, and died 06 Jan 1921 in Waterdown, Wentworth Co. Ontario. He married **Ann Decker** 20 May 1871 in Guelph, Wellington Co. Ontario, daughter of N. Decker and Susan Irons. She was born 09 Feb 1854 in Ontario, and died Aft. 1911.

Notes for David King:
Name: David King
Birth Place: Canada
Age: 27
Father Name: David King
Mother Name: Mary Bell
Estimated Birth Year: abt 1844
Spouse Name: Ann Dicker
Spouse's Age: 19
Spouse Birth Place: Canada
Spouse Father Name: W H Dicker
Spouse Mother Name : Susan Irons Dicker
Marriage Date: 30 May 1871
Marriage Place: Wellington
Marriage County: Wellington
Source: Indexed by: Ancestry.com

1881   Census Place: Puslinch, Wellington South, Ontario, Canada
    Source: FHL Film 1375894 NAC C-13258 Dist 151 SubDist A Div 1 Page 4
Family 14
    Sex Marr   Age   Origin Birthplace
David KING   M   M   37   English   Ontario   Occ: Farmer
    Religion: Church of England

Ann KING   F   M   29   German   Ontario   Religion:
    Church of England
William H. KING   M   7   English   Ontario   Religion:
    Church of England
Susan I. KING F   5   English   Ontario   Religion: Church of
England
Celeste KING   F   3   English   Ontario   Religion: Church of
England
Freeman KING   M   <1   English   Ontario   Religion:
    Church of England   Born: Aug; 9/12
Joseph BELL   M   20   English   Ontario   Occ: Farmer Religion:
    Church of England

1891 census Guelph City, Div 1 p 4 Rell T-6377
King David, 48 b Ontario father and mother b Eng, Church of England, Cattle Dealer
Ann, 39 b ontario father b USA, mother b Eng
William Henry 17 b Ont
Susan ida 15 b Ont\
Celista 13 b Ont
Freeman 10 b Ont
Rachel Ann 8 b Ont
Lydia Maud 6 b Ont
Elmer 8/12 b Ont

1901 census
27 King David M   Head M Feb 28 1843 58
8   27 King Ann F   Wife M Feb 9 1854 47
9   27 King William M   Son S Dec 13 1873 27
10   27 King Susan F   Daughter S Dec 4 1875 25
11   27 King Clestila F   Daughter S Mar 13 1878 23
12   27 King Freeman M   Son S Jul 23 1880 20
13   27 King Rachel F   Daughter S Nov 26 1882 18
14   27 King Maud F   Daughter S Jan 26 1885 16
15   27 King Elmer M   Son S Aug 3 1890 10
16   27 King Merlie F   Daughter S Aug 10 1892 8
17   27 King Clifton M   Son S Nov 12 1894
District: Ontario WENTWORTH (South/Sud) (#128)
Subdistrict: Flamboro (West/Ouest) f-3 Page 3
Details: Schedule 1 Microfilm T-6506

1911 Census of Canada
about David King
Name: David King
Gender: Male
Marital Status: Married
Age: 68

Birth Date: Feb 1843
Birthplace: Ontario
Family Number: 5
Relation to Head of House: Head
Spouse's Name: Ann
Tribal: English
Province: Ontario
District: Wentworth
District Number: 135
Sub-District: Flamborough East
Sub-District Number: 30
Place of Habitation: E Flambro
Census Year: 1911
Page: 1
Household Members: Name Age
David King 68
Ann King 59
Freeman King 30
Sarah E King 23
Elmer A King 20
Merlie King 19
Clifton D King 16
Harold Bevans 20 servant born England Feb. 1891

Children of David King and Ann Decker are:

135   i.   Mary Jane[5] King, born Mar 1872 in Arkell, Puslinch Tp. Wellington
               Co. Ontario; died 30 Aug 1874 in Arkell, Puslinch Tp. Wellington Co.
               Ontario.
136   ii.   William Henry King, born 13 Dec 1873 in Arkell, Puslinch Tp.
               Wellington Co. Ontario; died 26 May 1906 in Puslinch Tp. Wellington
               Co. Ontario. He married x.
137   iii. Susan Ida King, born 04 Dec 1875 in Wellington Co. Ontario.
138   iv.   Sarah G. King, born 1876. She married Marshall Lyons 04 Mar 1903
               in Wentworth Co. Ontario.

               Notes for Sarah G. King:
               Ontario, Canada Marriages, 1857-1924
               about Sarah G King
               Name: Sarah G King
               Birth Place: Canada
               Age: 27
               Estimated Birth Year: abt 1876
               Father Name: Dane King
               Mother Name: Ann Decker
               Spouse Name: Marshall Lyons
               Spouse's Age: 33

Spouse Estimated Birth Year: abt 1870
Spouse Birth Place: Canada
Spouse Father Name: John Lyons
Spouse Mother Name: Elizea Ralsberry
Marriage Date: 4 Mar 1903
Marriage Place: Wentworth
Marriage County: Wentworth
Family History Library Microfilm: MS932_112

139   v.   Celista King, born 13 Mar 1878 in Wellington Co. Ontario.

140   vi. Freeman King, born 23 Jul 1880 in Wellington Co. Ontario; died Aft. 1911. He married Sarah Edna Hood 25 Jan 1910 in Wentworth Co. Ontario; born May 1887 in Ontario.

Notes for Freeman King:
Ontario, Canada Marriages, 1857-1924
Name: Freeman King
Age: 29
Estimated Birth Year: abt 1881
Father Name: David King
Mother Name: Ann Dicker [sic]
Spouse Name: Sarah Edna Hood
Spouse's Age: 22
Spouse Estimated Birth Year: abt 1888
Spouse Father Name: John Hood
Spouse Mother Name: Elizabeth Ellen Hamilton Hood
Marriage Date: 25 Jan 1910
Marriage Place: Wentworth
Marriage County: Wentworth
Family History Library Microfilm: MS932_151

141   vii. Rachel Ann King, born 26 Nov 1882 in Wellington Co. Ontario. She married William John Mann 26 Jan 1909 in Wentworth Co. Ontario; born Abt. 1884.

Notes for Rachel Ann King:
Ontario, Canada Marriages, 1857-1924
about Rachel A King
Name: Rachel A King
Age: 26
Estimated Birth Year: abt 1883
Father Name: David King
Mother Name: Annie Decker

Spouse Name: William John Mann
Spouse's Age: 25
Spouse Estimated Birth Year: abt 1884
Spouse Father Name: Joseph Mann
Spouse Mother Name: Sarah Isles
Marriage Date: 26 Jan 1909
Marriage Place: Wentworth
Marriage County: Wentworth
Family History Library Microfilm: MS932_144

142 viii. Lydia Maud (Maud) King, born 26 Jan 1885 in Wellington Co. Ontario; died Aft. 1909. She married Milton Elwood Rymal 26 Jan 1909 in Wentworth Co. Ontario; born Abt. 1888.

Notes for Lydia Maud (Maud) King:
Ontario, Canada Marriages, 1857-1924
about Lydia Mande King
Name: Lydia Mande King
Age: 24
Estimated Birth Year: abt 1885
Father Name: David King
Mother Name: Annie Decker
Spouse Name: Milton Elwood Rymal
Spouse's Age: 21
Spouse Estimated Birth Year: abt 1888
Spouse Father Name: Charles M Rymal
Spouse Mother Name: Lizzie Dyment Rymal
Marriage Date: 26 Jan 1909
Marriage Place: Wentworth
Marriage County: Wentworth
Family History Library Microfilm: MS932_144

143 ix. Elmer Alvin King, born 03 Aug 1890 in Wellington Co. Ontario; died Aft. 1911. He married Gertrude Marie Markle 17 Sep 1919 in Wentworth Co. Ontario; born Abt. 1898 in West Flamboro.

Notes for Elmer Alvin King:
Ontario, Canada Marriages, 1857-1924
about Elmer Alvin King
Name: Elmer Alvin King
Birth Place: Pushlinch Tp Wellington CO
Age: 29
Estimated Birth Year: abt 1890

Father Name: David King
Mother Name: Anna Decker
Spouse Name: Gertrude Marie Markle
Spouse's Age: 21
Spouse Estimated Birth Year: abt 1898
Spouse Birth Place: West Flamboro
Spouse Father Name: Miles Markle
Spouse Mother Name: Edna Cummins
Marriage Date: 17 Sep 1919
Marriage Place: Wentworth
Marriage County: Wentworth
Family History Library Microfilm: MS932_509

144   x.   Merlie King, born 10 Aug 1892 in Wellington Co. Ontario; died Aft. 1911.

145   xi.   Clifton Dawson King, born 12 Nov 1894 in Arkell, Wellington Co. Ontario; died Aft. 1911. He married Mary Arlotta Featherston 30 Oct 1922 in Wentworth Co. Ontario; born Abt. 1897 in Waterdown Ontario.

Notes for Clifton Dawson King:
Ontario, Canada Marriages, 1857-1924
about Clifton Dawson King
Name: Clifton Dawson King
Birth Place: Arkell Ont
Age: 27
Estimated Birth Year: abt 1895
Father Name: David King
Mother Name: Anne Decker
Spouse Name: Mary Arlotta Featherston
Spouse's Age: 25
Spouse Estimated Birth Year: abt 1897
Spouse Birth Place: Waterdown Ont
Spouse Father Name: Wm Featherston
Spouse Mother Name: Arlotta Edwards
Marriage Date: 30 Oct 1922
Marriage Place: Wentworth
Marriage County: Wentworth
Family History Library Microfilm: MS932_629

69. Harriet[4] King (David[3], Thomas[2], James[1]) was born 19 Aug 1847 in Arkell, Puslinch Tp. Wellington Co. Ontario, and died 19 Jan 1928 in Guelph, Wellington Co.

Ontario. She married **Alexander McGinnis** 06 Sep 1876 in Puslinch Tp. Wellington Co. Ontario, son of Joseph McGinnis and Frances Downey. He was born 03 Nov 1849 in Arkell, Puslinch Tp. Wellington Co. Ontario, and died 1935 in Morriston, Wellington Co. Ontario.

Notes for Harriet King:
Name: Harriet King
Birth Place: Puslinch
Age: 28
Father Name: David King
Mother Name: Mary Bell
Estimated Birth Year: abt 1848
Spouse Name: Aleer McGinnis
Spouse's Age: 22
Spouse Birth Place: Canada
Spouse Father Name: Joseph McGinnis
Spouse Mother Name : Frances Downey
Marriage Date: 6 Sep 1876
Marriage Place: Wellington
Marriage County: Wellington
Source: Indexed by: Ancestry.com

1901 census Guelph, Wellington Co. Ontario E-3 p 7
McGinnis, Harriet, f, white, head, widow [sic], b 12 Aug 1851, age 49, English, Methodist, General Servant
Mary A. dau. b 19 Oct. 1877, 23, weaver
Joseph, son b 21 Dec 1878, 22, carriage maker
Daniel, son, 21 Apr 1881, 19 carriage Maker
Henry, son, 2 Apr 1887, 13
living at 120 Farquhar St.
==========================
Mcginnis/McGinnis, Harriet ……...F Head W S 12 Aug 1851 -49 Ont r English Meth General Servant 4 mos $12 [entry 44 63-68]
Mcginnis/McGinnis, Mary A. F Dau S 19 Oct 1877 -23 Ont r English Meth Weaver 12 mos $144
Mcginnis/McGinnis, Joseph M Son S 21 Dec 1878 -22 Ont r English Meth Carriage Maker 12 mos $300
Mcginnis/McGinnis, Danial M Son S 21 Sept 1881 -19 Ont r English Meth Carriage Maker 12 mos $200
Mcginnis/McGinnis, Henry M Son S 2 apr 1887 13 Ont r English Meth Student

1911 Census of Canada
Name: Harriett Mc Ginnis
Gender: Female
Marital Status: Married
Age: 58
Birth Date: Aug 1852

Birthplace: Ontario
Family Number: 144
Relation to Head of House: Head
Tribal: English
Province: Ontario
District: Wellington South
District Number: 134
Sub-District: Guelph
Sub-District Number: 46
Place of Habitation: 3 Wellington St
Census Year: 1911
Page: 13
Household Members: Name Age
Harriett Mc Ginnis 58 no occ
Henery Mc Ginnis 24 Apr 1887 single, carriage trimmer at carriage shop

Tovell Funeral Homes lists her death as 19 Jan 1928, funeral on 21 Jan 1928 and her age as 85 years 6 months, making her d.o.b. 1843

Tovell Funeral Home Records, Tovell Funeral Home Records, John A. Sherwood, 177 Neeve St, Guelph d 19 Jan, 1928, 177 Neeve St. age 85 years, 5 months.

Notes for Alexander McGinnis:
From Jan 1863 to March 1871, Alexander, Margaret, Annie and Daniel McGinnis are on a list of pupils at SS # 12, Puslinch

1881 Census Guelph Ontario p 23:
McINNES:
Alexander, 30, Irish, Catholic, b. Ontario, Labourer
Harriet, 34, Methodist,
MaryAnn, 4
Joseph, 3
Fanny Sept. 1880 birth

Census Place: Puslinch, Wellington South, Ontario, Canada
    Source: FHL Film 1375894 NAC C-13258 Dist 151 SubDist A Div 1 Page 23
Family 98
    Sex Marr   Age   Origin Birthplace
Alexander MCINNES M M   30   Irish   Ontario   Occ: Labourer
    Religion: Catholic
Harriet MCINNES   F M   34   English   Ontario   Religion: C.
Methodist
Maryann MCINNES F   4   Irish   Ontario Religion: C. Methodist

Joseph MCINNES   M   3   Irish   Ontario   Religion: C. Methodist
Fanny MCINNES   F <1   Irish   Ontario   Religion: C. Methodist   Born:
    Sep; 6/12

1891 census Puslinch Tp. Wellington Co.:
p. 28 W 1/3 141 line 19

McGINNIS:
Alexander, 41 b. Ont, father and mother b Ont., [sic] Roman Catholic
Harriet, 44, Methodist
MaryAnn, 14 Methodist
Fanny, 11 Methodist
Daniel 7 Methodist
Henry 4 Methodist

1901 Census see his mother and sister

1911 census Morriston, Puslinch Tp page 15 District 134 Wellington Subdistrict 23
Brown, Solomon, head, Badenoch St, single, Oct 1856, 54 yrs b On, German, Methodist
Brown, Bernard, brother May 1862, 49, hotel keeper
Brown, Mary, sister in law, June 1862, 49 b Ontario, catholic
McGinnis [no first name but it is Alexander], head, Badenoch St, [no month] 1848, 62
yrs, b On, Irish, Catholic, labourer

1915: Alex McGinnis, living Morriston, Puslinch Tp., farmer, Conc B, Lot 29

Buried Crown Cemetery, East side of Highway on Lot 28 front Conc 8, a half mile from
Morriston, Wellington Co. Ontario

Children of Harriet King and Alexander McGinnis are:
    146   i.   Mary Ann[5] McGinnis, born 19 Oct 1876 in Arkell, Puslinch Tp
                   Wellington Co. Ontario; died 26 Jul 1966 in Guelph, Wellington Co.
                   Ontario. She married John Alfred (Jack) Sheward 16 Apr 1906 in
                   Guelph, Wellington Co. Ontario; born 26 Jan 1874 in Kidderminster,
                   Worcestershire, England; died 19 May 1955 in Guelph, Wellington
                   Co. Ontario.

                   Notes for Mary Ann McGinnis:
                   Name: Mary Ann McGinis
                   Birth Place: Township of Guelph
                   Age: 29
                   Father Name: Alce McGinis
                   Mother Name: Harriet King
                   Estimated Birth Year: abt 1877
                   Spouse Name: John Alfred Steward
                   Spouse's Age: 32
                   Spouse Birth Place: Kiddermerter Eng

Spouse Father Name: Edwin Sheward
Spouse Mother Name : Emma Kilchen
Marriage Date: 16 Apr 1906
Marriage Place: Wellington
Marriage County: Wellington
Source: Indexed by: Ancestry.com

Mary married John Alfred SHEWARD, son of Edwin SHEWARD and Emma KITCHEN, on 16 Apr 1906 in Guelph, Ontario, Canada 1. (John Alfred SHEWARD was born on 26 Jan 1874 in Kidderminster, Worcester Co, England and died on 19 May 1955 in Guelph, Ontario, Canada 5 6.)

1910 Census Place: Freehold, Monmouth, New Jersey; Series: T624; Roll: 900; Page: 71B; Enumeration District: 70; Part: 2; Line: 38.
McNINNIE, Frank, head
SHEWARD, John A, 35 b England, boarder imm 1890, naturalized, weaver in carpet mill
Mary, b Canada, 24 boarder md 4 years, no children, imm 1910
Edwin, 49 b England boarder md 25 years, 3 children, none living, imm 1904, weaver in carpet mill
Nellie, b England 45 boarder, imm 1904
Harold b England 13 boarder, imm 1904 (he is found as Harold G. Sheward, living in Amsterdam, Montgomery Co. New York in the 1930 census with wife Edith J. and 3 children. He says he immigrated in 1912, is not naturalized and is a cutter in a silk mill. He is also found in WW1 Draft Registrations for USA as Harold George Sheward)

Name: Harold George Sheward
City: Amsterdam
County: Montgomery
State: New York
Birthplace: England
Birth Date: 21 Apr 1897
Roll: 1711956
DraftBoard: 0
He gives his next of kin as Mrs. Ella Sherwood of Amsterdam New York

1920 United States Federal Census > New York > Montgomery Co > Amsterdam Twp> District 81
SHEWARD, John A. b England, 46 imm 1886, Naturalized, Weaver in Carpet Mill
Mary Ann b Canada, 43, imm. 1904, Naturalized

Lorine McGinnis Schulze aka Massey has pictures of "Aunt Mary and Uncle Jack" She remembers going to visit them in Guelph with her father when she was a little girl. She was always afraid of them, as they had no children of their own and weren't overly friendly towards her. They seemed very dour to her.

Sources sent to Lorine McGinnis Schulze

1 Ontario Vital Statistics, Marriage certificate for John Alfred Sheward and Mary Ann McGinnis, (Repository: Family History Center, Kitchener, Ontario, Canada).

2 Ontario Vital Statistics, Death record for William Thomas Holyman, (Repository: Family History Center, Kitchener, Ontario, Canada). 202298.

3 Woodlawn Cemetery, Woodlawn Cemetery burial records, (Repository: Woodlawn Cemetery, Guelph, Ontario, Canada). Mary Ann McGinnis Sheward.

4 ? Funeral Home, Burial Record for Mary Ann McGinnis, (Repository: Guelph, Ontario, Canada).

5 Woodlawn Cemetery, Tombstone for John Alfred Sheward, (Repository: Woodlawn Cemetery, Guelph, Ontario, Canada).

6 Woodlawn Cemetery, Woodlawn Cemetery burial records, (Repository: Woodlawn Cemetery, Guelph, Ontario, Canada). John Alfred Sheward.

Notes for John Alfred (Jack) Sheward:
1. Residence; 1881; Kidderminster, Worcester Co, England. 4
Edward SHEWARD   Head   45   Kidder, Worcester, England
Worsted Carpet Weaver
Emma SHEWARD   Wife   44   Bewdley Forest, Worcester, England
Herbert SHEWARD   Son 16   Kidderr, Worcester, England   Worsted
Creeler
Laura Edith SHEWARD   19   Kidderr, Worcester, England
Worsted Winder
Ann Sarah SHEWARD   11   Kidderr, Worcester, England   Scholar
Alfred John SHEWARD   7   Kidderr, Worcester, England   Scholar
Charles Arthur SHEWARD   4   Kidderr, Worcester, England
Scholar Albert George SHEWARD   14   Kidderr, Worcester,
England   Designers Apprentice
Emma SHEWARD   18   Kidderr, Worcester, England   Worsted
Winder

Edwin SHEWARD   20   Bham, Warwick, England   Creeler

Source Information:
  Dwelling   55 Hoo Road
  Census Place Kidderminster Foreign, Worcester, England
  Family History Library Film   1341696
  Public Records Office Reference   RG11
  Piece / Folio   2902 / 144
  Page Number   46

World War I Draft Registration Cards, 1917-1918
Name: John Alfred Sheward
County: Montgomery
State: New York
Birth Date: 24 Dec 1873
Race: White
Roll: 1753846
DraftBoard: 0
John signed up on 12 Sept. 1915. His wife is Mary Ann Sheward of
Amsterdam New York. He is a carpet weaver working for
Hudderswood? Carpets in Amsterdam New York

From Ann Winder Sheward, 2001:
2. Arrived in America; 1886; Philadelphia, Philadelphia Co, PA. 5
Aboard The Ship "Lord Gough" From Liverpool. Lorine's Note: See
his father Edwin for dates and details.

3. Residence; 1899; Philadelphia, Philadelphia Co, PA. 6

4. Residence; Between 1903-1909; Guelph, Wellington Co, Ontario,
Canada. 7 8

5. Residence; Between 1912-1914; Peterborough, Ontario, Canada. 9
10

6. Residence; 1919; NJ. 11

7. Residence; Between 1921-1955; Guelph, Wellington Co, Ontario,
Canada. 12

8. Occupation; Carpet Weaver.

1 Ontario Vital Statistics, Marriage certificate for John Alfred
Sheward and Mary Ann McGinnis, (Repository: Family History
Center, Kitchener, Ontario, Canada).

2 Woodlawn Cemetery, Tombstone for John Alfred Sheward, (Repository: Woodlawn Cemetery, Guelph, Ontario, Canada).

3 Woodlawn Cemetery, Woodlawn Cemetery burial records, (Repository: Woodlawn Cemetery, Guelph, Ontario, Canada), John Alfred Sheward.

4 1881 British Census, Kidderminster, Worcester Co, England, (Repository: Family History Center, Salt Lake City, UT), Pg 46, schedule 215, 55 Hoo Road.

5 Philadelphia, PA, Passenger Lists for Philadelphia, (Repository: National Archives, Philadelpha, PA), 1886.

6 Philadelphia, PA, Philadelphia City Directories, (Repository: Pennsylvania Historical Library, Philadelphia, PA), 1899.

7 Guelph, Ontario, Canada, Guelph City Directories, (Repository: Guelph Public Library, Guelph, Ontario, Canada), 1903-1905.

8 Ibid, 1908-1909.

9 Peterborough, Ontario, Canada, Peterborough City Directories, (Repository: Peterborough Public Library, Peterborough, Ontario, Canada), 1912.

10 Ibid, 1913-1914.

11 Marjorie Briggs Bertolet, Marjorie Briggs Bertolet, (September, 1997). Margaret Briggs and Edwin Sheward spent their honeymoon at the home of Jack and Mary Ann Sheward somewhere in NJ.

12 Guelph, Ontario, Canada, Guelph City Directories, (Repository: Guelph Public Library, Guelph, Ontario, Canada), 1921.

13 Ontario Vital Statistics, Death record for William Thomas Holyman, (Repository: Family History Center, Kitchener, Ontario, Canada), 202298.

14 Woodlawn Cemetery, Woodlawn Cemetery burial records, (Repository: Woodlawn Cemetery, Guelph, Ontario, Canada), Mary Ann McGinnis Sheward.

15 ? Funeral Home, Burial Record for Mary Ann McGinnis, (Repository: Guelph, Ontario, Canada).

+   147   ii.   Joseph McGinnis, born 21 Dec 1877 in Arkell, Puslinch Tp.

Wellington Co. Ontario; died 08 Jan 1937 in Guelph, Wellington Co. Ontario.

+ 148 iii. Fanny McGinnis, born Sep 1880 in Arkell, Puslinch Tp Wellington Co. Ontario; died Aft. 1902.

+ 149 iv. Dan McGinnis, born 21 Nov 1880 in Arkell, Puslinch Tp Wellington Co. Ontario; died Aug 1937 in Sault Ste. Marie, Ontario.

+ 150 v. Henry McGinnis, born 02 Apr 1887 in Guelph, Wellington Co. Ontario; died Aug 1968 in Guelph, Wellington Co. Ontario.

70. John (David John?)[4] King (David[3], Thomas[2], James[1]) was born Abt. 1852 in Puslinch Tp Wellington Co. Ontario, and died Bet. 1897 - 1930. He married **Susanna Fife** 20 Jan 1874 in Wellington Co. Ontario, daughter of John Fife and Eliza Pallister. She was born 13 Oct 1854 in Guelph Ontario, and died 10 Mar 1930 in Toronto, Ontario.

Notes for John (David John?) King:
Name: Susanna Fife
Birth Place: Guelph
Age: 23
Father Name: John Fife
Mother Name: Eliza Pallister
Estimated Birth Year: abt 1851
Spouse Name: John King
Spouse's Age: 23
Spouse Birth Place: Puslinch
Spouse Father Name: David King
Spouse Mother Name : Mary Bell
Marriage Date: 20 Jan 1874
Marriage Place: Wellington
Marriage County: Wellington
Source: Indexed by: Ancestry.com

1881 Census
Name Marital Status Gender Ethnic Origin Age Birthplace Occupation Religion
John KING M Male English 28 Ontario Farmer Presbyterian
Susannah KING M Female Scottish 28 Ontario   Presbyterian
Mary C. KING   Female English 6 Ontario   Presbyterian
Eliza J. KING   Female English 4 Ontario   Presbyterian
Berthie F. KING   Female English 1 Ontario   Presbyterian
Source Information: Census Place Peel, Wellington Centre, Ontario
  Family History Library Film 1375895
  NA Film Number C-13259
  District 152
  Sub-district E
  Division 3
  Page Number 44
  Household Number 200

1891 Census of Canada
Name: Susannah King
Gender: Female
Marital Status: Married
Age: 37
Birth Year: abt 1854
Birthplace: Ontario
Relation to Head of House: Wife
Religion: Church of England
French Canadian: No
Father's Birth Place: Scotland
Mother's Birth Place: England
Province: Ontario
District Number: 126
District: Wellington North
Subdistrict: Arthur Village
Archive Roll #: T-6376
Household Members: Name Age
John King 37
Susannah King 37
Berthan T King 11
Anna M King 4

Is this John?
9 46 98 King John M   Head M Dec 15 1852 48
9 47 98 King Hattie F   Wife M Jan 21 1856 44
9 48 98 King Arthur M   Son S Mar 7 1881 19
10 1 98 King Harry M   Son S Apr 2 1879 21
Source Information: 1901 Census of Canada
Subdistrict: Sault Ste. Marie, ALGOMA, ONTARIO
District Number: 44
Subdistrict Number: a(1)-2
Archives Microfilm: T-6458

Notes for Susanna Fife:
1901 Census Amaranth, WELLINGTON (North/Nord), ONTARIO
6 30   59 Fyfe Robert M   Head M Apr 24 1887 24
6 31   59 King Susan F   Sister M Oct 1 1855 46 married
6 32   59 King M. Hanah F   Niece S Apr 21 1888 13
6 33   59 King William M   Nephew S Jun 10 1890 9
6 34   59 King Lily F   Niece S Mar   1898 4
District Number: 125 Subdistrict Number: a-2 Archives Microfilm: T-6504

Name : Susan King

Death date : 10 Mar 1930
Age at death : 76 years
Death place : Toronto, York, Ontario, Canada
Birth place : Guelph Twp
Gender : Female
Marital status : Widowed
Race (Term on Certificate) : English
Race : White
Ethnicity : English
Father name : John Fife
Mother name : Eliza Pallister
GSU film number : 2313239
Digital GS number : 4000632
Image number : 00223
Certificate number : 2686
Collection : Ontario Deaths 1869-1947

Children of John King and Susanna Fife are:

| 151 | i. | Mary Christina⁵ King, born 11 Dec 1874 in Eramosa Tp, Wellington Co. Ontario. |

Children of John King and Susanna Fife are:
- 151   i.   Mary Christina⁵ King, born 11 Dec 1874 in Eramosa Tp, Wellington Co. Ontario.
- 152   ii.   Eliza J. King, born Abt. 1877.
- 153   iii.   Bertha Heff King, born 11 Jan 1880 in Drayton, Wellington Co. Ontario. She married John J W Hayward 11 Feb 1914 in York Co. Ontario; born Abt. 1893 in England.

         Notes for Bertha Heff King:
         Ontario, Canada Marriages, 1857-1922
         Name: Berthe King
         Birth Place: Peel CO Ont
         Age: 31
         Father Name: John King
         Mother Name: Susan File
         Estimated birth year: abt 1883
         Spouse Name: John J W Hayward
         Spouse's Age: 21
         Spouse Birth Place: England
         Spouse Father Name: James Hayward
         Spouse Mother Name : Kate Lomax
         Marriage Date: 11 Feb 1914
         Marriage Place: York
         Marriage County: York
         Source: Indexed by: Ancestry.com

- 154   iv.   David John King, born 26 May 1885 in Petherton, Arthur Tp,

Wellington Co. Ontario.

155   v.   Annie (Hannah) May King, born 26 May 1887 in Arthur Village, Wellington Co. Ontario; died Aft. 1901. She married Thomas J Rodgers 23 Dec 1914 in Wellington Co. Ontario.

Notes for Annie (Hannah) May King:
Ontario, Canada Marriages, 1857-1924
about Hanna May King
Name: Hanna May King
Age: 27
Estimated Birth Year: abt 1887
Father Name: John King
Mother Name: Susan Fyfe
Spouse Name: Thomas J Rodgers
Spouse's Age: 27
Spouse Estimated Birth Year: abt 1887
Spouse Father Name: James Rodgers
Spouse Mother Name: Margaret Kirk
Marriage Date: 23 Dec 1914
Marriage Place: Wellington
Marriage County: Wellington
Family History Library Microfilm: MS932_324

156   vi.   William Robert King, born 19 Jun 1891 in Arthur Village, Wellington Co. Ontario; died Aft. 1901.

157   vii.   Lillian Ivean King, born 02 Mar 1898 in Amaranth, Wellington Co. Ontario; died Aft. 1950. She married Frank James Edwin Quance 02 Jun 1920 in York Co. Ontario; born Abt. 1893 in Barrie, Simcoe Co. Ontario.

Notes for Lillian Ivean King:
1901 Census of Canada
about Lily King
Name: Lily King
Gender: Female
Marital Status: Single
Age: 4
Birth Date: !! Mar 1898
Birthplace: Ontario
Relation to Head of House: Niece
Racial or Tribal Origin: Scottish (Scotish)
Nationality: Canadian
Province: Ontario
District: Wellington (North/Nord)
District Number: 125

Sub-District: Amaranth
Sub-District Number: A-2
Family Number: 59
Page: 6
Neighbors: View others on page
Household Members: Name Age
Robert Fife, head,
Susan King Oct 1855, 46 married
M Hannah King 21 Apr 18xx, 13 niece
William King 10 June 18xx, 9 nephew
Lily King March 1898, 4 niece

Ontario, Canada Marriages, 1857-1922
about Frank James Edwin Quance
Name: Frank James Edwin Quance
Birth Place: Barrie Ontario
Age: 27
Father Name: George Quance
Mother Name: Ette Eliza Tracey Quance
Estimated birth year: abt 1893
Spouse Name: Lillian Ivean King
Spouse's Age: 22
Spouse Birth Place: Palmerston Ont
Spouse Father Name: John King
Spouse Mother Name : Susan Fife
Marriage Date: 2 Jun 1920
Marriage Place: York
Marriage County: York
Source: Indexed by: Ancestry.com

71. Joseph[4] King (David[3], Thomas[2], James[1]) was born 15 Nov 1851 in Ontario, and died 09 Mar 1922 in Johnson, Algoma District. He married **Margaret Hatten**, daughter of Thomas Hatten and unknown. She was born 05 Jul 1857 in Ontario, and died 1906.

Notes for Joseph King:
1881   Census Place: Puslinch, Wellington South, Ontario, Canada
     Source: FHL Film 1375894 NAC C-13258 Dist 151 SubDist A Div 1 Page 3
Family 12
     Sex Marr   Age   Origin Birthplace
Joseph KING M   M   29   English   Ontario
     Occ: Farmer Religion: Weslyan Methodist
Margret KING F   M   24   English   Ontario
                Religion: Weslyan Methodist

2 40   19 King Joseph M   Head M Nov 15 1851 49
2 41   19 King Margaret F   Wife M Jul 5 1857 43
2 42   19 King Norman M   Son S May 16 1881 19
2 43   19 King Lorne M   Son S Oct 13 1892 18
2 44   19 King Thomas B M   Son S Aug 25 1885 15
2 45   19 King Mary A F   Daughter S Apr 9 1887 14
2 46   19 King Violet B F   Daughter S Aug 21 1892 8
2 47   19 King Minnie T F   Daughter S Apr 18 1896 4
2 48   19 Hatten Thomas F   father-in-law W Sep 24 1820 80
2 49   19 Hatten George M   Lodger S Jan 29 1855 46

Source Information: 1901 Census of Canada
Subdistrict: Desert Lake, ALGOMA, ONTARIO
District Number: 44
Subdistrict Number: h
Archives Microfilm: T-6457

Children of Joseph King and Margaret Hatten are:
158   i.   Norman⁵ King, born 16 May 1881 in Arkell Wellington Co. Ontario;
                died 1966 in Algoma District. He married Eliza Eakatt 24 Mar 1909 in
                Algoma Ontario; born 17 Sep 1886 in Guelph, Wellington Co.
                Ontario.

                Notes for Norman King:
                Ontario, Canada Marriages, 1857-1922
                Name: Norman King
                Age: 27
                Father Name: Joseph King
                Mother Name: Margaret Hatton
                Estimated birth year: abt 1882
                Spouse Name: Eliza Eakatt
                Spouse's Age: 22
                Spouse Father Name: Robert Eakatt
                Spouse Mother Name : Ellen Groom
                Marriage Date: 24 Mar 1909
                Marriage Place: Algoma District
                Marriage County: Algoma
                Source: Indexed by: Ancestry.com

                From: "Mrs Nickle" <nickle@netidea.com>
                Subject: Re: [OXF] Ewelme Parish Records
                Date: Sun, 29 Feb 2004 19:17:17 -0800

                Hi Andy,

My g'father, was a KING. Norman KING 16 may 1881 (Arkell, Puslinch twp., Wellington county,Ontario, Canada) -- 1966 (Bruce Mines, Algoma dist, Ontario)
His g'father, David KING, believed b. 10 Nov 1817 somewhere in England. He
died 24 Apr. 1907 in Ontario (possibly Wellington co.).

Does this ring any bells with your KINGs? I'd like to find his birth place
& family in England. Believe he was a young man when he came over as he
married in Ontario.

tia,
Margaret
British Columbia, Canada

159   ii.   Thomas Bertram King, born 25 Aug 1885 in Algoma District, Ontario. He married Olive Mary Dempster 18 Feb 1914 in Algoma District, Ontario; born Abt. 1891.

                Notes for Thomas Bertram King:
                Ontario, Canada Marriages, 1857-1924
                Name: Thos Bertram King
                Age: 28
                Estimated Birth Year: abt 1886
                Father Name: Joseph King
                Mother Name: Margaret Hatten
                Spouse Name: Olive Mary Dempster
                Spouse's Age: 23
                Spouse Estimated Birth Year: abt 1891
                Spouse Father Name: Alex Dempster
                Spouse Mother Name: Mary Jane Richardson Dempster
                Marriage Date: 18 Feb 1914
                Marriage Place: Algoma District
                Marriage County: Algoma
                Family History Library Microfilm: MS932_301

160   iii.   Mary Ann King, born 09 Apr 1887 in Algoma District Ontario. She married William John McLeod 1912 in Algoma Ontario.

                Notes for Mary Ann King:
                Name: Mary Ann King

Age: 25
Father Name: Joseph King
Mother Name: Margaret Hatton
Estimated birth year: abt 1887
Spouse Name: William John McLeod
Spouse's Age: 32
Spouse Father Name: John J McLeod
Spouse Mother Name : Annie McLeod
Marriage Date: 4 Sep 1912
Marriage Place: Algoma District
Marriage County: Algoma
Source: Indexed by: Ancestry.com

161   iv.   Violet Vera King, born 21 Aug 1892 in Algoma District, Ontario.
162   v.   Lorne King, born 13 Oct 1892 in Arkell Wellington Co. Ontario. He
             married (1) Mary Elizabeth Agnes Linklater 28 Oct 1914 in Algoma
             District, Ontario; born Abt. 1896 in Green Lake Ontario. He married
             (2) Maud Robertson 16 Jun 1920 in Algoma District, Ontario.

             Notes for Lorne King:
             Ontario, Canada Marriages, 1857-1924
             Name: Lorn King
             Birth Place: Arkell Ont
             Age: 31
             Estimated Birth Year: abt 1883
             Father Name: Joseph King
             Mother Name: Maggie Hatten
             Spouse Name: Mary Elizabeth Agnes Linklater
             Spouse's Age: 18
             Spouse Estimated Birth Year: abt 1896
             Spouse Birth Place: Green Lake Ont
             Spouse Father Name: George Linklater
             Spouse Mother Name: Mary ??AR??S
             Marriage Date: 28 Oct 1914
             Marriage Place: Algoma District
             Marriage County: Algoma
             Family History Library Microfilm: MS932_301

             Ontario, Canada Marriages, 1857-1924
             about Lorne King
             Name: Lorne King
             Birth Place: Guelph Ontario
             Age: 37
             Estimated Birth Year: abt 1883
             Father Name: Joseph King
             Mother Name: Margaret Hatten

Spouse Name: Maud Robertson
Spouse's Age: 29
Spouse Estimated Birth Year: abt 1891
Spouse Birth Place: Toronto Ontario
Spouse Father Name: James Robertson
Spouse Mother Name: Mary Eaket
Marriage Date: 16 Jun 1920
Marriage Place: Algoma District
Marriage County: Algoma
Family History Library Microfilm: MS932_525

163   vi.   Minnie Taverna Lawrence King, born 18 Apr 1896 in Desbarats, Johnson Tp, Algoma District, Ontario; died 03 Nov 1965 in Sault Ste Marie, Algoma, Ontario. She married George Bye 27 Jun 1917 in Echo Bay, Algoma District, Ontario; born 09 Nov 1896 in Inglewood Ontario.

Notes for Minnie Taverna Lawrence King:
Ontario, Canada Marriages, 1857-1924
about Minnie Lawrence King
Name: Minnie Lawrence King
Birth Place: Desbarats Ont
Age: 21
Estimated Birth Year: abt 1896
Father Name: Joseph King
Mother Name: Margaret Hatten
Spouse Name: George Bye
Spouse's Age: 20
Spouse Estimated Birth Year: abt 1897
Spouse Birth Place: Inglewood Ont
Spouse Father Name: Francis Clay Bye
Spouse Mother Name: Fannie Eakett Bye
Marriage Date: 27 Jun 1917
Marriage Place: Algoma District
Marriage County: Algoma
Family History Library Microfilm: MS932_413

According to the online family tree, Minne and George had 5 children. George married for a second time. No first names are provided (ktaylor6@cogeco.ca)

72. George⁴ King (David³, Thomas², James¹) was born 31 Aug 1855 in Ontario, and died Aft. 05 Nov 1913 in Blind River, Algoma?. He married **Eliza Jane Robinson** 03 Jul 1878 in Wellington Co. Ontario, daughter of Edward Robinson and Mary Flewellyn. She was born 17 Jan 1853 in Puslinch Tp, Wellington Co. Ontario, and died 04 Nov 1913 in Blind River, Algoma Ontario.

Notes for George King:
Name: Eliza Jane Robbinson
Birth Place: Puslinch
Age: 24
Father Name: Edward Robbinson
Mother Name: Mary Flewellyn
Estimated Birth Year: abt 1854
Spouse Name: George King
Spouse's Age: 22
Spouse Birth Place: Puslinch
Spouse Father Name: David King
Spouse Mother Name : Mary Bell
Marriage Date: 3 Jul 1878
Marriage Place: Wellington
Marriage County: Wellington
Source: Indexed by: Ancestry.com

1881 Census Place: Puslinch, Wellington South, Ontario, Canada
     Source: FHL Film 1375894 NAC C-13258 Dist 151 SubDist A Div 1 Page 27
Family 112

Sex	Marr	Age	Origin	Birthplace
George KING M	M	25	English	Ontario
Occ:	Farmer	Religion:	C. Methodist	
Elisa J. KING F	M	27	English	Ontario
	Religion:	C. Methodist		
George E. KING M		1	English	Ontario
	Religion:	C. Methodist		

1901 Census of Canada
Name: George King
Gender: Male
Marital Status: Married
Age: 45
Birth Date: 31 Aug 1855
Birthplace: Ontario
Relation to Head of House: Head
Spouse's Name: Liza H
Racial or Tribal Origin: English
Nationality: Canadian
Religion: Methodist
Occupation: Night Watch Man
Province: Ontario
District: Nipissing
District Number: 92
Sub-District: Cooks Mills

Sub-District Number: R-1
Family Number: 22
Page: 3
Neighbors: View others on page
Household Members: Name Age
George King 45
Liza H [J] King 48
William King 16
Rubby King 9

George was in Rainy River by 1922

Children of George King and Eliza Robinson are:

+ 164   i.   George Edward[5] King, born 13 Sep 1879 in Wellington Co. Ontario; died 14 Oct 1912 in Algoma District Ontario.

   165   ii.   William David Freeman King, born 01 Mar 1885 in Wellington Co. Ontario. He married Florence Adelia Cook 03 Oct 1916 in Algoma Ontario.

         Notes for William David Freeman King:
         Name: Wm David Freeman King
         Birth Place: Guelph
         Age: 31
         Father Name: George King
         Mother Name: E Robbison
         Estimated birth year: abt 1885
         Spouse Name: Florence Adelia Cook
         Spouse's Age: 29
         Spouse Birth Place: Dean Lake
         Spouse Father Name: James Cook
         Spouse Mother Name : Annie Everett
         Marriage Date: 3 Oct 1916
         Marriage Place: Algoma District
         Marriage County: Algoma
         Source: Indexed by: Ancestry.com

   166   iii.   Mary Pearl Everetta King, born 30 Mar 1887 in Wellington Co. Ontario; died Bef. 1901.

   167   iv.   Ruby King, born 06 Mar 1892 in Wellington Co. Ontario. She married W G Stimpson 1916 in Algoma Ontario.

         Notes for Ruby King:
         Name: Ruby King

Birth Place: Guelph Ontario
Age: 23
Father Name: George King
Mother Name: Eliza Jane Robinson King
Estimated birth year: abt 1893
Spouse Name: W G Stimpson
Spouse's Age: 32
Spouse Birth Place: London England
Spouse Father Name: Wm Geo Stimpson
Spouse Mother Name : Mary Jane Degnerd Stimpson
Marriage Date: 29 Aug 1916
Marriage Place: Algoma District
Marriage County: Algoma
Source: Indexed by: Ancestry.com

Generation No. 5

92. Henry George (Harry)[5] King (James Parker[4], George A.[3], Lewis[2], James[1]) was born 10 Feb 1888 in Wellington Co. Ontario, and died Aft. 1916. He married **Thelma**. She was born Abt. 1893 in Ontario.

Child of Henry King and Thelma is:

    168   i.   Thelma[6] King, born Abt. 1912 in British Columbia.

123. George W.[5] King (George Lewis[4], Thomas William[3], Lewis[2], James[1]) was born 28 Dec 1912 in Huron Co. Michigan, and died 31 Dec 1999 in Cass City, Michigan. He married **Elsie May Jackson** 19 Sep 1932 in Huron Co. Michigan. She died 17 May 1997.

Notes for George W. King:
Cass City Chronicle, Wed. Jan 5, 2000 page 9. OBITUARY
George W. King Sr., 87, of Cass City, died Friday, Dec. 3 1, 1999, in his home.
He was born Dec. 28, 1912,in Huron County, to GeorgeL. and Hattie (Kirkpatrick)
King and lived in the area hiswhole life. He married ElsieMay Jackson Sept. 19, 1932,
in Huron County. She diedMay 17, 1997.He farmed most of his life.He is survived by his children,
George W. (Phyllis)King Jr. of Cass City, BctteLou (Calvin) Hunt of Ubly,Glen L. (Janet) King of Auburn,
Jerry (Bev) King ofBridgeport, James L. King ofCass City; 15 grandchildren;3 1 great-grandchildren; a
brother, William King of Lexington, and many nieces and nephews.
He was preceded in death by 3 brothers, Herbert,Russell and James; 7 sisters,Helen Smithers, Nellie
Apley, Hattie Wellock,Velma Wills, Dora Etzler,Bertha Wills Campbell, andVera Paison.
Funeral services were heldSunday in Kranz FuneralHome, Cass City, withChuck

Emmert of Novesta

Church of Christ officiating.Interment was in ElklandTownship Cemetery, CassCity.
Memorials may be made tothe Family DiscretionaryFund.

Children of George King and Elsie Jackson are:

169	i.	George W.[6] King.
170	ii.	Bette Lou King.
171	iii.	Glen L. King.
172	iv.	Jerry King.
173	v.	James L. King.

133. Marion[5] King (Thomas William[4], David[3], Thomas[2], James[1]) was born Abt. 1879.
She married **William McArthur** 27 Mar 1901 in Algoma Ontario, son of Neil McArthur
and Margaret McLeod. He was born Abt. 1874.

Notes for Marion King:
Ontario, Canada Marriages, 1857-1924
Name: Marion King
Age: 22
Estimated Birth Year: abt 1879
Father Name: Thos King
Mother Name: Mary Ann Ramsay King
Spouse Name: Wm McArthur
Spouse's Age: 27
Spouse Estimated Birth Year: abt 1874
Spouse Father Name: Neil McArthur
Spouse Mother Name: Margaret McLeod
Marriage Date: 27 Mar 1901
Marriage Place: Algoma District
Marriage County: Algoma
Family History Library Microfilm: MS932_103

Warren Mcarthur 5 Sep 1903 Male Algoma Wm McArthur Marion King

Child of Marion King and William McArthur is:
    174   i.   Warren[6] McArthur, born 05 Sep 1903 in Algoma, Ontario.

147. Joseph[5] McGinnis (Harriet[4] King, David[3], Thomas[2], James[1]) was born 21 Dec
1877 in Arkell, Puslinch Tp. Wellington Co. Ontario, and died 08 Jan 1937 in Guelph,
Wellington Co. Ontario. He married **Olive Lohilda Peer** 02 Sep 1905 in Guelph,
Wellington Co. Ontario, daughter of Stephen Peer and Mary Vollick. She was born 15
Jun 1880 in Kilbride, Nelson Tp. Halton Co. Ontario, and died 25 May 1961 in Guelph,
Wellington Co. Ontario.

Notes for Joseph McGinnis:
1891 census Puslinch Tp. Wellington Co:

McGinnis, Joseph, 13, b. Ont, father and mother b On. Methodist, farm labourer, could read but not write. Working on Carter farm

4 Sept. 1905:

Groom Joseph McGinnis, 28, residence Guelph, born Arkel, bachelor. Occupation Labourer. Parents Alex McGinnis and Harriet King
Bride Olive Peer, 26, residence Guelph, born Kilbride, spinster. Parents Stephen Peer and Mary Vollick.
Witnesses: Wm. C. MacArthur residence Bruce Mines and Mary A. McGinnis, Guelph.
Place of marriage: Guelph
Religion: both Methodist
Married by S.E. Marshall, by license registered 15 Sept. 1905. Reg. # 019916 from Marriages - Division of the City of Guelph, Schedule B, County of Wellington, page 92

1911 Census Guelph
Name: Joseph Mc Ginnis
Gender: Male
Marital Status: Married
Age: 33
Birth Date: December 1877
Birthplace: Ontario
Family Number: 6
Relation to Head of House: Head
Tribal: Canadian
Province: Ontario
District: Wellington South
District Number: 134
Sub-District: Guelph
Sub-District Number: 31
Place of Habitation: 16 Waterloo St E
Census Year: 1911
Page: 9
Household Members: Name Birth Year
Joseph Mc Ginnis 1877 contractor, foreman, Methodist
Olive Mc Ginnis 1880
Clarence Mc Ginnis 1906
Lindsay Mc Ginnis 1908

1917 Directory for Guelph
Joseph McGinnis, 76 Water St. works at Page-Hersey Co.

Page-Hersey had a long history that began with the merger of five companies in

Montreal; the J.C. Hodgson Company, Pillow-Hersey manufacturing Company (directed by Mr. Randolph Hersey), Cohoes Rolling Mill Company (Directed by Mr. George Henry Page), Page-Hersey Iron and Tube Company and Montreal Rolling Mills. Pillow-Hersey Company and Cohoes Rolling Mill Company merged under Page-Hersey Iron and Tube Company in 1898. Montreal Rolling Mills absorbed Page-Hersey Iron and Tube Company in 1902. The Secretary- treasurer of Pillow-Hersey Manufacturing Company, Mr. W.W. Near, took the name and started up in Guelph that same year, incorporated under Page-Hersey Iron and Tubes Company Limited. Production of two-inch butt weld pipes began at the Guelph factory in 1903. By 1906 the factory had the capability to manufacture twelve-inch butt weld pipes.

Obit Guelph Mercury 9 Jan 1937:
Deaths: McGinnis - At St. Joseph's Hospital on Fri, Jan 8, 1937, Joseph, dearly beloved husband of Olive Peer, in his 60th year. Funeral services Monday at his late residence 76 Water St. at 2 pm. Burial Woodlawn Cemetery, Guelph.

Woodlawn Cemetery, Guelph Ontario Block P Row 56 Stone 807:
In/Loving memory of/Joseph McGINNIS/Died Jan. 8, 1937/aged 59 years/at rest

Notes for Olive Lohilda Peer:
BIRTH: Birth certificate photocopy in possession of Lorine McGinnis Schulze. Birth Certificate Microfilm Reel 1845398 Reg. # 10116

Olive Lohilda Peer born 15 June 1880, Nelson Tp. Halton Co. to Steven [sic] Edward Peer and Mary E. Vollick. Father a carpenter.

John McCrae (1872-1918) the author of In Flanders Fields, lived one or two doors away from my grandmother Olive Peer, on Water Street in Guelph. John was the son of David McCrae and Janet Simpson Eckford

Children of Joseph McGinnis and Olive Peer are:
> 175   i.   Clarence Elmer[6] McGinnis, born 29 Jul 1906 in Guelph Wellington Co. Ontario; died 14 Jan 1980 in Hamilton, Ontario.
>
>   Notes for Clarence Elmer McGinnis:
>   Burial Woodlawn Cemetery, Guelph Ontario. Block P Row 24 Stone #321:
>
>   McGINNIS/Clarence E./July 29, 1906/Jan. 14,1980/Son of Joseph and Olive/
>
> 176   ii.   Lindsay Lorne McGinnis, born 23 Jun 1908 in Guelph Wellington Co. Ontario; died 07 Dec 1924 in Guelph Wellington Co. Ontario.

Notes for Lindsay Lorne McGinnis:
Name: Lorne McGur Lindsay
Date of Birth: 23 Jun 1908
Gender: Male
Birth County: Wellington
Father's name: Joseph McGinnis
Mother's name: Olive Peer
Roll Number: VRBCAN1908_102540

Buried Woodlawn Cemetery, Guelph Ontario
Block K, Ci

Death certificate:
#033769
Lindsay Lorne McGinnis, school boy, born Guelph 23 June 1908
died age 16 yrs 5 months 14 days
Father Joseph McGinnis born Arkell Ontario
Mother Olive Lohilda Peer born Kilbride Ontario
Dr. F. Walsh
Informant Clarence E. McGinnis, 76 Water St. Guelph, brother
Buried Union Cemetery, Guelph on 9 Dec. 1924
Undertaker Alfred Tovell, 44 Quebec St. Guelph Ontario
Date of death 7 Dec. 1924
Cause of death Convulsions caused by acute Bright's disease, kidneys
Date of start of medical treatment 10 Sept. 1924

177   iii.   Cecil Norman McGinnis, born 15 May 1912 in Guelph, Wellington
               Co. Ontario; died 25 Dec 1960 in Oshawa, Ontario. He married Joan
               Dorien Edith Fuller 11 Apr 1936 in Guelph, Wellington Co. Ontario;
               born 02 Sep 1916 in Guelph, Wellington Co. Ontario; died 22 Jan 2009
               in Bowmanville, Ontario.

               Notes for Cecil Norman McGinnis:
               Cecil and Joan were married in a double wedding with Lillian Fuller
               & James Nevill Bonar at St. James Anglican Church. They lived 127
               Division St. Guelph, Rockwood and then 32 Cedar St. Ajax.

               Cecil was a Lieut. in Signal Corps WW11, and was in England from
               1941-1945. Joan and her sister Lillian lived together with Larry,
               David, Charleen, & Lillian's son Charlie. Joan worked in a munitions
               factory until Cecil's return 1945, while Lillian cared for the four
               children. After Cec's return, Lilian, a widow now that her own
               husband had been killed in the War, took her son Charlie to
               Woodstock to live.

               Cecil, Joan and their children (their last child Lorine was born after

Cec's return) lived in Ajax until two years after Cecil's death. Cecil died in Oshawa General Hospital on Christmas Day 1960 after a few months illness with cancer of the pancreas. Cecil was cremated at St. James Crematorium, Toronto, Ont. Joan, her daughter Lorine, and Joan's sister Lillian moved to London, Ontario in 1965.

St. James Crematorium

Your father - was he Cecil Norman McGinnis - who died December 25th, 1960?

If he is, his ashes are indeed buried in a common ground -BUT the lot where his urn is - can be identified.

The remains are in Common Ground Lot 119, Section "Q" -Vault #1.

I asked the question directly: can the remains be identified and removed so that a marker can be placed - and I was told the answer was - yes!

Might I suggest that if you wish to explore this matter further you call either Bob Turvey or Bob Hollands at the Cemetery: 416-964-9194.

Notes for Joan Dorien Edith Fuller:
Mr. & Mrs. Charles H. Fuller announce the egagements of their daughters, Lillian to J. Nevin Bonar, son of Mr. and Mrs. james Bonar, 16 Lawrence Avenue; and Joan to Cecil N. McGinnis son of Mr. and Mrs. Joseph McGinnis, 76 Water Street, the weddings to take place at St. James Church on April 11

Joan died at 5:15 am

178   iv.   Royal Nelson McGinnis, born 13 Apr 1914 in Guelph Wellington Co. Ontario; died Feb 1993 in Guelph Wellington Co. Ontario. He married Marjorie Beatrice Cahoe; died 17 Sep 1999 in Guelph, Wellington Co. Ontario.

Notes for Marjorie Beatrice Cahoe:
20 Sep 1999: The funeral is on
Tuesday at 1:30p.m. at Wall & Custance Funeral Home in Guelph. It's located at 206 Norfolk St. at what is known as 5 points corner.

179   v.   Frank Edward McGinnis, born 06 May 1917 in Guelph Wellington
                Co. Ontario; died 03 Oct 1926 in Guelph Wellington Co. Ontario.

                Notes for Frank Edward McGinnis:
                buried Woodlawn Cemetery Guelph Ontario "Frankie McGinnis"
                Block K, Ci

                Name : Frank Edward Mcginnis
                Titles :
                Death date : 03 Oct 1926
                Estimated death year :
                Age at death : 9 years
                Death place : Wellington, Ontario
                Birth date : 1917
                Estimated birth year : 1917
                Birth place :
                Gender : Male
                Marital status :
                Race (Term on Certificate) :
                Race :
                Ethnicity :
                Spouse name :
                Spouse titles :
                Father name : Joseph Mcginnis
                Father titles :
                Mother name : Olive Peer
                Mother titles :
                GSU film number : 2079859
                Digital GS number : 4171426
                Image number : 999
                Reference number : 035990
                Collection : Ontario Deaths 1869-1947

180   vi.   Joseph McGinnis, born 06 Apr 1925 in Guelph Wellington Co.
                Ontario; died 19 Apr 1992 in Guelph Wellington Co. Ontario. He
                married Rose Marie Muller; born Abt. 1909 in Germany; died 31 Aug
                2005 in Elora, Ontario.

                Notes for Joseph McGinnis:
                Joseph's ashes were taken to Walle, Co. Verden in Germany by his
                widow Rose and he is buried there.

                Notes for Rose Marie Muller:
                Rose McGinnis passed away last evening at around 8:30pm.

Wednesday Aug.
31st 2005. She had been ill for a while and family members didn't think she last the weekend. Visitation is on Friday from 4 to 8pm and the funeral is in Elora on Saturday. She is to be cremated and her ashes taken to Germany at a later date.

148. Fanny⁵ McGinnis (Harriet⁴ King, David³, Thomas², James¹) was born Sep 1880 in Arkell, Puslinch Tp Wellington Co. Ontario, and died Aft. 1902. She married **James G. Howard** 17 Jun 1899 in Waterloo Ontario, son of William Howard and Margaret. He was born 12 Mar 1877 in Guelph Ontario, and died Aft. 1902.

Notes for Fanny McGinnis:
1901 Census of Canada Page Information
District: Ontario WELLINGTON (South/Sud) (#126)
Subdistrict: Guelph (City/Cité) E-1 Page 20
Details: Schedule 1 Microfilm T-6505
Transcriber: Lorne MacFarlane
Proof reader: J. David Thomas
34   197 Howard James M   Head M Mar 12 1877 24
 35   197 Howard Fannie F   Wife M Oct 9 1880 20
 36   197 Howard William R M   Son S Aug 4 1900 8 mos

Name: Fanny McGinnis
Birth Place: Arthur
Age: 19
Father Name: Alex McGinnis
Mother Name: Mary McGinnis
Estimated Birth Year: abt 1880
Spouse Name: James G Howard
Spouse's Age: 21
Spouse Birth Place: Guelph
Spouse Father Name: Wm Howard
Spouse Mother Name : Margaret Howard
Marriage Date: 17 Jun 1899
Marriage Place: Waterloo
Marriage County: Waterloo
Source: Indexed by: Ancestry.com

Letter from Uncle Clare, 1960s: "My Aunt Fannie, Mrs. James Howard, lived in St. Catharines for many years. ON Berryman Ave and Church St. She may be in the Oddfellows Lodge Home in either Barrie or Orillia if she is still alive. She was born in 1880, same year as your grandmother"

Children of Fanny McGinnis and James Howard are:

181   i.   William R.[6] Howard, born 04 Aug 1900 in Guelph, Wellington Co. Ontario.

182   ii.   Ivy Nellie May Howard, born 20 Jun 1902 in Wellington Co. Ontario.

149. Dan[5] McGinnis (Harriet[4] King, David[3], Thomas[2], James[1]) was born 21 Nov 1880 in Arkell, Puslinch Tp Wellington Co. Ontario, and died Aug 1937 in Sault Ste. Marie, Ontario. He married **Maggie Olive Hatten** 26 Mar 1919 in Algoma Ontario, daughter of William Hatten and Louisa Ferguson. She was born 19 Oct 1893 in Portlock, Johnston Tp Ontario, and died 1971.

Notes for Dan McGinnis:
CEF database, signed up 5 Nov 1914 in Kingston Ontario. date of birth crossed out. Gives next of kin as Mother, Harriet McGinnis, 64 Kent St, Guelph Ontario. He is a blacksmith, born Wellington County

Notes for Maggie Olive Hatten:
Name: Maggie Olive "Ollie" HATTEN
Birth: 19 OCT 1893 in Johnson Twp., Ontario 1
Father: William "Bill" HATTEN b: 24 FEB 1863 in Erin, Eramosa County, Ontario
Mother: Louisa FERGUSON b: 12 SEP 1874 in Lucknow, Kinloss Twp., Ontario

ID: I0526
Name: William "Bill" HATTEN
Birth: 24 FEB 1863 in Erin, Eramosa County, Ontario 1
Death: 24 SEP 1939 in Desbarats, Johnson Twp., Ontario 1
Burial: 26 SEP 1939 Desbarats Cemetery, Desbarats, Johnson Twp., Ontario 1
Reference Number: 526

Father: Thomas HATTEN b: 24 SEP 1820 in England
Mother: Ann EAKETT b: 22 FEB 1821 in England

Marriage 1 Louisa FERGUSON b: 12 SEP 1874 in Lucknow, Kinloss Twp., Ontario
Married: 18 DEC 1889 in Johnson Twp. Ontario 2
Children
John Elmer HATTEN b: 25 OCT 1890 in Tarbutt Twp. Ontario
Mary Ann "Mary" HATTEN b: 4 DEC 1891 in Tarbutt, Ontario
George Orton "Orton" HATTEN b: 19 OCT 1893 in Johnson Twp., Ontario
Maggie Olive "Ollie" HATTEN b: 19 OCT 1893 in Johnson Twp., Ontario
Myrtle I. HATTEN b: 18 FEB 1896
Robert Stanley "Bob" HATTEN b: 7 MAR 1899
Beatrice Mildred HATTEN b: ABT. 1901
William Lorne HATTEN b: ABT. 9 DEC 1902
Bertram "Bert" HATTEN b: 6 JAN 1904 in Johnson Twp., Ontario

Hazel HATTEN b: 1906
William Harvey "Harvey" HATTEN b: 1906
Valentine "Tiny" HATTEN b: 14 FEB 1909
Thelma Victoria HATTEN b: 8 MAR 1912 in Tarbutt Twp., Ontario
Ruby Ellen "Nellie" HATTEN b: 24 JUL 1915

Children of Dan McGinnis and Maggie Hatten are:

> 183   i.   Daniel[6] McGinnis, born 16 Apr 1920 in Koah, Algoma Ontario; died 16 Apr 1920 in Korah, Algoma, Ontario.
>
> Notes for Daniel McGinnis:
> Name : Daniel Mcginnis
> Titles :
> Death date : 16 Apr 1920
> Estimated death year :
> Age at death : 1 day
> Death place : Karah, Algoma, Ontario
> Birth date : 16 Apr 1920
> Estimated birth year :
> Birth place : Koah Twp.
> Gender : Male
> Marital status : Single
> Race (Term on Certificate) :
> Race :
> Ethnicity :
> Spouse name :
> Spouse titles :
> Father name : Dan Mcginnis
> Father titles :
> Mother name : Maggie Olive Hatten
> Mother titles :
> GSU film number : 1863283
> Digital GS number : 4170930
> Image number : 188
> Reference number : yr 1920 cn 9021
> Collection : Ontario Deaths 1869-1947

> 184   ii.   Melitta McGinnis, born 13 Apr 1921 in Guelph Ontario.
> 185   iii.   Donald McGinnis, born 16 Mar 1923.
> 186   iv.   Vina McGinnis, born 15 Feb 1925 in Guelph Ontario.
> 187   v.   Ruby McGinnis, born 11 Mar 1927 in Guelph Ontario.
> 188   vi.   Warren McGinnis, born 31 Mar 1929 in Guelph Ontario; died 1990 in Sault Ste. Marie Ontario. He married Gladys Matiland 11 Jun 1952.
> 189   vii.   John Elmer McGinnis, born 08 Mar 1931 in Guelph Ontario.
> 190   viii. Lily McGinnis, born 02 Sep 1932 in Guelph Ontario.
> 191   ix.   Melinda McGinnis, born 1935 in Guelph Ontario.

150. Henry⁵ McGinnis (Harriet⁴ King, David³, Thomas², James¹) was born 02 Apr 1887 in Guelph, Wellington Co. Ontario, and died Aug 1968 in Guelph, Wellington Co. Ontario. He married **Eunice G. Cole** 13 Jan 1913 in Wellington Co. Ontario, daughter of Barney Cole and Mary Tirrell. She was born Abt. 1894 in Charlotte Michigan, and died in Guelph, Wellington Co. Ontario.

Notes for Henry McGinnis:
Detroit Border Crossings and Passenger and Crew Lists, 1905-1957
about Eunice Mc Ginnis
Name: Eunice Mc Ginnis
Arrival Date: 21 Sep 1917
Age: 23
Birth Date: abt 1894
Birthplace: Charlotte Mi
Gender: Female
Race/Nationality: English
Port of Arrival: Detroit, Michigan
Departure Contact: Husband Henry Mcginniss, 64 Kent St, Guelph Ontario
Arrival Contact: Sister Sarah Burglaund 1054 4th St, Detroit Michigan
was in USA from 1894-1907, in Jackson Michigan
5' 4" medium complexion, brown hair, blue eyes
Microfilm Roll Number: M1478_59

Name: Henry McGinnis
Age: 26
Estimated Birth Year: abt 1887
Spouse Name: Unice Cole
Spouse's Age: 20
Marriage Date: 1913
Marriage Place: Wellington
Marriage County: Wellington
Source: Indexed by: Ancestry.com

buried Woodlawn Cemetery, Guelph Ontario Block D2

Notes for Eunice G. Cole:
buried Woodlawn Cemetery, Guelph Block D2 Eunice G. McGinnis

Children of Henry McGinnis and Eunice Cole are:
> 192   i.   Albert⁶ McGinnis, born 27 Oct 1914 in Guelph Ontario. He married Doris Savage; born 29 May 1915; died 18 Oct 1980.

193	ii.	John McGinnis, born 02 Feb 1916 in Guelph Ontario. He married Eileen Bleach.
194	iii.	Marie McGinnis, born 11 Jul 1918 in Guelph Ontario. She married John Ridd.
195	iv.	Russel Ernest McGinnis, born 19 Mar 1921 in Guelph, Ontario; died 06 Jun 1988 in Guelph, Ontario. He married Elsie Boyle; born 1923; died 2007.

Notes for Russel Ernest McGinnis:
Converted to Catholicism

buried Marymount Cemetery, Section 2, Guelph Ontario

164. George Edward[5] King (George[4], David[3], Thomas[2], James[1]) was born 13 Sep 1879 in Wellington Co. Ontario, and died 14 Oct 1912 in Algoma District Ontario. He married **Sarah A. Jackson**, daughter of David Jackson. She was born 20 Feb 1880 in Quebec.

Notes for George Edward King:
1901 Census of Canada
Name: George E King
Gender: Male
Marital Status: Married
Age: 21
Birth Date: 13 Sep 1879
Birthplace: Ontario
Relation to Head of House: Head
Spouse's Name: Sarah A
Racial or Tribal Origin: English
Nationality: Canadian
Religion: Methodist
Occupation: Mill Man
Province: Ontario
District: Nipissing
District Number: 92
Sub-District: Cooks Mills
Sub-District Number: R-1
Family Number: 20
Page: 2
Household Members: Name Age
George E King 21
Sarah A King 21
Grace E King 2
David Jackson 47

Ontario, Canada Births, 1869-1909
Name: Elgin George King
[Lloyd George Elgin King]
Date of Birth: 27 Mar 1908
Gender: Male
Birth County: Algoma District
Father's name: George E King
Mother's name: Sarah A Sands

Children of George King and Sarah Jackson are:
     196   i.   Grace E.[6] King, born 18 Sep 1898 in Ontario.
     197   ii.   Lloyd George Elgin King, born 1908 in Merrit, Algoma, Ontario.

2. Lewis King 1793-1873 married Elizabeth Smith ca 1800-1871

April 3, 1834 Lewis is shown as the owner of the Crown Lands front half Lot 5 Conc 10, Arkell, Puslinch Tp. Wellington Co. Ontario. ID 5, Sale Clergy Land Archival Reference 01 C1113 001 008. Source: CLRI

1843 Assessment Puslinch Twp. Lewis & George King are on Conc 10 Lot 5, with 30 acres uncultivated and 70 cultivated. Beside them on Conc 10 Lot 6 are Lewis' brother Thomas and son David. Lewis has 2 horses 2 years old or older, 2 Oxen, 3 milk cows and 3 young cattle. His assessment was 92 pounds

1840 Census Puslinch tp Wellington County Gore District [MS 700-2]:
Heads of Families/ Males under 10/ Males over 10/ Females under 10/ Females over 10/ Deaf and Dumb/ Insane / Total in family / Church of England

----

William Hewer -/1/-/1/-/-/2/2 (m. #4)
James Hewer 1/3/-/2/-/-/6/6/
Lues [sic] King 2/2/2/1/-/-/7/7/
Thomas King -/2/1/1/-/-/4/4 (his brother)
Peter Bell 1/2/-/2/-/-/5/5/ (Thomas' son David's father in law)

Lues [sic] King, head of a family of 7, consisting of 2 males over 16, 2 males under 16, 2 females under 16 and 1 female over 16. Church of England. This means he had one son born before 1826 (George), 2 sons born 1826-1842 (Thomas & James), 2 daughters born 1826-1842 (Hannah & Jane)

1842 Census Puslinch. Lewis is head of family of 8 (6 born in England, 2 in Canada) He has 1 son under 5; 2 sons 5-14; 3 daughters 5-14; 1 married man 30-60 and 1 married woman 14-45. They are Wesleyan Methodists. Lewis has been in the Province for 10 years, making his year of immigration circa 1832. Lewis' daughter Sarah showed her immgration to Canada as 1831 in the 1901 census. No ships passenger list has been found but manifests of passengers bound for Canada did not have to be archived before 1865. There seems to be a missing son aged 5-14.

Guelph Mercury April 1994
HEWERS OF ARKELL MADE THEIR MARK
..the Hewer family who settled at Arkell in the 1830s. Mr. James Hewer was one of a company of men from England who arrived at the present site of Arkell in 1831. These pioneers had travelled on foot all the way from the Port of New York, much of the distance through virgin forest. In addtion to James Hewer, the following men are known to have been in that party: John and Thomas Arkell; F.W. Stone; John Outin; Henry Haines; James Carter; Joseph Dory; Charles Willoughby; **Peter Bell;** **Louis King** *and others from Farnham England. Thomas Arkell's acreage was known as Farnham Plains. The Arkell United Church stands on a plot of gournd donated by Charles Willoughby. Rev. Douglas Rudd*

	Males.		Females.					
Printed at Ruthven's BOOK AND JOB OFFICE, HAMILTON, Upper-Canada. **HEADS** of **FAMILIES.**	Under 16	Over 16	Under 16	Over 16	Deaf and Dumb.	Insane.	Total in each Family.	Church of England.
→ Robert Thatcher	·	1	2	1			4	4
Thomas Arkel	2	1	1	1			5	5
Danel Comens	2	1	3	1			7	
James Farland		2	1	3			6	
William Hamilton	·	2	·	2			4	
John Coufield	3	2	1	3			9	9
Sameuel Willson		1		1			2	
Joseph Soumes	2	1	1	1			5	
Charles Willoby	1	1	2	1			5	5
Sameuel Akot	1	1	1	1			3	3
William Hewer		1		1			2	2
James Hewer	1	3		2			6	6
Robert Cook	3	1	2	1			7	·
Lues King	2	2	2	1			7	7
Thomas King	·	2	1	1			4	4
Peter Bell	1	2	·	2			5	5

" . . . *Minutes of the yearly school meeting held at the school house on Wednesday the 13th day of January, 1858. Moved by Mr. John Caulfield, Seconded by Mr. Henry Haines, that Mr. John Iles be appointed Chairman. Moved by Mr. John Caulfield, Seconded by Mr. James Hewer, that James Coleman be appointed Secretary. Moved by Mr. Thomas Carter, Seconded by Mr. Louis King, that Mr. James Fulton be appointed trustee. Moved by Mr. Adam Hume, Seconded by Mr. William Scott, that Mr. James Orme be appointed trustee. On a show of hands being called for, it was decided that Mr. James Fulton had the majority; he was therefore declared elected. Moved by Mr. Peter Orme, Seconded by Mr. Robert Cook, that the school be conducted in the free system for this year. Carried unanimously.*"

2. Lewis King 1793-1873 (cont'd)

1851 census Puslinch Tp Wellington Co. Ontario
Lewis King, farmer b Eng WM, 55
Elizabeth King, b Eng, WM 52
James King labourer b C.W Wm 14
Jane King b CW WM 9
- one storey log cabin next door to his son George and family

1861 census for Arkell p 16: Lewis age 63, farmer and "Mrs." age 55 are living with their son Thomas, age 25 and his wife "Mrs"] and their son Lewis age 2 months. Also living with them is Lewis' daughter Jane aged 18.

1871 census for Arkell, Puslinch Tp, Wellington South:
Lewis King, 75 b England Wesleyan Methodist
Elizabeth 71 b England
George 27 b Canada, C. Presbyterian, farmer (grandson)
Jane 24, b Canada, C. Presbyterian (George's wife)
Lewis and Elizabeth are on Lot 5, Conc 10, Arkell. Microfilm C-9945 Division 4 Page 24

Ontario Death Registrations. Elizabeth King died Sept. 4, 1871, 71 years old, born England. Died of dysentery had for 10 days

Arkell United Church Cemetery, Arkell Ontario, Sacred to the memory of [Elizabeth], wife of Louis King, who died Sept. 3 [sic] 1871, age 71 years.

Arkell United Church Cemetery, Arkell Ontario In memory of Lewis King who died Nov. 29, 1873, 78 years. A native of Suffolk England.

Obit in Guelph Evening Mercury of Sat. Nov. 29, 1873:
KING: In Puslinch on 29th inst, Mr. Lewis King age 78 years. Deceased was one of the earliest settlers in Puslinch and was widely known and respected. His death was hastened by the bite of a dog on his hand a few days ago.

Unto the Surrogate Court of the County of Wellington
The Petition of Thomas Parker of the Town of Sarnia in the
County of Lambton Carpenter, — Humbly Sheweth: — That
Lewis King late of the Township of Puslinch in the County of
Wellington Yeoman deceased died on or about the first day of
December in the year of our Lord one thousand eight hundred and
seventy three at the Township of Puslinch in the County of Wellington that the said Deceased at the time of his death had a
fixed place of abode at the Township of Puslinch in the said County
of Wellington. That the said Deceased in his lifetime duly made
his last Will and Testament bearing date the fifteenth day of
of October in the year of our Lord one thousand eight hundred and
sixty eight. That your Petitioner Thomas Parker the executor named
in the said Will That the value of the personal Estate and effects
of the said Deceased which he in any way died possessed of or
entitled to and for and in respect to which a Probate of the
said Will is to be granted are of or about the value of one
hundred Dollars to the best of your Petitioners Knowledge and
belief

Whereof your Petitioner prays that Probate of the said Will
of the said deceased may be granted to Thomas Parker by this
Honorable Court
Dated this seventeenth day of December 1874

Will
in King

This is the last Will and Testament of me Lewis King of
the Township of Puslinch in the County of Wellington Yeoman I
I give and bequeath to my children Sarah Louisa Harriet Alice

144

James and Jane share and share alike certain moneys being the
hundred and seventy five dollars payable under a certain Indenture of
Rent Charge and Mortgage of the South West or front half of lot number
two in the tenth concession of the said Township of Pickering dated the
fifteenth day of October one thousand eight hundred and sixty eight
made between George King of the First part Elizabeth his wife of the
second part me the said Amos King of the Third part and my
wife Elizabeth of the Fourth part 3rd I give devise and bequeath
to my wife Elizabeth all other property of which I may die
seized possessed of or otherwise entitled to, to hold to her own use forever
forever 3rd I appoint Thomas Parker of the said Township of
Pickering Farmer Executor of this my last Will and Testament
4th I hereby revoke all former Wills heretofore made by me
In witness whereof I have hereunto set my hand seal this
fifteenth day of October in the year of our Lord one thousand
eight hundred and sixty eight.

Signed by the said Testator as his last
Will and Testament in the presence of us
present at the same time who at his
request, in his presence and in the presence (signed
of each other have subscribed

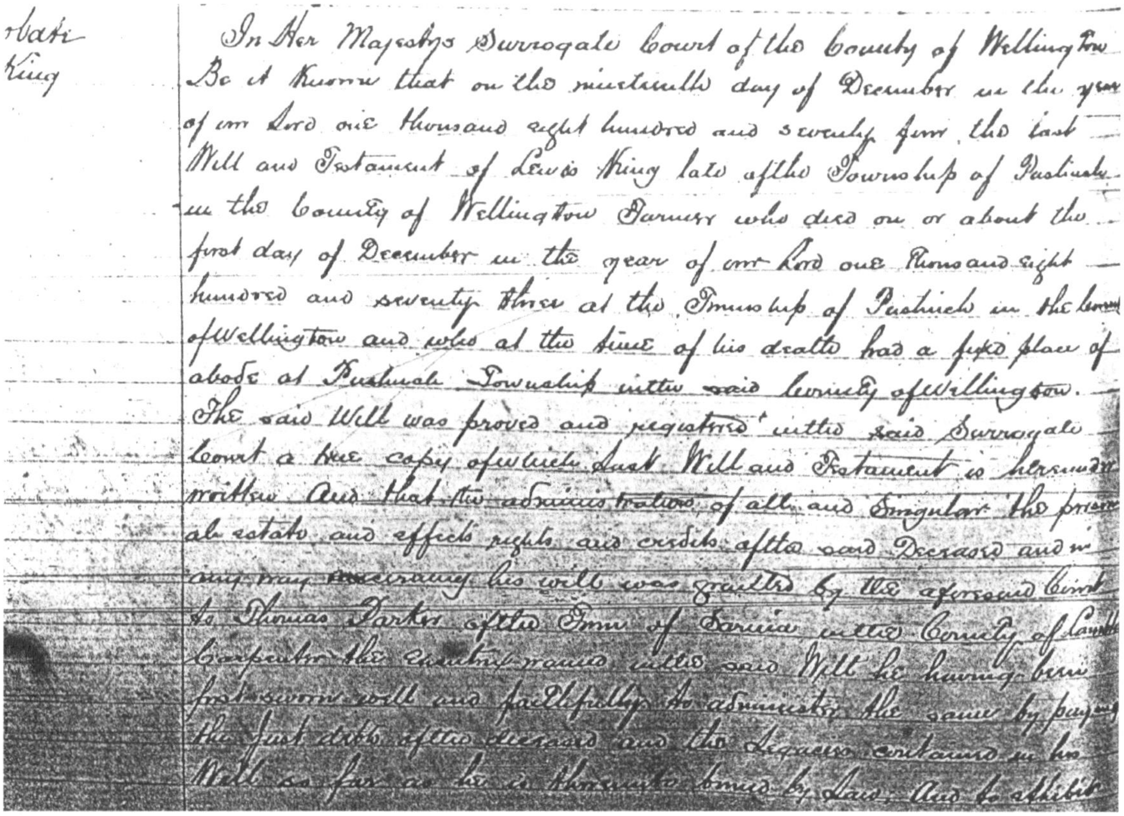

Probate King

In Her Majesty's Surrogate Court of the County of Wellington
Be it Known that on the nineteenth day of December in the year
of our Lord one thousand eight hundred and seventy four, the last
Will and Testament of Lewis King late of the Township of Puslinch
in the County of Wellington Farmer who died on or about the
first day of December in the year of our Lord one thousand eight
hundred and seventy three at the Township of Puslinch in the County
of Wellington and who at the time of his death had a fixed place of
abode at Puslinch Township in the said County of Wellington.
The said Will was proved and registered in the said Surrogate
Court a true copy of which last Will and Testament is hereunto
written And that the administration of all and singular the personal estate and effects rights and credits of the said Deceased and in
any way concerning his will was granted by the aforesaid Court
to Thomas Parker of the Town of Sarnia in the County of Lambton
Carpenter the executor named in the said Will he having been
first sworn well and faithfully to administer the same by paying
the just debts of the deceased and the legacies contained in his
Will so far as he is thereunto bound by Law And to exhibit

Surrogate Court Records, 1874-1877 Wellington County. Reel 6-705, p 133. Will written 15 Oct. 1868, probated 17 Dec. 1871. In Lewis King's will he bequeaths equal shares of money from his estate to his children Sarah, Louisa, Hannah, Thomas, James and Jane. His son-in-law Thomas Parker is named as executor. He also names his wife Elizabeth and won George in the will.

3. Thomas King 1796-1863 married Harriet Dawson 1797-1854
married Elizabeth Gow ca 1834-?

1840 Census Puslinch tp Wellington County Gore District [MS 700-2]
Heads of Families/ Males - 10/Males + 10/ Females - 10/ Females + 10/ Deaf & Dumb/ Insane / Total in family / Church of England
----
Lues [sic] King 2/2/2/1/-/-/7/7/(his brother)
Thomas King -/2/1/1/-/-/4/4
Peter Bell 1/2/-/2/-/-/5/5/ (Thomas' son David's father in law)

Thomas King is the head of a house of 4 people - 2 males over 16 (Thomas and son David), one female under 16 (unknown), and one female over 16 (Harriet). All 4 are Church of England. This gives Thomas & Harriet an unknown daughter born 1826 - 1842.

Jan. 8, 1847: Thomas is the owner of the Crown Land on front half, Conc. 10, Lot 6, Arkell, Puslinch Tp. Wellington Co. ID 6, Sale, Clergy Land 01 C1113 002 212 Source: CLRI

1861 census Puslinch twp Wellington Co. Ward #5 King, Thomas, innkeeper b Eng, 65 wife Elizabeth 27, sons Thomas 6 & James 4

Frostenden, Suffolk Co. England Parish Registers. Burial 19 Dec 1793 Elizabeth Dawson [late Baldry] age 32 wife of William. [William's first wife]
Banns were read on 27 Apr, 4 May & 11 May 1794 William Dawson widower & Sarah Smith, single of Uggeshall.
Baptism: Harriet Dawson 17 Mar 1797 born 14 Mar 1797 d/o William & Sarah [late Smith].
Marriage: Thomas King, single man, married Harriet Dawson, single woman, 19 May 1817 with consent of parents. Witnesses Sarah Jisk & John Harvey.

1843 Assessment of Puslinch Tp Wellington Co. Thomas & David King, front 100 acres of Lot 6 Concession 10. 30 acres are uncultivated, 70 acres culitivated. They have 3 horses, 2 oxen, 7 milk cows and were assessed for 129 L

1842 census Puslinch Tp., in the Gore District [MS 700-2]
Thomas King is the head of a house of 6 people - 1 males under 5 (David's son Thomas), one female 5-14 (?), 1 married man 21-30 (David) , 1 married man 30-60 (Thomas) , 2 married women 14-45 (Harriet & Mary). We still see the unknown daughter for Thomas & Harriet - her date of birth now narrowed to 1828-1837. Since 4 of the 6 are said to be born in England, and 2 in Canada, we know that this daughter was born in Canada probably sometime after 1831. They have been in the Province for 10 years (circa 1832)

Arkell Pioneer Cemetery, Puslinch Tp. Wellington Co. Ontario: In memory of Harriet, wife of Thomas King, who died Apr. 14, 1851 [4?], aged 57 years

Surrogate Court Records 1859-1864 Reel 6-703 pp 633-634
1863: Thomas died intestate but his widow Elizabeth filed papers in court re his property. She named 3 children David, Thomas and James

Arkell Pioneer Cemetery, Puslinch Tp. Wellington Co. Ontario: In memory of Thomas King, who died 18 June 1863, aged 62 years

County Marriage Register 1858-1869 Wellington Co. John Huhn, 27 of Clifford b Germany s/o Wm. Huhn and Elizabeth Fischer - Elizabeth King 25 of Aberfoyle b Canada d/o Jas. Gow and Christina Ferguson m 10 Nov 1868 by Rev Kenneth McDonald of E Puslinch, Canada Presbyterian Church Wit JB Johnston Aberfoyle.

In the goods of Thomas King, deceased… The petition of Elizabeth King, Puslinch Twp, Wellington Co, widow of Thomas King deceased…. who died on or about the 18th day of June 1863… The petition states that Thomas died without a will, that the value of his goods is about $400.00 and that he has "kindred living in Upper Canada" namely the widow, and three children – David King, Thomas King & James King. Elizabeth King, the widow, signs with her mark X

Elizabeth, widow of Thomas King signs July 1863 that she has been sworn in.

Affidavit of Value of Property signed by Elizabeth, widow of Thomas King 23 July 1863. Property worth about $400.00 which Elizabeth wishes to administer

Affidavit signed by Elizabeth, widow of Thomas King, 23 July 1863.

Oath for Administration signed by Elizabeth 23 July 1863. Says Thomas died without a will, that she is his lawful widow. His debts will be (or have been) paid, etc.

Wellington King Regis... deceased, who died on or about the eighteenth
day of June AD 1863, at the Township of Puslinch in the County of Wellington
Intestate, and had at the time of his death a fixed place of abode at the Township
of Puslinch in the said County of Wellington. These presents granted
by the Magistrates Surrogate Court of the County of Wellington to ...
King of the Township of Puslinch in the County of Wellington, the ...
of the said Intestate, he having been first sworn faithfully to administer
the same by paying his just debts and distributing the residue (if any)
of his Personal Estate and effects according to Law, and to exhibit a true and
perfect Inventory of all and singular the said Personal Estate and effects, goods
and Credits, and to render a just and true account thereof whenever required
by Law so to do,:—

Tho.S Keating
Registrar

Letters of Administration

Ontario Archives. Reel 6-703, pp 633-635 Thomas King

4. Sarah Catherine King 1817-1910 married William Hewer ca 1818-1888

1861 census Puslinch Tp Wellington Co.
William Hewer, Miller, b England, 41
Mrs. Hewer b Eng 31
John Hewer, labourer b Canada 17
Elizabeth Hewer b Canada 15
Jane Hewer b Canada 13
James Hewer b Canada 7
Jemima Hewer b Canada 5
Johanna Hewer b Canada 3
Richard Hewer b Canada 1

Death Certificate, #023010 p 339 Div. of Guelph, Co. of Wellington Sarah Catherine HEWER, female, English, d Jan 11, 1910 b Aug 7 1817 in "Bain" in Suffolk, Eng, 92 years, 5 mos, 4 days, lived 406 Paisley Rd Guelph. Retired, Widowed. Father Louis King of Suffolk England Mother Elizabeth Smith England. Dr. Savage, notified by Mrs. Joan Marriott (daughter) 406 Paisley Rd died of arterio-sclerosis/apoplexy, 3 days, Guelph. Dr. Savage

1901 census City of Guelph
124 Paisley Rd

1871 census Puslinch Tp Wellington Co.
William Hewer, 52 b Engl farmer and shoemaker
Sarah 50 b England
William 17 b Ont. farmer [I believe he is James on 1861 census]
Richard 10 b On
Henery 9 b On
Thomas 2 b on
Jane 22 b On
Jemima 15 b On
Joanna 13 b On
Margret Jane 4 b On
Thomas 2
James Hewer, 77 (father), b England Methodist, farmer
Elizabeth Hewer, 71

> *Sarah Catherine King's grandchildren were the Marriott Twins of the Downie Bros. circus They were famous trapeze artists. Sarah Catherine Kings's in-law, Christina Hewer McPhee, owned the Downie Bros. circus with her husband. She, too, was in the circus as a trapeze artist. Sarah was living with her grand-children when she died*

William Hewer came to Canada at the age of 16 with his parents, James Hewer and Sarah Hill. The family sailed on the Ship Bristol, from Bristol England to New York on 10 November 1834. Their intended place of residence was given as United States

========>

5. George A. King ca 1817-1881 married (1) Mary Anne Harrison ca 1815-1858 married (2) Sarah Thompson 1841-1864 married (3) Elizabeth Parker 1835-Bet. 1900-1910

1851 census Puslinch Tp Wellington Co. Ontario C 11743
beside Lewis and Elizabeth King and family

George King farmer b England WM 34
Mary Ann King b Eng 37
George King b CW 8
Francis King b CW 6
Lewis King b CW 5
Elizabeth King b CW 2
living 1 1/2 storey log cabin

1858 Barton Twp Assessment Roll -
George King, Conc 5, Pl 13 25 acres,
dairyman

County Marriage Register 1858-1869 Vol. 1 Wellington Co., Ref 1: 165
George King, 46 of Puslinch b Eng s/o Lewis and Elizabeth King to Elizabeth parker, 30 of Puslinch b England d/o Francis and Rachel Parker. married 27 Sept 1865 by Rev William Newton of Guelph, Primitive Methodist. Wit Thomas Parker of Puslinch.

Directory of Wellington County, 1867 Puslinch Tp. Residents
KING
David C 10 L 56 Free
George C 10 L5 Free
Thomas W. C 9 L 7 Householder

Marriage Registration 27 Sep 1865 Guelph, Wellington Co. Ontario
Name: George King
Birth Place: England
Residence: Puslinch Township
Age: 46
Father Name: Lewis King
Mother Name: Elizabeth King
Spouse Name: Elizabeth Parker
Spouse's Age: 30
Spouse Birth Place: England
Spouse Residence: Puslinch Township
Spouse Father Name: Francis Parker
Spouse Mother Name : Rachel Parker
Family History Library Microfilm: 1030067

County Marriage Registers of Wentworth, 1858-1869, Ref 25. George King, 36, of Barton, b England s/o Lewis & Elizabeth King, m Sarah Thompson, 20, of Barton, b Canada d/o Thomas Dec 16, 1859 Rev Geroge A Bull Church of England Wit A J Glen of Hamilton.

1871 Census Guelph, south ward
George KING, 52 b Eng WM, milkman
Elizabeth 36 b England
Lewis 23 b Ontario
Martha 19 b Ont
Albert 10 b Ont
female (name not clear) 9 b Ont
Thomas 7 b Ont
James 4 b ont
Mary L. 1 b Ont

5. George A. King ca 1817-1881 (cont'd)

1881 Census Place:Guelph, Wellington South, Ontario, Canada
Source:FHL Film 1375894 NAC C-13258 Dist 151 SubDist C Div 4 Page 75 Family 362

	Sex Marr Age	Origin	Birthplace			
George KING M	M	62	English	England	Occ:Farmer	Religion:C. Methodist
Elisabeth KING F	M	45	English	England	Religion:	C. Methodist
Lewis KING M		30	English	Ontario	Occ: Laborer	Religion: C. Methodist
Albert KING M		20	English	Ontario	Occ: Laborer	Religion: C. Methodist
Thomas KING M		17	English	Ontario	Occ: Moulder	Religion: C. Methodist
James KING	M	14	English	Ontario	Religion:	C. Methodist
Louisa KING	F	11	English	Ontario	Religion:	C. Methodist
William KING	M	9	English	Ontario	Religion:	C. Methodist
Frederick KING	M	6	English	Ontario	Religion:	C. Methodist
Charles KING	M	3	English	Ontario	Religion:	C. Methodist

Christian Guardian, Death Notices 1851-1860, Mrs. George A. King, [Mary Anne Harrison] d/o Mr. and Mrs Edward Harrison b Yorkshire England. Came to Canada at age 10. Married Mr. King in 1841. Died in Nelson Tp March 12 1858 in 37th year. Pre deceased by child in 1852. Survived by husband, 1 daughter and 3 sons. (May 12 1858 p 126 obits).

1891 census City of Guelph Div 5 p 57 N 1/5, 263

King Elizabeth 55 widow b Eng father and mother b Eng Meth
William 19 b Ontario father and mother b England, moulder
Ferderick 16 b Ontario ditto
Louisa 21 b Ontario ditto
Charles 13 b Ontario ditto

1900 United States Federal Census Detroit City, Ward 5, Wayne, Michigan

Elizabeth King 64 born Aug. 1835 England, immigrated 1892, head of house, parents born England, mother of 6 children, 5 living, widow
Louisa King 29
Fredrick King 25
Charles King 22 b. Mar 1878 imm 1892

6. Louisa King 1825-1917 married Carter Whiting ca 1829-1902

1851 Census of Canada East, Canada West, New Brunswick, and Nova Scotia
Province: Canada West (Ontario) District: Hamilton City District Number: 45 Sub-District: St Lawrence Sub-District Number: 439 Page: 109 Line: 1 Roll: C_11767 Schedule: A

Carter Whiting, 29, carpenter born England
Louisa Whiting, 23 born England
Malvina Turnbul, 11 born England
Elizabeth Whiting 1 born Canada
Thomas King, 18, born Canada, residence Puslinch

Frame house, 1 1/2 storey, 5 family members, 1/5 of an acre

New South Wales, Australia, Unassisted Immigrant Passenger Lists, 1826-1922
Name: Mr. Whiting
Port of Departure: Melbourne
Port of Arrival: Sydney, New South Wales
Voyage Arrival Date: 1 Mar 1873
Vessel Name: Dandenong

New South Wales, Australia, Unassisted Immigrant Passenger Lists, 1826-1922
Name: Carter Whiting
Port of Departure: Melbourne
Port of Arrival: Sydney, New South Wales
Voyage Arrival Date: 1 Feb 1876
Vessel Name: Dandenong

Australian Electoral Rolls, 1901-1936
Name: Carter Whiting
Electoral Year: 1856
State: Victoria
District: Melbourne
Subdistrict: University
St. Mary's Division
Living Rathdown St
Occupation carpenter

1881 Census Place: Oakville, Halton, Ontario, Canada
Source:FHL Film 1375893 NAC C-13257 Dist 150
SubDist D Page 16 Family 80

	Sex Marr	Age	Origin	Birthplace
Carter WHITING		50	English	England
Occ:Carpenter	Religion:		Methodist	Canada
Louisa WHITING		50	English	England
Religion:	Methodist	Canada		
Malvina WHITING		16	English	Australia
Religion:	Methodist	Canada		

1891 Census of Canada Province: Ontario
District Number: 119 District: Toronto City
Subdistrict: St Patricks Ward Archive Roll #: T-6372

Household Members: Name Age
Carter Whiting 65 b. England, Methodist, parents born England
Louisa Whiting 60 b England, Methodist, parents born England

1901 Census of Canada District: Ontario Wellington (South/Sud) (#126) Subdistrict: Guelph (City/Cité) E-14 Page 12 Details: Schedule 1 Microfilm T-6505
Whiting Louisa F Head M Apr 10 1825 75

8. Thomas William King 1834-aft 1910 married (1) Helen/Ellen Daville ca 1835- bet 1888-1900 married (2) Amelia Lightall Lamb ca 1852-?

Ontario Canada Marriages
Name: Thomas William King
Birth Place: Canada
Residence: Nelson Township
Age: 23
Father Name: Louis
Mother Name: Elizabeth
Estimated Birth Year: 1835
Spouse Name: Helen Daville
Spouse's Age: 18
Spouse Birth Place: England
Spouse Residence: Nelson Township
Spouse Estimated Birth Year: 1840
Spouse Father Name: William
Spouse Mother Name : Sarah
Marriage Date: 9 Jan 1858
Marriage County: Halton
Family History Library Microfilm: 1030057

Michigan Marriages 1868-1925
Groom name: Thomas King
Groom age: 65 years
Groom birth year: 1835
Groom birth place: Canada
Bride name: Amelia Lighthall Lamb
Bride age: 48 years
Bride birth year: 1852
Bride birth place: Canada
Marriage date: 10 May 1900
Marriage place: Port Austin, Huron, Michigan
Father of groom name: Louis
Mother of groom name: Elizabeth Smith
Father of bride name: Unknown
Mother of bride name: Unknown
Film number: 2342515
Digital GS number: 4208648
Reference number: v 2 p 233 rn 83

1851 Census Nelson Tp Halton Co. Pt 1
http://data2.collectionscanada.ca/1851_pdf/e095/e00235
2702.pdf
Daville, William b England 43 tanner
Sarah b England 34
Ellen b England 34 [numbers are messed up and crossed out - this probably should be 14]
Elizabeth b England 11
Francis J b Upper Canada 61 [sic - should be 6?] (male)
Sarah b Upper Canada 2

1880 United States Federal Census Huron, Huron, Michigan
Household Members: Name Age
Thomas King 47 farmer b NY, parents b New York
Ellen King 40 b Ohio, parents b Ohio [sic]
James King 21 works out, b Ohio [sic]
William King 18 works out, b Ohio [sic]
Ellen King 16 b Michigan
Thomas King 12 b Michigan
Viola King 8 b Michigan
George King 10M Michigan
Note the incorrect locations of birth. It is possible however that Thomas was born in New York, as that is the likely port of arrival for his father Lewis.

1900 United States Federal Census Hume, Huron, Michigan
Residence : Huron & Gore Townships, Huron, Michigan

Household Members: Name Age
Thomas King 66 b Apri 1834 Canada English, immigrated 1879 parents born England.Married 1900
Amelia King 47 hybe 1852 Can. Eng, immigrated 1880
Orville King 12 Jan 1888 Michigan, son
Winford Carey 17 hired man

1910 United States Federal Census Port Austin, Huron, Michigan

Household Members: Name Age
Thomas W King 76 b Canada English, parents born England, immigrated 1875
Amelia A King 68

10. Harriet Jane King 1842-? married Thomas Parker ca 1840-aft 1901

[handwritten baptismal register form]

Township of Puslinch *Wellington Dist.* 367

NAME OF PERSON BAPTIZED.	NAMES OF PARENTS.	Place of Parents' Residence.	Born Where.	Born When.	Baptized Where.	Baptized Where.	Minister Baptizing.
2. Harriet Jane King	Lewis & Eliz	do	do	31 May 1842		do	do

United Church Archives Wesleyan Methodist Baptismal Register, Vol 1 p. 367
Harriet Jane King daughter of Lewis & Elizabeth born 31 May 1842 baptised 6 July 1842 in Puslinch

1871 Census District: Halton (038) Sub-district: Nelson (A) Division: 3 Page: 66 Microfilm reel: C-9955

Parker Thomas, 32, b Eng, English origin, sawyer Wesleyan Methodist
Harriet Jane 28 B Ont
Elizabeth A. 7 b Ont
Mary Louise 5 b Ont
Fanny Jane 3 b Ont
Rachel b 1870 d Feb 1871
living C 2 Lot 8 1/4 acre, tenants

1891 Census of Canada
Province: Ontario
District Number: 82
District: Lambton West
Subdistrict: Sarnia Town
Archive Roll #: T-6348
Household Members: Name Age
Thomas Parker 50 b England, Congregationalist parents born England, married, Occ: Wharfinger [sic]
William F Parker 14 b. Ontario, single mother born Ontario

1891 Census of Canada
Province: Ontario
District Number: 90
District: Middlesex East
Subdistrict: London
Archive Roll #: T-6352
Household Members: Name Age
Harriet Parker 48 married born Ontario, Congregationalist

1901 Census of Canada
Province: Ontario District: Middlesex (East/est) District Number: 87 Sub-District: London Sub-District Number: C-7 Family Number: 11 Page: 6 Hospital for the Insane.

Harriet Jane Parker, Married Age: 58 Birthplace: Ontario, Patient, English origin,   Religion: Congregationalist Occupation: Housekeeper

1901 Census of Canada
Province: Ontario
District: Lambton (West/Ouest)
District Number: 79
Sub-District: Sarnia (Town/Ville)
Sub-District Number: F-4
Family Number: 15
Page: 1
Household Members: Name Age
Thomas Parker 60 b 29 Mar 1844 England, Occ: Warfinger. Methodist, Immigrated 1860. Married

11. David King 1817-1907 married Mary Bell 1819-1885

Names of Inmates.	Profession, Trade or Occupation.	Place of Birth.	Religion.	Residence if out of limits.	Age next birth day.	Male.	Female.
1	2	3	4	5	6	7	8
David King	Farmer	England	Church of England		34	1	
Mary King		Do	Do		32		1
Thos W King		C W	Methodist		9	1	
David King		Do	Do		7	1	
Mary Anne King		Do	Do		5		1
Harriett King		Do	Do		4		1
John King		Do	Do		2	1	
Joseph King		Do	Do		1	1	
Thos King		Do	Do		18	1	

1851 Census Puslinch Tp. Wellington Co. Ontario
David King, farmer, born England, Church of England, 34
Mary born England, Church of England, 32
Thomas born C. W. (Canada West), Methodist, 9
David born C. W. (Canada West), Methodist, 7
Mary Anne born C. W. (Canada West), Methodist, 5
Harriet born C. W. (Canada West), Methodist, 4
John born C. W. (Canada West), Methodist, 2
Joseph born C. W. (Canada West), Methodist, 1
George born C. W. (Canada West), Methodist, 18
Living 1 1/2 storey log cabin near his uncle Lewis King and
cousins

1843 Assessment of Puslinch Tp Wellington Co.
Thomas & David King, front 100 acres of Lot
6 Concession 10. 30 acres are uncultivated,
70 acres are culitivated. They have 3
horses, 2 oxen, 7 milk cows and were
assessed for 129 L

Directory of Wellington County, 1867
Puslinch Tp. Residents
KING
David C 10 L 56 Free
George C 10 L5 Free
Thomas W. C 9 L 7 Householder
BELL
Joseph C 10 L7 Free

3 December 1831. Passenger list of the Brig Charles Joseph sailing from Liverpool to New York. Among the passengers are Mary Bell, age 10, her siblings Joseph, Peter, Phoebe and Ann, and her mother Elizabeth age 45 and grandmother Frances Higginson age 65, carpenter's wife. The ship left Liverpool on 21 or 27 of September.

11. David King 1817-1907 (cont'd)

1871 Census Puslinch Tp, Wellington Co. Ontario
David King, 53, farmer, b England WM,
Mary, 51, b England WM
Thomas, 29 farmer widower with 5 [?] kids
Richard, 27, butcher
Harriet, 23
John, 21, farmer
Joseph 19 farmer
George 16 farmer

The agricultural portion of the 1871 census shows David and his family living on 100 acres, Concession 10 Lot 6 with 1 house, 3 barns, 4 carriages, 3 wagons, 2 ploughs, 1 reaper, 1 horse rake and 1 fanning mill. Livestock consisted of 3 horses, 3 colts, 3 cows, 5 bulls, 5 sheep, and 10 pigs. They made 3 lb of butter and had 20 acres of pasture, 3 acres of garden, 7 acres of wheat, 20 acres of spring wehat, 30 acres of fall wheat, 1 acre of potatoes and 12 acres of hay. They harvested 200 bushels of barley, 300 bushels of oats, 200 bushels of peas, 100 bushels of potatoes, 3,000 bushels of turnips and 300 bushels of apples.

Death Registration 1907 Algoma District
David King, died 24 May 1907, age 89. Living S 1/2 Lot 1, Concession 3, Johnson's. Widower, Methodist, born England. Died of La Grippe [flu] which he had for 3 days. Informant Joseph King [his son]

Grave, Arkell Pioneer Cemetery
Mary, beloved wife of David King
died Decr 3, 1885 aged 66 years

18. Elizabeth Hewer 1847-Aft. 1901 married John Marriott 1834-?

There were two children from this marriage called the
MARRIOTT TWINS who were world famous trapeze
artists. See #86. Albert George Marriott

1891 Census Guelph, Wellington Co. Ontario
District Number: 127 Archive Roll #: T-6377

Household Members: Name Age
John Marriott 54 b England, Methodist, parents born
England
Elizabeth Marriott 44
William Marriott 23
Fredrick Marriott 17
Ada Marriott 15
Bertha Marriott 12
Minard Marriott 8
Albert Marriott 8
Kate W Marriott 6

27. George King 1844-1903 married Jane Scott 1848-1920

1871 Census Wellington South, Puslinch Division: 4
Page: 24 Microfilm reel: C-9945
Lewis King, 75 b England WM
Elizabeth 71 b Eng
George 27 b Canada, C. Presbyterian, farmer
Jane 24, b Canada, C. Presbyterian
George and his wife Jane are with his grandparents Lewis
and Elizabeth King

Ontario Deaths 1869-1947
Name : George King
Death date : 10 May 1903
Age at death : 59 years
Death place : Keppel, Grey, Ontario
Birth date : 1844
Birth place : Ontario
Gender : Male
Marital status : Married
GSU film number : 1854188
Digital GS number : 4175424
Image number : 741
Certificate number : yr 1903 cn 10786

1901 Census of Canada District: Grey (North/Nord)
District Number: 65 Sub-District: Keppel Sub-District
Number: C-7 Family Number: 10 Page: 2
Geo King 56   24 Feb 1844 Ontario, farmer Presbyterian
Jean King 53 Mar 1847 Ontario Scotch
James King 31 14 Sep 1869 single
Mary King 25 11 Oct 1875 single

Ontario Deaths 1869-1947
Name: Jean Scott King
Death date: 29 Feb 1920
Age at death: 71 years 11 months
Death place: Owen Sound, Grey Co., Ontario
Birth date: 18 Mar 1848
Birth place: Wellington County
Gender: Female
Marital status: Widowed
Father name: James Scott
Mother name: Margaret Anderson
GSU film number: 1863285
Digital GS number: 4170968
Reference number: yr 1920 cn 16975

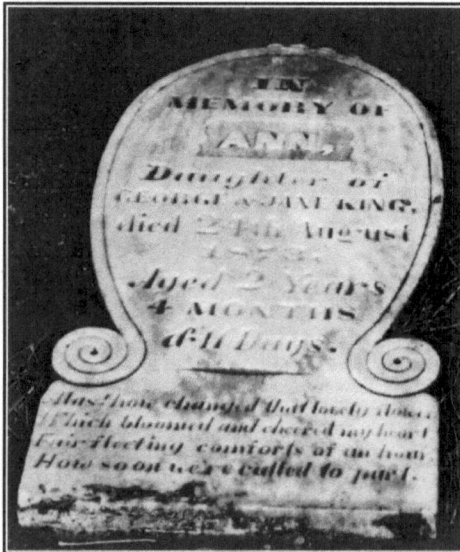

Arkell United Church Cemetery, Arkell
Ontario, Ann d/o George and Jane King died 24
Aug 1873 aged 2 yrs 4 ms 11 days.

30. Elizabeth King ca. 1849-? married James Henry Hall ca. 1847-?

Marriage Registration 1881
Name: James Henry Hall
Birth Place: Pilkington
Age: 34
Father Name: Joseph Hall
Mother Name: Maria Hall
Estimated Birth Year: abt 1847
Spouse Name: Elizabeth King
Spouse's Age: 30
Spouse Birth Place: Arkell
Spouse Father Name: George King
Spouse Mother Name : Ann L King
Marriage Date: 14 Mar 1881
Marriage Place: Wellington
Marriage County: Wellington
Source: Indexed by: Ancestry.com

1901 Census of Canada
District: Toronto (Centre) (City/Cité)
District Number: 116
Sub-District: Toronto (Centre)
(City/Cité) Ward/Quartier No 3
Sub-District Number: A-32
Family Number: 14
Page: 2

Household Members: Name Age
MRS Elizabeth Hall 53 Widowed Birth
Date: 25 Sep 1847 Ontario , Methodist
Ethel Hall 16
Fred B Hall 25
May Hall 21
Thomas Hall 23

31. Martha King ca 1853-1879 married James Henry Hall ca1847-?

Marriage Registration 1872
Name: James Henry Hall
Birth Place: Pilkington
Age: 24
Father Name: Joseph Hall
Mother Name: Maria Hall
Spouse Name: Martha King
Spouse's Age: 19
Spouse Birth Place: Puslinch
Spouse Father Name: George King
Spouse Mother Name : Ann King
Marriage Date: 1 May 1872
Marriage Place: Wellington
Marriage County: Wellington
Source: Indexed by: Ancestry.com

Ontario Deaths 1869-1947
Name: Martha H. Hall
Death date: 28 Jan 1879
Estimated death year:
Age at death: 26 years
Death place: Wellington, Guelph,
Birth date: 1853
Cause of death: Rupture of gall bladder
GSU film number: 1853228
Digital GS number: 4171353
Image number: 403
Reference number: p 156

32. Albert E. King 1860-1932 married Mary Ann unknown ca 1869-aft 1932

1891 census city of Guelph, Wellington Co. Div 4 p 15
B 1/5, 75. King Albert, 30 b Ontaro father and mother b England, methodist, groom and labourer
Mary Ann 22 b England Father b England mother b Scotland, Church of England

1901 census Guelph, Wellington Co. E-14 page 13
King, Albert E. b 4 Sept. 1860, 40, b Ontario , Eng, Meth, Gardener
Mary A. born 5 July 1868, 32 b. Eng, imm 1884, Eng. Meth

Death Certificate. Albert King, 29 Ashbury St. Fairbanks Ontario. Informant Mary Ann King, same address, says Albert's date of birth was 15 July 1861. father George King born England mother P. Sarah Thompson? [ink faded, hard to read] born Ontario. Cause of death 15 Jul 1932 sudden heart attack.

35. James Parker King 1867-Aft. 1916 married Clara Gertrude Partridge 1869-Aft. 1916

Name: James Parker King
Birth Place: Arkell
Age: 21
Father Name: George King
Mother Name: Elizabeth King
Estimated Birth Year: abt 1866
Spouse Name: Clara Gertrude Partridge
Spouse's Age: 18
Spouse Birth Place: Ashby England
Spouse Father Name: Wm H Partridge
Spouse Mother Name : Martha Partridge
Marriage Date: 27 Apr 1887
Marriage Place: Wellington
Marriage County: Wellington
Source: Indexed by: Ancestry.com

1911 Census of Canada
Province: Alberta District: Red Deer
District Number: 5 Sub-District Number: 63
Page: 8 Family Number: 139

Household Members: Name Age
James P King 45 b. Oct 1866 Ontario
Clara King 43 Mar 1868 Ontario

1916 Canada Census of Manitoba, Saskatchewan, and Alberta
Home in 1916: Alberta, Red Deer, 01
Address: 35, 12, 4, Whiteside
Household Members: Name Age
Harry King 28 md b 1881 Ontario, head
Thelma King 23 md b Ontario, wife
Thelma King 4 b BC, daughter
James P King 51 b. Ontario, father
Clara King 48, mother

Alberta Homestead Records 1870-1930
KING, James Parker
Section 7 Township 35 Range 12 Meridian 4
Film # 2882 in Accession # 1970.313 at Provincial Archives of Alberta
File # 1829084

1900 census Detroit Michigan with William King, her brother in law
Clara King 28 Jul 1871 can. imm 1891 sis in law b Eng (hubby b Can)
Florence King 9 Aug 1890 Ontario clara's dau
Agnes King 7 June 1892 michigan

1901 Census of Canada
Province: The Territories District: Alberta
District Number: 202 Sub-District: Ponoka
Sub-District Number: Q3-1
Family Number: 200 Page: 18

Household Members: Name Age
James P King 33 b. 19 jul 1867 Ontario. immigrated 1900. Methodist, farmer
Clara G King 31
Henry G King 13
Flossie M King 11
Agnes G King 8

37. William H. King 1873-aft 1930 married Margaret House 1873-aft 1950

1900 United States Federal Census Detroit Ward 7, Wayne, Michigan

Household Members: Name Age
William King 27 b Mar 1873 Canada English, immigrated 1892, parents born England. Married 5 years (1895)
Margaret King 26 aug 1872 par b Can
Clarence J King 4
Olive M King 1
Henry G King 3/12
Clara King 28 Jul 1871 can. imm 1891 sis in law b Eng (hubby b Can)
Florence King 9 aug 1890 Ontario clara's dau
Agnes King 7 june 1892 michigan

Detroit Border Crossings and Passenger and Crew Lists, 1905-1957
Name: Margaret King; Arrival Date: 29 Oct 1908
Age: 36; Birth Date: abt 1872
Birthplace: Guelph Ontario; Race/Nationality: German
Port of Arrival: Detroit, Michigan
Accompanied by: Husband William H and 6 children; Son Clarence; Son George; Son Albert; Son Spencer; Daughter Olive; Daughter Myrtle
last residence Ponoka Alberta
Departure Contact: Brother Joseph House, Yorktown, Sask
Arrival Contact: Brother-in-law Fred King 340 Gratiot Ave Detroit MI farmer
1896-Oct 1900 lived Laconia NH and Detroit MI 5"7" fair, lt brown hair, blue eyes
Microfilm Roll Number: M1478_38

1930 United States Federal Census Detroit, Wayne, Michigan

Household Members: Name Age
William H King 59 b Canada imm 1894 PA (first papers) gardener at private house
Margaret King 59
Clarence J King 32
Albert J King 26
Frances King 21
Harold King 18
Spencer King 23

Detroit Border Crossings and Passenger and Crew Lists, 1905-1957
Name: Margaret M King; Arrival Date: 7 Sep 1950 ;Age: 78; Birth Date: 5 Aug 1872
Birthplace: Guelph Ontario; Race/Nationality: Canadian
Port of Arrival: Detroit, Michigan
Microfilm Roll Number: M1478_38

1901 Census of Canada
Province: The Territories District: Alberta
District Number: 202 Sub-District: Ponoka
Sub-District Number: Q3-1 Family Number: 199
Page: 18

Household Members: Name Age
William H King 28 b. 9 Mar 1873 Ontario. Immigrated 1900, farmer, English Origin
Margaret M King 27 5 Aug 1873, R.C. German origin
Clarence J King 4 14 Apr 1896 USA
Olive M King 2 14 Aug 1898 USA
Henry G King 1 6 Feb 1899 USA

1910 United States Federal Census Redford, Wayne Co, Michigan

Household Members: Name Age
William H King 38 b. Canada English, parents born Canada English, immigrated 1892
Margaret King 38
Clarence King 14
Olive King 10
George King 10
Albert King 6
Spencer King 3
Francis King 1 8/12 abt 1908 daughter

1920 United States Federal Census Redford, Wayne Co, Michigan

Household Members: Name Age
William H King 46 b. Canada, Parents b. England. Immigrated 1909, Owns his home, can read and write.
Margret King 46
Clarence King 23
Olive King 21
George King 19
Albert King 16
Spencer King 13
Frances King 11
Harold King 8 6/12
Elmer Lefevre 21

38. Frederick Temple King 1874-aft 1930 married Alice Maude Moynes 1879-aft 1950

Michigan Marriages 1868-1925
Groom name: Frederick T. King
Groom age: 27 years
Groom birth year: 1875
Groom birth place: Canada
Bride name: Alice N. Moynes
Bride age: 23 years
Bride birth year: 1879
Bride birth place: Canada
Marriage date: 18 Feb 1902
Marriage place: Detroit, Wayne, Michigan
Father of groom name: George
Mother of groom name: Elizabeth Parker
Film number: 2342523
Digital GS number: 4001634
Image number: 250
Reference number: v 4 p 451 rn 35605

1920 United States Federal Census Detroit Ward 21, Wayne, Michigan

Household Members: Name Age
Fred T King 42 born Canada, parents born England, rents his home, immigrated 1890, can read and write
Alice King 40
Clerance King 15
Gladys King 17

1910 United States Federal Census Detroit Ward 5, Wayne, Michigan

Household Members: Name Age
Fred King 35 b. Canada English, parents born England, immigrated 1892
Alice King 32
Clarence King 5
Gladys King 7

World War I Draft Registration Cards, 1917-1918
Name: Fredrick Temple King
City: Detroit
County: Wayne
State: Michigan
Birth Date: 9 Aug 1874
Race: White
Roll: 2032764
DraftBoard: 26
Naturalized. Relative Alice Maude King, 450 Mamotique, Detroit Michigan. Retail Shoe Merchant, self employed at 316 Gratiot Ave, Detroit Michigan. Medium height, blue eyes, brown hair, enlistment Sept 12, 1918

1930 United States Federal Census Detroit, Wayne, Michigan

Household Members: Name Age
Frederick T King 53 b. Canada, imm 1895, naturalized, merchant, shoe store
Alice King 52 b. unknown, immigrated 1883, naturalized
Clarence King 25 sales clerk, shoe store
James Powell 26 roomer

39. Charles Joseph King 1878-aft 1920 married Etta E. unknown ca 1880-aft 1920

1910 United States Federal Census Farmington, Oakland, Michigan

<u>Household Members: Name Age</u>
Charles J King 35 b. Canada English, parents born England, Immigrated 1887
Etta E King 33
Dora J King 9
Shiney R King 7
Francis F King 5
Maude E King 4
Alfred C King 2

World War I Draft Registration Cards, 1917-1918
Name: Charles Joseph King
City: Detroit
County: Wayne
State: Michigan
Birth Date: 17 Mar 1878
Race: White
Roll: 2032418
DraftBoard: 15
Sept 1918. Shoe Business, self-employed 1175 Gratiot Ave (also his residence). Nearest relative Mrs Elizabeth King (his mother?), Redford Michigan

1920 United States Federal Census Detroit Ward 13, Wayne, Michigan

<u>Household Members: Name Age</u>
Charles J King 43., born Canada, parents born England. Immigrated 1889. Can read and write. Rents his home
Etta King 43
Dora King 18
Shirley King 17
Francis King 15
Maud King 13
Alfred King 11
Esther King 5

41. Northrup Whiting 1852-1929 married (1) Mary Nichols Calver 1853-1922 married (2) Minnie Schofield Hawarth ca 1869-?

1891 Census of Canada Province: Ontario District Number: 88 District: Lincoln and Niagara Subdistrict: St Catharines Archive Roll #: T-6351

Household Members: Name Age
Northup Whiting 38 b. USA, Methodist, parents b. England, gardener
Mary E Whiting 38 b Ontario parents b England
Chas Whiting 13 b. Ontario
James Whiting 12 b. Ontario
Sarah Whiting 6 b. Ontario

1911 Census of Canada Province: Ontario District: Lincoln District Number: 93 Sub-District: St. Catherines Sub-District Number: 46 Place of Habitation: 11 Fitzgerald Page: 13

Household Members: Name Age
Northop Whiting 59 b Dec. 1852 United States of America   Immigrated 1874
Mary E Whiting 59 b May 1852 Ontario

1901 Census of Canada Province: Ontario District: Lincoln & Niagara District Number: 85 Sub-District: St Catharines (City/Cité) Sub-District Number: K-3 Family Number: 40 Page: 4

Household Members: Name Age
Northup Whiting 48 b 11 Dec 1852 England. Immigrated 1868. American nationality, florist, Protestant
Mary Whiting 48 b 12 May 1852 Ontario
Charles Whiting 23
Sarah Whiting 16
Sidney Trapnell 22 b. 27 Sep 1878, lodger

Marriage Registration 1 March 1876

Northrup Whiting, 23 years old, living Guelph, born New York City, labourer, son of Carter & Louisa Whiting

Mary Elizabeth Nichols Calver, 24 years old, living Guelph, born Guelph, daughter of Samuel & Sarah Calver

42. Malvina Whiting 1856-1903 married Charles Welch ca 1869-?

1891 Census of Canada Province: Ontario District Number: 103 District: Ottawa City Subdistrict: St Georges Ward Archive Roll #: T-6359

Household Members: Name Age
Charles Welsh 22 b England, parents born England, Church of England
Malvine Welsh 26 b Australia
Charles Mills 22 b England, lodger

Ontario Death Registration. Malvina Welch, age 36 died May 13, 1903. Married. Born Australia. Cause of death Acute Anaemia following a miscarriage 2 weeks earlier

Registry of Births, Deaths, Marriages, Victoria Australia at
https://online.justice.vic.gov.au/bdm/
Family Name: WHITING
Given Name(s):   Malvina
Sex: Unknown
Event: BIRTH
Father's Name: Carter
Mother's Name: KING - Louisa
Birth Place: BEEC
Registration Year: 1865
Registration Number: 790

746

SCHEDULE C.
County of Carleton

Left Side page
Malvina --->

	NAME OF DECEASED. (Surname First.)	Sex. (M. or F.)	Date of Death. Month.	Year.	Age.	RESIDENCE. No. or House or Lot.	Concession or Street.	OCCUPATION. occ MARRIED OR SINGLE.
485	Armstrong James	M.	8 May 1903		82 yrs.	Prot. Home for Aged		occ Laborer M. or S.
	Wickware Janet	F.	11		64	355	Cooper	occ M. or S. W
	Welch Malvina		13		36	118	Ottawa	occ M. or S. M occ

747

DEATHS.
Division of Ottawa

Right Side page
Malvina --->

Where Born.	Cause of Death. Length of Illness.	Name of Physician in Attendance.	Religious Denomination.	Name of Person Making Return.	Date of Registration.
Ireland	Paralysis - 2/2	Dr Beamans	Meth.	W.D. Jokney	8 May 1903	037299
Scotland	Asthma - 1 yr.	Cooke		J.P. Cooke, 27/12	007300
Australia	Acute anaemia following miscarriage - 2 wks	Brown	the deceased / E.H. Brown	13	007301
					007302

169

43. Lewis Whiting 1857-? married (1) Mary Fimpel ca 1859-aft 1925 married (2) Ellen Villeneuve

1881 Census St Catherines, Lincoln, Ontario
Name Marital Status Gender Ethnic Origin Age Birthplace Occupation Religion
Lewis WHITING M Male English 23 Australia Laborer Weslyan Methodist
Mary WHITING M Female German 22 Ontario Weslyan Methodist

Source Information: Family History Library Film 1375890 NA Film Number C-13254 District 145 Sub-district A Division 3 Page Number 50 Household Number 258

10833-87 (Renfrew Co) Louis WHITING, 29, traveler, Reachworth? Victoria Australia, Toronto, s/o Carter WHITING & Louisa WHITING married Ellen VILLENEUVE, 19, Westmeath, Renfrew, d/o (Francis & Melvina?), witn, unreadable, 1887, Eganville [very faded reg'n]

1891 Census of Canada Province: Ontario District Number: 72 District: Hamilton City Subdistrict: Ward 1 Archive Roll #: T-6341

The 3 older boys were in a Boy's Home in Ward 1, Hamilton run by Mary Shaw, Matron. Their little brother Harry was in Ward 3 in an Infant Home

Household Members: Name Age
Charles Whiting 10 b. Ontario, Church of England, parents born Ontario
Lewis Whiting 8 b. Ontario, Church of England, parents born Ontario
Frank Whiting 7 b. Ontario, Church of England, parents born Ontario

Boys Home 23 Duke street

The birth registrations of her sons Frank and Harry state mother is "Mary Fimple" It is printed above as FIMPLE, then crossed out and replaced with FIMPEL. A starmp says "corrected by VSA 1919 and declaration dated 21/5/25 by Mary Whiting, mother"

1891 Census of Canada Province: Ontario District Number: 72 District: Hamilton City Subdistrict: Ward 4 Archive Roll #: T-6341

Household Members: Name Age
Ben Scratch 49
Malinda Scratch 44
John H Scratch 23
Erions E Scratch 17
Ben A Scratch 16
Walter Scratch 13
Arthur Scratch 10
Annie Scratch 5
Mary Whiting 29 Widowed, lodger, Baptist, parents born Germany

1891 Census of Canada District Number: 72 District: Hamilton City Subdistrict: Ward 3 Archive Roll #: T-6341

Little Harry was placed in the Home for the Friendless & Infant Home in Hamilton. Helen Mair was the Matron in 1891. The children in this Home were under age 5. His older brother's were placed in a Boy's Home for older children

Household Members: Name Age
Harry Whiting 4 b. Ontario, Baptist, parents born Ontario

Home of the Friendless and Infants Home, Caroline street south.

1901 Census of Canada Province: Ontario District: Hamilton (City/Cité) District Number: 69 Sub-District: Hamilton (City/Cité) Ward/Quartier No 4 Sub-District Number: D-4 Family Number: 139 Page: 13

Household Members: Name Age
Mary Whiting 42 b 28 Feb 1859 Ontario, German origin, widow, tailoress, Baptist
Lewie Whiting 18 20 Feb 1883 Ontario, shoe finisher
Harry W Whiting 14 b. 24 Jul 1886, tea packer

52. William D. King ca 1863-aft 1920 married (1) Margaret Jenks ca 1868-?
married (2) Nellie Peel ca 1892-?

Michigan Marriages 1868-1925
Groom name: William D King
Groom age: 38 years
Groom birth year: 1866
Groom birth place: Canada
Bride name: Margaret Jarks
Bride age: 36 years
Bride birth year: 1868
Bride birth place: Germany
Marriage date: 05 Jul 1904
Marriage place: Delray, Wayne, Michigan
Father of groom name: Thomas
Mother of groom name: Ellen King
Father of bride name: Unknown
Mother of bride name: Unknown
Film number: 2342669
Digital GS number: 4208698
Reference number: vol 4 p 529 rn 43098

Michigan Marriages 1868-1925
Groom name: William D. King
Groom age: 50 years
Groom birth year: 1865
Groom birth place: Canda
Bride name: Nellie Peel
Bride age: 23 years
Bride birth year: 1892
Bride birth place: Michigan
Marriage date: 08 Jun 1915
Marriage place: L'Anse, Baraga, Michigan
Father of groom name: Thomas K...
Mother of groom name: ...elen Devalle
Father of bride name: Alfred Pee...
Mother of bride name: Unknown
Film number: 2342709
Digital GS number: 4209290
Reference number: v 1 p 76 rn 26

1910 United States Federal Census Negaunee Ward 3, Marquette, Michigan
Household Members: Name Age
William D King 48 b Canada English, parents born Canada English. Immigrated 1877
Margaret E King 46
Note that the following are all boarders
Thomas Blendell 30
John Canary 24
Arthur Canary 18
Fabian Page 30
Duncan R A Fox 26
William Ditz 22
Clyde Defrance 19
Oscar Peterson 41
Hordan W Bloise 56
John Gertz 26
Morse Herman 20
Alfred Erickson 41
Dolph Lavamie 48
Alexander Turcott 39
Robert Fox 58
Nellie Peel 17
Leda Witlund 19
Marie Lumphrey 19
Lily Pazq 15

1920 United States Federal Census Detroit Ward 10, Wayne, Michigan

Household Members: Name Age
William King 57 naturalized in 1900, b Canada, parents born England, immigrated 1890, owns his home, can read and write
Ellen King 57

57. Viola King 1873-aft 1930 married (1) John Sturck ca 1837-between 1913-1920 married (2) Henry Manning Shepherd ca 1800-? married (3) James McNeal ca 1872-?

Michigan Marriages 1868-1925
Groom name: John Stuck
Groom age: 61 years
Groom birth place: Canada
Bride name: Viola King
Bride race or color (on document):
Bride age: 26 years
Bride birth place: Michigan
Marriage date: 19 Dec 1898
Marriage place: Port Austin, Huron, Michigan
Father of groom name: Jno. Stuck
Mother of groom name: Betsy Hauspiller
Father of bride name: Thos. King
Mother of bride name: Helen Davill
Film number: 2342509
Digital GS number: 4208258
Reference number: p 213 rn 238

Michigan Marriages 1868-1925
Groom name: Henry Manning Shepherd
Groom age: 37 years
Groom birth place: Michigan
Bride name: Viola Sturk
Bride age: 40 years
Bride birth place: Canada
Marriage date: 15 Jul 1920
Marriage place: Corunna, Shiawassee, Michigan
Father of groom name: John Shepherd
Mother of groom name: Anna Bersett
Father of bride name: Thomas King
Mother of bride name: Helen Deville
Film number: 2342739
Digital GS number: 4032439
Reference number: v 7 p 226 rn 11027

1930 United States Federal Census Rush, Shiawassee, Michigan
Household Members: Name Age
James McNail 54 b Michigan
Viola McNail 57
Russell G McNail 16
Dora V McNail 1 3/12 dau
Howard D Sturk 17 stepson b ca 1913 MI

1900 United States Federal Census Dwight Township, Huron, Michigan

Household Members: Name Age
John Sturk 62 b. Sep. 1827 Canada English, immigrated 1880, parents b. Canada. Married 2 years (1898)
Viola Sturk 28 b Can. Eng. Jul 1871 imm 1890 father b Can, mother b Eng mother of 1 living child, md 1898
Verney Sturk 3 b Apr 1897 Michigan
Ellen Sturk 1 b Oct 1899 MIchigan
Lottie Sturk 11 b Apr 1889 location unknown, adopted daughter

1910 United States Federal Census Dwight, Huron, Michigan
Household Members: Name Age
John Sturk 72 born Canada English, parents born Canada English. Immigrated 1889
Viola Sturk 38
Vernon Sturk 13
Helen Sturk 10

Michigan Marriages 1868-1925
Groom name: James Mcneal
Groom age: 47 years
Groom birth place: Michigan
Bride name: Viola King Sturk
Bride age: 51 years
Bride birth place: Canada
Marriage date: 30 Oct 1923
Marriage place: Corunna, Shiawassee, Michigan
Mother of groom name: ...ary Stringham
Father of bride name: T. King
Film number: 2342757
Digital GS number: 4210120
Reference number: v 9 rn 272

58. George Lewis King 1879-1966 married Hattie Kirkpatrick 1879-1937

1900 United States Federal Census Egleston, Emmet, Michigan
Household Members: Name Age
George King 24 b Michigan, parents born Canada English. married 3 years (1897)
Hattie King 20 b Nov 1879 MI parents b Canada
Herbert King 1 son

1930 United States Federal Census Sheridan, Huron, Michigan
Household Members: Name Age
George L King 50 b. Michigan
Hattie King 50
Bertha King 19
George King 17
Vera King 15
Hattie King 12
James King 10
William King 4

1910 United States Federal Census Colfax, Huron, Michigan
Household Members: Name Age
George L King 31 b. Michigan, parents b. Canada English
Hattie King 31
Herbert King 11 son
Nellie King 9 b 1901 MI daughter
Helen King 7 b 1903 MI daughter
Rusel King 5 b 1905 MI son
Velma King 3 b 1908 MI daughter

World War I Draft Registration Cards, 1917-1918
Name: George Lewis King
City: Not Stated [Bad Axe] County: Huron
State: Michigan Birth Date: 6 Aug 1879
Race: White Roll: 1675754 DraftBoard: 0
Res: 3 Bad Axe, Huron MI
Occ: farming, self employed. Relative Hattie King
Medium height and build, blue eyes brown hair

Cass City Chronicle, Wed. Jan 5, 2000 page 9. OBITUARY
George W. King Sr., 87, of Cass City, died Friday, Dec. 3 1, 1999, in his home. He was born Dec. 28, 1912, in Huron County, to GeorgeL. and Hattie (Kirkpatrick) King and lived in the area hiswhole life. He married ElsieMay Jackson Sept. 19, 1932, in Huron County. She diedMay 17, 1997.He farmed most of his life.He is survived by his children, George W. (Phyllis)King Jr. of Cass City, BctteLou (Calvin) Hunt of Ubly,Glen L. (Janet) King of Auburn, Jerry (Bev) King ofBridgeport, James L. King ofCass City; 15 grandchildren;3 1 great-grandchildren; a brother, William King of Lexington, and many nieces and nephews. He was preceded in death by 3 brothers, Herbert, Russell and James; 7 sisters,Helen Smithers, Nellie Apley, Hattie Wellock,Velma Wills, Dora Etzler, Bertha Wills Campbell, andV era Paison. Funeral services were heldSunday in Kranz FuneralHome, Cass City, withChuck Emmert of Novesta Church of Christ officiating.Interment was in ElklandTownship Cemetery, CassCity. Memorials may be made to the Family Discretionary Fund.

Cass City Chronicle, Feb. 24, 1966
Funeral services for George L. King, 87, lifelong resident of the Thumb, were held Saturday in Bad Axe funeral home. Rev. J. Arthur Murfin, pastor of the Baptist Church m Port Huron,officiated and burial was in Colfax Cemetery. Mr. King died Tuesday night, Feb. 15, in Huron Community Health Center after a long illness. Born Aug. 6, 1878, near Huron City, Mr. King was a farmer for many years. He also operated a service station at M-53 and M-81, Cass City. He and Miss Hattie Kirkpatrick were married April 23, 1898, at Bad Axe. Mrs. King died Feb. 4, 1937. Two daughters also preceded him in death.He is survived by five sons,Herbert King of Lapeer, Russell King of Trenton, George King Jr. and James King, both of Cass City,and William King of Port Huron;five daughters, Mrs. Robert Smithers of Toledo, Mrs. Stanley Wills of Cass City, Mrs. Robert Etzler of Port Austin, Mrs. Wilford Willsof Ubly and Mrs. William Paison of Lapeer, and four generations of grandchildren.

1920 United States Federal Census Bingham, Huron, Michigan

Household Members: Name Age
George L King 40 b Michigan, parents b. Canada. Rents his home, can read and write
Hattie King 40
Helen King 17
Russell King 14
Velma King 12
Dora King 11
Bertha King 9
George King 7
Vera King 5
Hattie King 2 7/12
James King 4/12

66. Thomas William King 1841-1906 married (1) Mary Ann Kemble ca 1844-1869 married (2) Mary Ann Ramsey ca 1842-between 1882-1901 married (3) Margaret Brugess ca 1868-?

367

United Church Archives Wesleyan Methodist Baptismal Register, Vol 1 p. 367
Thomas William King son of David & Mary born 15 Aug. 1841 bpt 4 Jan 1842 Puslinch

Pioneer Cemetery, Arkell Ontario: "Joseph, son of Thomas W. and Mary A. King, d. Oct 2, 1873 aged 11 mos 9 days"

Arkell United Church Cemetery, Arkell Ontario, Double grave with one marker:
Mary Ann d. Dec. 13, 1870 age 1 yr. 2 mos 2 days
Catherine d. Dec. 9, 1870 age 5 yrs 7 mos 16 days
Children of Thomas W. and Mary A. King.

1881 Census Puslinch, Wellington South, Ontario, Canada FHL Film 1375894 NAC C-13258 Dist 151 SubDist A Div 1 Page 43

	Marr	Age	Origin	Birthplace
David KING | M | 63 | English; England | Occ:Gentleman
Religion:C. Methodist
Mary KING | M | 61 | English;England | Religion:C. Methodist
Thomas H KING | M | 39 | English Ontario | Occ:Farmer Religion:C. Methodist
Maryann KING | M | 39 | Irish | Ontario Religion:C. Presbyterian
Marion KING | | 2 | English;Ontario Religion:C. Presbyterian

Directory of Wellington County, 1867
1867 Puslinch Tp. Residents
KING David C 10 L 56 Free
KING George C 10 L5 Free
KING Thomas W. C 9 L 7 Householder

Thomas King's first wife, Mary Ann Kemble, died in 1869, quite likely in childbirth. Her daughter Mary Ann was born 11 Oct. 1869.

Pioneer Cemetery, Arkell Ontario: "Our darling Mary d. Oct. 12, 1876 age 7 mos, daughter of Thomas W. and Mary A. King. Sleep on my Mary in calm repose, though parted for awhile, To _ _ _ _ _ on _ _ _ will join praise And grace your happy smile"

1891 Census of Canada Province: Ontario District Number: 46 District: Algoma Subdistrict: Port Findlay Archive Roll #: T-6323
Household Members: Name Age
Thomas King 49, b Ontario, Free Church, parents born England
Maryann King 49 wife
Marion King 12 daughter
Stella King 8 daughter

1901 Census of Canada
King Thomas M Head W Sep 15 1841 59
King Estella F Daughter S Sep 17 1882 18
Subdistrict: Tarbutt, Algoma, Ontario
District Number: 44 Subdistrict Number: c-1
Archives Microfilm: T-6458

67. David King 1843-1921 married Ann Decker 1854-aft 1911

Township of Puslinch Wellington Dist. 367

NAME OF PERSON BAPTIZED.	NAMES OF PARENTS.	Place of Parents' Residence.	Born Where.	Born When.	Baptized Where.	Baptized Where.	Minister Baptizing.
David King	David Mary	do.	do.	28 Feb.	do.	do.	do.

United Church Archives Wesleyan Methodist
Baptismal Register, Vol 1 p. 367
David King son of David & Mary born 28 Feb.
1843 bpt 16 April 1843 in Puslinch

1891 census Guelph City, Div 1 p 4 Rell T-6377
King David, 48 b Ontario father and mother b
Eng, Church of England, Cattle Dealer
Ann, 39 b ontario father b USA, mother b Eng
William Henry 17 b Ont
Susan ida 15 b Ont
Celista 13 b Ont
Freeman 10 b Ont
Rachel Ann 8 b Ont
Lydia Maud 6 b Ont
Elmer 8/12 b Ont

**1901 census Ontario WENTWORTH (South/Sud)
(#128) Subdistrict: Flamboro (West/Ouest) f-3
Page 3 Details: Schedule 1 Microfilm T-6506**

King David M   Head M Feb 28 1843 58
King Ann F   Wife M Feb 9 1854 47
King William M   Son S Dec 13 1873 27
King Susan F   Daughter S Dec 4 1875 25
King Clestila F   Daughter S Mar 13 1878 23
King Freeman M   Son S Jul 23 1880 20
King Rachel F   Daughter S Nov 26 1882 18
King Maud F   Daughter S Jan 26 1885 16
King Elmer M   Son S Aug 3 1890 10
King Merlie F   Daughter S Aug 10 1892 8
King Clifton M   Son S Nov 12 1894

**1881 Census Place:Puslinch, Wellington South, Ontario,
Canada. FHL Film 1375894 NAC C-13258 Dist 151
SubDist A Div 1 Page 4 Family 14**

	Sex	Marr	Age	Origin	Birthplace
David KING	M	M	37	English, born Ontario	
Occ:Farmer Religion:Church of England					
Ann KING	F	M	29	German, born	Ontario
Religion:Church of England					
William H. KING	M		7	English, born	Ontario
Religion:Church of England					
Susan I. KING	F		5	English, born Ontario	
Religion:Church of England					
Celeste KING	F		3	English , born Ontario	
Religion:Church of England					
Freeman KING	M		9 mos.	English , born Ontario	
Religion:Church of England, Born:Aug;					
Joseph BELL	M		20	English, born Ontario	Occ:
Farmer Religion:Church of England					

**1911 Census of Canada, Province: Ontario District:
Wentworth District Number: 135 Sub-District:
Flamborough East Sub-District Number: 30
Place of Habitation: E Flambro**

Household Members: Name Age
David King 68, born Feb. 1843 Ontario, English origin
Ann King 59
Freeman King 30
Sarah E King 23
Elmer A King 20
Merlie King 19
Clifton D King 16
Harold Bevans 20 servant born England Feb. 1891

69. Harriet King 1847-1928 married Alexander McGinnis 1849-1935

United Church of Canada, Victoria University Archives, Fonds 5, Series 8, Vol. 3, Wesleyan Methodist Baptism Registers, Vol. 1 p 367
Harriet d/o David and Mary King. Parents living Puslinch, child born Puslinch 19 Aug 1847, baptised 24 Oct. 1847.

Registers of Church of Our Lady, Guelph Ontario, 1850.
Alexander born on the 3rd of November [February was written in then scratched out] 1849 [the year has been altered, it appears the priest began writing 185 then changed the 5 to a 4 and continued with a 9] baptised on the 3 Feb. 1850 is the son of Joseph McGinnis and his wife Fanny. Sponsors were James McNorton and Ann Grant.

NAME or PERSON BAPTIZED.	NAMES OF PARENTS.	Place of Parents' Residence.	Born Where.	Born When.	Baptized When.	Baptized Where.	Minister Baptizing.
Harriet King	David, Mary	do	do	19 Aug 1847	24 Oct 1847	do	John Brown

CDV (photo) of Harriet King ca 1867

Alex McGinnis' Irish Catholic parents settled on Conc. 3 Lot 10 Puslinch Tp. Wellington County, on land owned by James McGinnis, a son of John McGinnis who owned Conc. 3 Lot 11. This land is swampy and not good farm land, although Joseph does not appear to have been a farmer.

Some time after arriving in Puslinch, Joseph rented a tavern called "Speed The Plow" at Conc 4 Lot 6 Puslinch Tp. on the River Speed. In 1851 and 1861 the family was living in a 2-storey log cabin in Puslinch Tp.

From Jan 1863 to March 1871, Alexander and his siblings Margaret, Annie and Daniel McGinnis are on a list of pupils attending School SS # 12, Puslinch. A frame school was built in 1847 and the stone schoolhouse was built in 1854 or 1856.

Alex and Hattie married one month before their daughter Mary was born. Family lore states that Mary's father and brothers came after Alex with a shotgun and forced him to marry a very pregnant Hattie.

1901 census Guelph, Wellington Co. Ontario E-3 p 7
McGinnis, Harriet, f, white, head, widow [sic], b 12 Aug 1851, age 49, English, Methodist, General Servant
Mary A. dau. b 19 Oct. 1877, 23, Methodist, weaver
Joseph, son b 21 Dec 1878, 22, Methodist, carriage maker
Daniel, son, 21 Apr 1881, 19, Methodist, carriage Maker
Henry, son, 2 Apr 1887, 13, Methodist, student living at 120 Farquhar St.

1901 census Morriston, Wellington Co. S. Ontario Dist. 126, f-3 p 15 Line 36 (T 6505)
Vogt, John, Head, b 30 Sept 1854, 46, Denmark. Imm. 1880 Naturalized 1884, Hotel Keeper
Vogt, Frances, wife, b 1855, 45, Ont. Irish
Vogt, Florance M. b 16 Nov. 1894, On. 6
McGinnis, Frances, widow, mother in law, b 1824 Ireland, age 76 imm. 1850
McGinnis, Alex, brother in law, married, b 1857 Ont. age 43, hosteler

69. Harriet King (Cont'd)

1881 Census Guelph Ontario p 23:
McINNES [sic] Alexander, 30, Irish, Catholic, b. Ontario, Labourer
Harriet, 34, Methodist, b. Ontario
MaryAnn, 4, Methodist, b. Ontario
Joseph, 3, Methodist, b. Ontario
Fanny b Sept. 1880, Methodist, b. Ontario

1891 census Puslinch Tp. Wellington Co. p. 28 W 1/3 141 line 19

McGINNIS Alexander, 41 b. Ont, father and mother b Ont., [sic] Roman Catholic
Harriet, 44, Methodist
MaryAnn, 14 Methodist
Fanny, 11 Methodist
Daniel 7 Methodist
Henry 4 Methodist

Photo of Harriet King ca 1920s

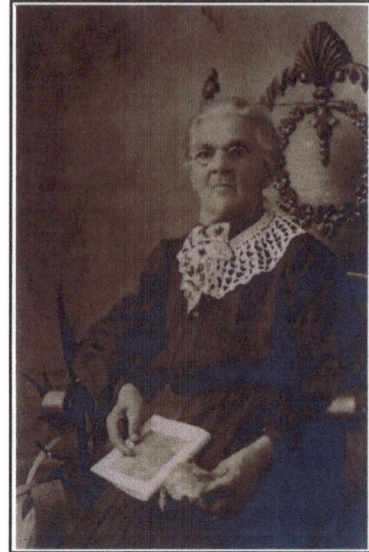

1911 census Morriston, Puslinch Tp page 15 District 134 Wellington Subdistrict 23
Brown, Solomon, head, Badenoch St, single, Oct 1856, 54 yrs b On, German, Methodist
Brown, Bernard, brother May 1862, 49, hotel keeper
Brown, Mary, sister in law, June 1862, 49 b Ontario, Catholic
McGinnis [no first name but it is Alexander], head, Badenoch St, [no month] 1848, 62 yrs, b On, Irish, Catholic, labourer

1911 Census of Canada, Province: Ontario District: Wellington South District Number: 134 Sub-District: Guelph Sub-District Number: 46
Place of Habitation: 3 Wellington St Page: 13
<u>Household Members: Name Age</u>
Harriett Mc Ginnis 58 no occupation, born Aug. 1852 Ontario. English origin
Henry Mc Ginnis 24 Apr 1887 single, carriage trimmer at carriage shop

Ontario Canada Deaths, Harriet McGinnis born Aug. 9, 1847 in Puslinch Tp, to David King and Mary Bell. She had senility adenomatous goitre and died of apolplexy of the brain. She lived at 44 Quebec St Guelph. Died Wellington County.

Alex is buried in Crown Cemetery, East side of Highway on Lot 28 front Conc 8, a half mile from Morriston, Wellington Co. Ontario. His stone has an incorrect year of birth, and was erected by his daughter Mary McGinnis Sheward

1915: Alex McGinnis was living in Morriston, Puslinch Tp., farmer, Conc B, Lot 29

Harriet is buried in Woodlawn Cemetery, Guelph Ontario

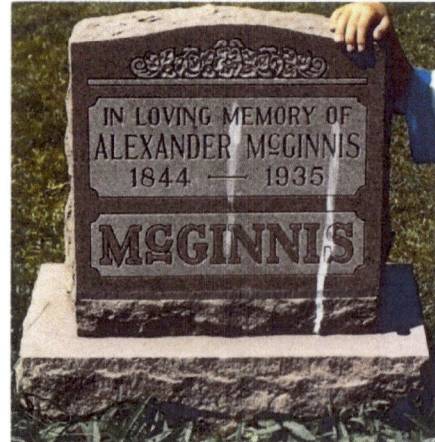

Tovell Funeral Homes lists Hattie's death as 19 Jan 1928, funeral on 21 Jan 1928 and her age as 85 years 6 months, making her d.o.b. 1843

70. John King ca 1852-aft. 1910 married (1) Susanna Fife 1854-1930 m (2) Iva L. Cox 1884-?

1881 Census Peel, Wellington Centre, Ontario

Name Marital Status Gender Ethnic Origin Age Birthplace Occupation Religion
John KING M Male English 28 Ontario Farmer Presbyterian
Susannah KING M Female Scottish 28 Ontario Presbyterian
Mary C. KING   Female English 6 Ontario Presbyterian
Eliza J. KING   Female English 4 Ontario Presbyterian
Berthie F. KING   Female English 1 Ontario Presbyterian
Family History Library Film 1375895 NA Film Number C-13259 District 152 Sub-district E Division 3 Page Number 44 Household Number 200

Photo of Susan Fife ca 1900, courtesy of David Rodgers

Ontario Deaths 1869-1947
Name : Susan King
Death date : 10 Mar 1930
Age at death : 76 years
Death place : Toronto, York, Ontario, Canada
Birth place : Guelph Twp
Marital status : Widowed
Ethnicity : English
Father name : John Fife
Mother name : Eliza Pallister

1891 Census of Canada District: Wellington North Subdistrict: Arthur Village District Number: 126 Archive Roll #: T-6376
Household Members: Name Age
John King 37
Susannah King 37 Church of England, parents born Scotland
Berthan T King 11
Anna M King 4

1901 Census Amaranth, WELLINGTON (North/Nord), ONTARIO
Fyfe Robert M   Head M Apr 24 1887 24
King Susan F Sister M Oct 1 1855 46 married
King M. Hanah F Niece S Apr 21 1888 13
King William M Nephew S Jun 10 1890 9
King Lily F Niece S Mar 1898 4
District Number: 125 Subdistrict Number: a-2
Archives Microfilm: T-6504

Michigan Marriages 1868-1925
Groom name: John King
Groom age: 42 years
Groom birth year: 1868
Groom birth place: Canada
Bride name: Iva Cox Cobler
Bride age: 26 years
Bride birth year: 1884
Bride birth place: Nebraska
Marriage date: 01 Aug 1910
Marriage place: Battle Creek, Calhoun, Michigan
Father of groom name: David King
Mother of groom name: Mary Bell
Father of bride name: Samuel Cox
Mother of bride name: Mary Frey
Film number: 2342688
Digital GS number: 4209131
Reference number: v 1 p 26 rn 355

1910 United States Federal Census Battle Creek Ward 5, Calhoun, Michigan

Household Members: Name Age
John King 42 m2x, b Can, father b Can, mother b. England, farmer
Iva King 26 m2x, b Nebraska father b Indiana, mother b Illinois

TWO ARRESTS ON CHARGE OF ARSON

MR. AND MRS. JOHN KING ACCUSED OF SETTING SPRAGUE BUILDINGS ON FIRE

Alleged That Tenants and Owner of Farm Had Trouble. Prosecutor Authorized Arrests

Charged with arson in connection with the burning of the buildings on the Wilbur Sprague farm in Emmet township on Saturday Sept. 1, Mr. and Mrs. John King of Battle Creek were arrested yesterday by Deputy Sheriff Frank Eddy and arraigned in court in that city. This caused a sensation as both are well known residents of the county. It is claimed that the woman with her husband's cognizance set fire to the barn. The house, two large barns, silos, and several outbuildings were destroyed at a loss of about $12,000. The Citizens Mutual Fire Insurance Co. adjusted and paid the loss, at the full insurance carried, $5,543.

The fire occurred shortly after noon. The Kings were tenant farmers working the Sprague farm on shares, they to have one-third interest in the revenues.

On the side King maintained an extensive milk route, but a short time ago he was arrested and convicted of adulterating the milk. Sprague refused to help him out and ordered him to vacate the house. A dispute over the settlement of the share due King arose, but the Kings ostensibly started to pack up. The fire on Labor day destroyed all their household goods, but it is alleged these had been more than covered by insurance taken out a few days before. It is said Mr. Sprague settled with Mr. King and paid him $300.

At the time of the fire Mr. King was in Battle Creek looking for a house so it is rumored. The officers believe that he had things fixed with his wife. She telephoned to the place where Mr. Sprague boarded and said a stranger was there to see him. She was informed that Sprague was not there. However in a few minutes she again phoned that the barn was on fire.

Secretary A. J. Murray reported the fire to State Fire Marshal Robinson and both conducted an investigation. Several witnesses were women and the testimony was laid before Prosecutor Kirschman, State Fire Marshal Robinson signing the complaint Saturday afternoon.

The officers who made the arrest charge that Mrs. King's object in setting the place on fire was double—to avenge fancied wrongs perpetrated by Sprague, and to get insurance money. Both Mr. and Mrs. King claim to be innocent. Several prominent people volunteered to go on their bonds, which were set at $1,000 each, after they had been arraigned, and demanded an examination.

Mrs. King claims a stranger was hanging around the place, and neighbors say she called them by telephone asking if Mr. King was there. The police assert she knew her husband was in town and that the stranger was a myth.

The examination of Mr. and Mrs. John King charged with arson, was adjourned in Justice Hart's court in Battle Creek this morning. They are alleged to have set fire to buildings on the farm of Wilbur Sprague, south of that city.

Evening Chronicle. Marshall, Michigan. 16 Sept. 1913 & 17 Sept. 1913

MRS. JOHN KING BREAKS DOWN

TELLS TWO DIFFERENT STORIES OF THE FIRE ON SPRAGUE FARM.

Hearing Is Continued Until Today by Deputy State Fire Marshal Robinson.

Secretary A. J. Murray of the Citizens Mutual Fire Ins. Co., met Deputy State Fire Marshal Robinson at Battle Creek Friday and they went out and looked over the loss on the Wilbur Sprague farm in Emmet. Mr. and Mrs. John King who resided on the place were subpoenaed before them and Mr. Robinson took the testimony of both. Mrs. King broke down when being examined. She tells two different stories in connection with the fire, one being that a strange man appeared at the place looking for Mr. Sprague and soon after the fire broke out in the barn and she called a neighbor by phone, first to ascertain if Mr. Sprague was there and then to notify the neighbor that the place was on fire. Mr. King was

Evening Chronicle. Marshall, Michigan. 8 Sept 1913

the place was on fire. Mr. King was in Battle Creek at the time the fire broke out. The hearing was continued until today and further testimony taken in Battle Creek. It is learned Mr. Sprague and Mr. King had some difficulties, one being over the milk. Mr. King was arrested at Battle Creek for watering the milk. He was working the Sprague farm on a one-third interest and got one third of the milk. After he was arrested it is said he declined to draw any more milk but Mr. Sprague insisted on it being drawn as he had sold it under contract. He finally settled with Mr. King, paying his about $300 and Mr. and Mrs. King were about to move off the place.

It is said they had a piano and some other household goods purchased on a contract and according to a report Mr. King sought to get the insurance on what he had in the residence increased recently.

A writ of error has been granted the Ohio Farmers' Insurance company in the suit brought against it by John and Iva King, who suffered the loss of considerable household effects in the fire on the W. W. Sprague fire in Emmet a year ago.

Marshall News Statesman, Michigan. 10 Sept. 1914

The examination of John and Iva L. King who were arrested on the charge of arson in connection with the fire on the Wilbur Sprague farm in Emmet Labor day, furnished bonds in the sum of $1,000 for an examination before Justice Hart at Battle Creek. It is said a fire insurance policy for $800 on furniture was taken out by Mr. and Mrs. King on July 19 in the Ohio Farmers' Insurance Co. They asked for a $1,000 policy, but it was refused by the Battle Creek agent. King, a few days after the fire went to the representative of the insurance company to collect insurance. The agent scented something wrong, and got in communication with Deputy State Fire Marshal Samuel Robinson. As a result of the latter's investigation Mr. and Mrs. King were arrested. If the couple are acquitted their insurance will be paid promptly. Otherwise the

Evening Chronicle. Marshall, Michigan. 17 Sept. 1913

Marshall News
Statesman. Michigan
1 June 1914

KINGS GET THEIR INSURANCE IN COURT

END OF CASE BROUGHT BY SPRAGUE FARM TENANTS FOR LOSS IN FIRE.

The case of John King vs. the Ohio Mutual Farmers' Insurance company, came to a close yesterday in Battle Creek when the jury returned a verdict of $816.67 in favor of the plaintiff, after being out 'ess than a half hour. The case has occupied the attention of the court for only a day.

The Kings, who resided on the Sprague farm had their household goods packed and ready to move to 'Battle Creek last year, the fore part of September, when the farm buildings caught fire. Mr. and Mrs. King were arrested and charged with arson following an investigation carried on by the state fire marshal, but later the cases were dismissed on account of lack of evidence. The Insurance company, however, refused to pay Mr. and Mrs. King the insurance said to be due, with the result that the matter was brought into court. The plaintiffs will receive $800 the face value of the policy, and $16.67 interest.

Evening Statesman, Marshall
Michigan. 23 Sept. 1913

Because Prosecuting Attorney Kirschman was busy in circuit court yesterday, the examination of Mr. and Mrs. John King, charged with arson, was adjourned until September 30 in Justice Hart's court. This case is attracting considerable attention, as it is not often that arrests are made on this charge, and a case must have considerable merit before such a complaint will be allowed. Mr. and Mrs. King were arrested as the result of a fire which destroyed the buildings on the Wilbur Sprague farm, south of Battle Creek. Labor day, last. Complaint was made by a deputy state fire marshall after he had made a thorough investigation. The prosecution will try to show, as a motive for the alleged crime, that there previously ensued a quarrel between the tenants and the owner of the farm. The prosecution will also try to show that but a comparatively short time before the fire, Mr. and Mrs. King had their furniture insured through a local dealer, in the Ohio Farmers' Insurance company, for $800, and that, at about this time, proceedings were started to put the Kings off the farm.

Evening Chronicle
Marshall Michigan
3 Oct. 1913

BIG ARSON CASE HAS COLLAPSED

STATE OFFICIAL WHO HAD MR. AND MRS JOHN KING ARRESTED FAILS TO SHOW UP.

This Has Happened So Often That Justice Hart Finally Dismisses the Defendants.

At the suggestion of Prosecuting Attorney Robert Kirschman, Mr. and Mrs. John King, held on a charge of arson, were dismissed in Justice Hart's court in Battle Creek yesterday morning, because of the failure of the complaining witness to put in an appearance or to have witnesses in court.

Labor day noon a fire broke out in the barn on the farm of Wilbur Sprague west of Ceresco. Mr. and Mrs. King were residing on this farm and, because they had previously had trouble with Sprague and he had instituted proceedings against them to have them ejected, suspicion fell upon the tenants.

A short time previous to this Mr. and Mrs. King had taken out insurance on some furniture for about $800 through a local agency. In the fire practically every building on the Sprague farm was destroyed, and the furniture of Mr. and Mrs. King was burned.

When they attempted to collect for their loss the representative of the Ohio Farmers' Insurance company, in which company the furniture had been insured and the directors of the Citizens' Mutual of Calhoun county in which company Mr. Sprague's buildings were insured, notified Deputy State Fire Marshal Samuel Robinson that he thought something was wrong. The fire marshal after making thorough investigation, swore out warrants before the prosecuting attorney, charging Mr. and Mrs. King with arson. Bonds were placed at $1,000 each when they were arraigned and they demanded an examination and these bonds were furnished.

Several times since their arraignment they have appeared for examination, but on each occasion the case was adjourned, owing to the failure or inability of the complaining witness and other interested parties to the case to be present.

Yesterday morning the case came up again for examination, and Prosecuting Attorney Kirschman decided to hold the examination or cause a dismissal. In the absence of any witnesses the prosecuting attorney made a suggestion to the court that the case be dismissed and the court took the suggestion kindly.

71. Joseph King 1851-1922 married Margaret Hatten 1857-?

1881 Census Place: Puslinch, Wellington South, Ontario, Canada
FHL Film 1375894 NAC C-13258 Dist 151 SubDist A
Div 1 Page 3 Family 12

	Sex	Marr	Age	Origin	Birthplace
Joseph KING	M	M	29	English	Ontario
Occ:	Farmer	Religion:Weslyan Methodist			
Margret KING	F	M	24	English	Ontario
		Religion:Weslyan Methodist			

1901 Census of Canada Subdistrict: Desert Lake, Algoma, Ontario
King Joseph M   Head M Nov 15 1851 49
King Margaret F   Wife M Jul 5 1857 43
King Norman M   Son S May 16 1881 19
King Lorne M   Son S Oct 13 1892 18
King Thomas B M   Son S Aug 25 1885 15
King Mary A F   Daughter S Apr 9 1887 14
King Violet B F   Daughter S Aug 21 1892 8
King Minnie T F   Daughter S Apr 18 1896 4
Hatten Thomas F   father-in-law W Sep 24 1820 80
Hatten George M   Lodger S Jan 29 1855 46

District Number: 44 Subdistrict Number: h
Archives Microfilm: T-6457

Ontario, Canada Deaths, 1869-1932, Algoma District
1922 - 101 Joseph King born Puslinch Ontario, living
Johnson Tp, English origin, 71 years old, born 1851,
Father David King born Succix [sic] England. Mother
Mary Bell born Towecther [?] England. Brother George
King of Rainy River was informant. Buried Desbarats
Ontario on 11 March 1922. Undertaker in Sault Ste
Marie. Died March 9 of chronic cardiac valvular
disease.

1891 Census of Canada, Province: Ontario District Number: 46 District: Algoma Subdistrict: Port Findlay Archive Roll #: T-6323

Household Members: Name Age
Joseph King 38 born Ontario, Free Church, father b.
England, mother b Nova Scotia [sic]
Margaret King 34 Free Church, parents born England
Norman King 10 born Ontario, Free Church
Lorn King 8 born Ontario, Free Church
Thomas King 5 born Ontario, Free Church
Maryann King 4 born Ontario, Free Church
Thomas Hatten 68 b England, father in law, parents
born England, blacksmith

1911 Census of Canada, Province: Ontario District: Algoma West District Number: 55 Sub-District: Johnston Sub-District Number: 5 Place of Habitation: Johnson Page: 9
Household Members: Name Age
Joseph King 59 b. Nov. 1851 Ontario.
Margaret King 53 b. July 1857 Ontario
Lorne King 28 b. Oct 1882 Ontario
Thomas B King 25 b. Aug 1885 Ontario
Mary Ann King 23 b. Apr 1887 Ontario
Violet V King 18 b. Aug 1892 Ontario
Minnie T King 14 b. Apr 1896 Ontario

72. George King 1855-aft. 1913 married Eliza Jane Robinson 1853-1913

1881 Census Puslinch, Wellington South, Ontario, FHL Film 1375894 NAC C-13258 Dist 151 SubDist A Div 1 Page 27 Family 112

	Sex	Marr	Age	Origin	Birthplace
George KING	M	M	25	English	Ontario
Occ:	Farmer	Religion:			C. Methodist
Elisa J. KING	F	M	27	English	Ontario
	Religion:				C. Methodist
George E. KING		M		1	English
Ontario		Religion:			C. Methodist

1911 Census of Canada, Province: Ontario District: Algoma East, District Number: 54, Sub-District: Blind River, Sub-District Number: 63, Page: 21

Household Members: Name Age
George King 53 Aug 1855 Ontario
Eliza King 52 b Jan. 1858
William D F King 26 b March 1885
Ruby King 19 b March 1892
Louise Moffit 24 lodger

1901 Census of Canada, Province: Ontario District: Nipissing District Number: 92 Sub-District: Cooks Mills Sub-District Number: R-1 Family Number: 22 Page: 3

Household Members: Name Age
George King 45 b. 31 Aug. 1855 Ontario, English origin, night watchman, Methodist
Liza H [J] King 48
William King 16
Ruby King 9

Ontario Canada Deaths 04 Nov 1913 Eliza died of heart failure. Age given as 61, place of birth Wellington Co. Her husband George was the informant. Parents Edward Robinson, Mary Fluellen [sic].

George was in Rainy River by 1922

86. Albert George Marriott 1882 -? married Maud Morrill 1884-?

Ontario, Canada Marriages, 1857-1924
Name: Albert Geo Marriott
Birth Place: Guelph
Age: 23
Father Name: John Marriott Marriott
Mother Name: Elizabeth Marriott
Spouse Name: Maud Morrill
Spouse's Age: 23
Spouse Birth Place: Midland
Spouse Father Name: Thomas Morrill
Spouse Mother Name: Phoebe Merrett
Marriage Date: 14 Mar 1907
Marriage Place: Wellington
Marriage County: Wellington
Family History Library Microfilm:
MS932_131

New York Passenger Lists, 1820-1957
3 Dec. 1907 sailing from Havana Cuba
to New York on board the Havana
Albert G. Marriot, 24 juggler, artist,
father John, non immigrant alien
Manet Marriot, 24 juggler

Microfilm Serial: T715
Microfilm Roll: T715_1053

1935 passenger list Albert and #87 brother
Minard aka Murray

1901 Census Guelph Ontario

Marriott John M   Head M Aug 14 1834 66
Marriott Elizabeth F   Wife M Nov 22 1847 53
Marriott Ada S. F   Daughter S Sep 13 1876 24
Marriott Albert G. M   Son S Jun 22 1882 18
Marriott Mes?? J. M   Son S Jun 22 1882 18
Marriott Kate W. F   Daughter S Nov 4 1885 15
District Number: 126
Subdistrict Number: e-14
Archives Microfilm: T-6505

U.S. Naturalization Records Indexes, 1794-1995
Name: Albert George Marriott
Birth Date: 2 Jul 1885
State: Michigan
Locality, Court: Detroit, District Court
Title: Index Cards to Naturalization Petitions for the
U.S. District Court for the Eastern District of Michigan,
Southern Division, Detroit, 1907-1995
Description: M-625 Series: M1917

1930 United States Federal Census
Pine Grove, Van Buren, Michigan

Household Members: Name Age
Albert G Marriott 45 born Canada immigrated 1902,
naturalized, vaudeville performer
Maude Marriott 44 born Canada, immigrated 1886, vaudeville
performer

"The Marriott Twins Scored World Fame"

1937 sailed from Japan to New York on Kongo Maru
Albert George, 54, Aerial Act, American,
Naturalized Circut Court Van Buren Co.
Paw Paw Michigan Jan 21, 1933. born
Guelph Ontario, Visa permit issued
Tokyo June 8, 1937, Residence Allegan
Michigan

Maude Morrill, 53, housewife, born
Barrie Ontario, US Passport 359567
issued Washington DC June 4, 1937
Microfilm Serial: T715
Microfilm Roll: T715_6006

_...Guelph's famous Marriott Twins. The winning of a baton contest
in the old Guelph skatin grink gave the Marriotts their start for 60
years in the show business, gaining them international fame._

_In 1896 they joined the Harry Lindely Dramatic Company, playing
in Canada up to tDawson City in the Yukon. Engagements with
other companies included the Andrew Downie Company of
Vancouver, Mrs. Downie was a former Guelph girl, Tena Hewer.
The Downies built up a creditble circus later sold to Charles Sparks,
becomign quite noted._

_It was with the Downie circus that the Marriotts orignated their
bicycle juggling act which they repeated at the opening of Tony
Pastor's Theatre in New York._

86. Albert George Marriott (cont'd) & 87. Minard Marriott

ANDREW DOWNIE'S CIRCUS made several successful visits around the turn of the century. For a one-ring show hauled overland by wagons, Downie achieved maximum results from 50 performers and a profusion of animals

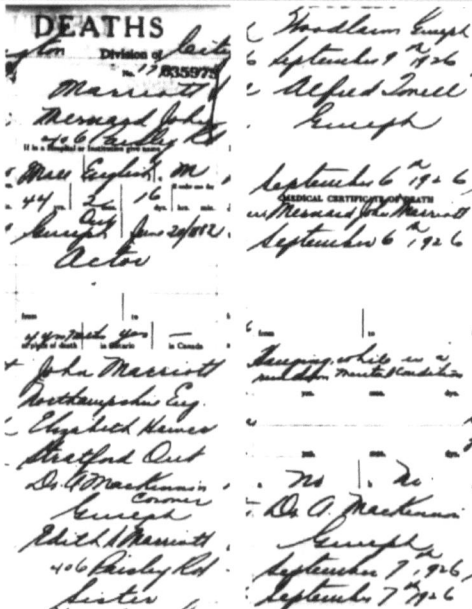

Guelph Mercury Sept 21, 1939
[letter from Al Marriott] ..."*We played with the Orrin Circus in Mexico for three years then going to the Million Dollar Theatre [note from Lorine - this was built in 1918 so we have a vague timeline] in Buenos Aires, Argentina for six months. Next came several months at theatres in Havana Cuba. On five occasions we played return engagement sin front of the grandstand at Toronto Exhibition and making appearnaces before the Prince of Wales*"

The Marriott Twins were booked for a world tour and played the large cities of Europe and other continents. Following this was a booking to represent the USA at th ePan-Pacific Peace Exposition at Nagoya Japan for six months.

Among the engagements was one with President Truman at a county fair in Missouri and the following week at Washington DC. There followed references in Al Marriott's letter to numreous other engagements including seven years at the Hippodrome in New York.

In later years with the coming of the aeroplane their act took the form of a large plane mounted on a high tower. The players performed on a trapeze hanging from the plane, as well as being fastened to the propeller. The home of Mr. and Mrs. Al Marriott is now Georgia

Death of Mernard John Marriott at 406 Paisley Rd, Guelph, Wellington County.44 years 2 months 16 days old, born Guelph 16 June 1882. Actor. Father John Marriott born Northampshire, England. Mother Elizabeth Hewer born Stratford Ontario. Informant: Edith S. Marriott, sister. Burial in Woodlawn Cemetery. Death was suicide and is noted as "hanging while in a run-down mental condition"

123. Charles Whiting 1877-? married Florence Piller ca 1876-

1911 Census of Canada Province: Ontario
District: Lincoln District Number: 93
Sub-District: Grantham Sub-District Number:
18
Place of Habitation: Grantham-15-2 Page: 4
Household Members: Name Age
Charles Whiting 34 b Sep 1876 Ontario
Florence Whiting 36 b Aug 1874 England,
immigrated 1890
Percy C Whiting 7 b Dec 1903
Arthur Whiting 4 b Sep 1906
Edna Clay Whiting 2 b Aug 1908
Myrtel Whiting 4 mos b Feb 1911

124. James Whiting 1879-

1911 Census of Canada
Name: James Whiting
Gender: Male
Marital Status: Married
Age: 32
Birth Date: abt 1879
Birthplace: Toronto
Family Number: 46
Province: Ontario
District: Wentworth
District Number: 135
Sub-District Number: 9
Place of Habitation: Lunatic Asylum
Page: 33

127. Charles Whiting 1881-1892

Ontario, Canada Deaths, 1869-1934
Name: Charles Whiting
Death Date: 2 Jan 1892
Death Location: Hamilton, Wentworth Co.
Age 9
Birth Location: Australia
Cause of death: Acute Embro Spinal Meningitis,
had for 5 days

128. Lewis Gordon Whiting 1883-? married Nellie Gillard

In 1891, 8 year old Nellie was living with her parents
Alfred and Anna and grandparents Joseph and Elizabeth
in Dereham, Norfolk County

Ontario, Canada Births, 1869-1909
Name: Infant Stillborn
Date of Birth: 20 May 1909
Gender: Female
Birth County: Wentworth
Father's Name: Lewis Gordon Whiting
Mother's Name: Nellie Gillard
Roll Number: VRBCAN1908_102549

**1911 Census of Canada, Province Ontario District: Hamilton West
District Number: 78 Sub-District: Ward four Sub-District
Number: 15 Place of Habitation: 296 King St-W Page: 5**

Household Members: Name Age
Robert Haygasth 45
Caroline Haygasth 39
Fredrick Haygasth 20
Louis Whiting 28 b May 1883 Ontario, lodger, English origin
Nellie Whiting 28 b Sep 1882 Ontario, wife

130. Harry Webber Whiting 1886-?

Border Crossings: From Canada to U.S., 1895-1956
Name: Harry W Whiting
Arrival Date: 7 Sep 1914
Age: 24 Birth Date: 16 Sep 1889
Birthplace: St Catharines Ont
Race/Nationality: German
Port of Arrival: Niagara Falls, New York, USA
Departure Contact: Mother Mary Whiting, 138 Beaconsfield, Toronto
Upholsterer
Was in USA previously in 9-5-1914 (5 Sept. 1914)
Medina New York
5'4" brown hair blue eyes

Border Crossings: From Canada to U.S., 1895-1956
Name: Harry W Whiting
Arrival Date: Sep 1914
Age: 28 Birth Date: abt 1886
Birth Country: Canada
Race/Nationality: German
Port of Arrival: Olcott, New York, USA
Mother Mary Whiting, Beaconsfield St. Toronto
Going to Medina New York
Upholsterer

Border Crossings: From Canada to U.S., 1895-1956
Name: Harry Whiting
Arrival Date: Aug 1916
Age: 30 Birth Date: abt 1886
Birth Country: Canada
Race/Nationality: English
Port of Arrival: Detroit, Michigan, USA
Auto-trimmer. Destination Toledo Ohio
Mother Mary Whiting, 15 Margaretta St. Toronto

LIST OR MANIFEST OF ALIEN PASSENGERS APPLYING FOR ADMISSION

PORT OF Detroit

World War I Draft Registration Cards, 1917-1918
Name: Harry W Whiting
2912 Lawrence Ave
City: Toledo County: Lucas State: Ohio
Birthplace: Ontario; Canada
Birth Date: 24 Jul 1886
Race: Caucasian (White)
Trimmer, partly supports his mother
Single
Roll: 1851236 DraftBoard: 3
June 5, 1917

Border Crossings: From Canada to U.S., 1895-1956
Name: Harry W Whiting
Arrival Date: Feb 1919
Age: 32
Birth Date: abt 1887
Birth Country: Canada
Race/Nationality: English
Port of Arrival: Detroit, Michigan, USA
Auto Trimmer. Last lived Toronto Ontario
Mother Mary Whiting, 15 Marguerite St. Toronto
Going to Toledo Ohio

166. Mary Ann McGinnis 1876-1966 married John Alfred (Jack) Sheward 1874-1955

World War I Draft Registration Cards, 1917-1918
Name: John Alfred Sheward
County: Montgomery
State: New York
Birth Date: 24 Dec 1873
Race: White
Roll: 1753846
DraftBoard: 0
John signed up on 12 Sept. 1915. His wife was Mary Ann Sheward of Amsterdam New York. He was a carpet weaver working for Hudderswood? Carpets in Amsterdam New York

Jack arrived in America as a 12 year old in 1886 at the port of Philadelphia, Philadelphia Co, PA. Aboard The Ship "Lord Gough" From Liverpool. His parents and siblings were on board.

Edwin Sheward last residence Ireland
Emma Sheward last residence Ireland
Arthur Sheward last residence England
George Sheward last residence England
Herbert Sheward last residence Ireland
John Sheward last residence England

1910 Census Freehold, Monmouth, New Jersey; Series: T624; Roll: 900; Page: 71B; Enumeration District: 70; Part: 2; Line: 38.
McNINNIE, Frank, head
SHEWARD, John A, 35 b England, boarder imm 1890, naturalized, weaver in carpet mill
Mary, b Canada, 24 boarder md 4 years, no children, imm 1910
Edwin, 49 b England boarder md 25 years, 3 children, none living, imm 1904, weaver in carpet mill
Nellie, b England 45 boarder, imm 1904
Harold b England 13 boarder, imm 1904 (he is found as Harold G. Sheward, living in Amsterdam, Montgomery Co. New York in the 1930 census with wife Edith J. and 3 children. He says he immigrated in 1912, is not naturalized and is a cutter in a silk mill. He is also found in WW1 Draft Registrations for USA as Harold George Sheward)

Tovell Funeral Home Records, Tovell Funeral Home Records, John A. Sherwood, 177 Neeve St, Guelph d 19 Jan, 1928, 177 Neeve St. age 85 years, 5 months.

Burial: Mary and John are buried in Woodlawn Cemetery, Guelph

1920 United States Federal Census > New York > Montgomery Co > Amsterdam Twp> District 81
SHEWARD, John A. b England, 46 imm 1886, Naturalized, Weaver in Carpet Mill
Mary Ann b Canada, 43, imm. 1904, Naturalized

167. Joseph McGinnis 1877-1937 married Olive Lohilda Peer 1905-1961

1891 census Puslinch Tp. Wellington Co:
McGinnis, Joseph, 13, b. Ont, father and mother b On. Methodist, farm labourer, could read but not write. Working on Carter farm

Birth Registration: Olive Lohilda Peer born 15 June 1880, Nelson Tp. Halton Co. to Steven [sic] Edward Peer and Mary E. Vollick. Father a carpenter.

Groom Joseph McGinnis, 28, residence Guelph, born Arkel, bachelor. Occupation Labourer. Parents Alex McGinnis and Harriet King
Bride Olive Peer, 26, residence Guelph, born Kilbride, spinster. Parents Stephen Peer and Mary Vollick.
Witnesses: Wm. C. MacArthur residence Bruce Mines and Mary A. McGinnis, Guelph.
Place of marriage: Guelph. Religion: both Methodist. Married by S.E. Marshall, by license registered 15 Sept. 1905.

1911 Census Guelph, Province: Ontario
District: Wellington South District Number: 134 Sub-District: Guelph Sub-District Number: 31 Place of Habitation: 16 Waterloo St E Page: 9
Household Members: Name Birth Year
Joseph Mc Ginnis b Dec. 1877 contractor, foreman, Methodist
Olive Mc Ginnis 1880
Clarence Mc Ginnis 1906
Lindsay Mc Ginnis 1908

1917 Directory for Guelph: Joseph McGinnis, 76 Water St. works at Page-Hersey Co. Production of two-inch butt weld pipes began at the Guelph factory in 1903. By 1906 the factory had the capability to manufacture twelve-inch butt weld pipes.

Woodlawn Cemetery, Guelph Ontario, Guelph Ontario Block P Row 56 Stone 807: In/Loving memory of/Joseph McGINNIS/Died Jan. 8, 1937/aged 59 years/at rest.

Obit Guelph Mercury 9 Jan 1937:
Deaths: McGinnis - At St. Joseph's Hospital on Fri, Jan 8, 1937, Joseph, dearly beloved husband of Olive Peer, in his 60th year. Funeral services Monday at his late residence 76 Water St. at 2 pm. Burial Woodlawn Cemetery, Guelph.

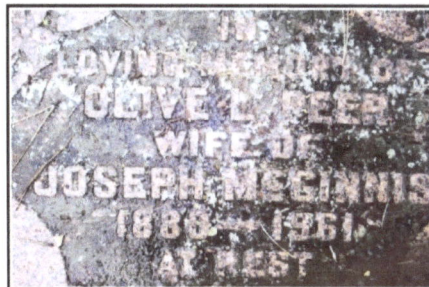

John McCrae (1872-1918) the author of In Flanders Fields, lived one or two doors away from my grandmother Olive Peer McGinnis, on Water Street in Guelph.

Woodlawn Cemetery, Guelph, Wellington Co. Ontario, Block P Row 35 Stone #500: In/Loving Memory of/Olive L. PEER/wife of/Joseph McGINNIS/1880-1961/at rest

168. Fanny McGinnis 1880-? married James Howard 1877-?

Registers of Church of Our Lady, Guelph Ontario, 27 Dec. 1881, Was baptised Ann, about 15 months old. Parents Alex. McGinnis & Harriet King (Protestant) Puslinch. Sponsors Mrs. McGinnis, mother of the father.

1911 Census of Canada, Province: Ontario District: Wellington South District Number: 134 Sub-District: Guelph Sub-District Number: 31 Place of Habitation: 31 Waterloo St Page: 10

Household Members: Name Age
James L Howard 33 b. March
Fannie Howard 30 b. Oct.
Willie Howard 11
Clifford Howard 6

1901 Census of Canada Page
District: Ontario WELLINGTON (South/Sud) (#126)
Subdistrict: Guelph (City/Cité) E-1 Page 20
Details: Schedule 1 Microfilm T-6505
Howard James M   Head M Mar 12 1877 24
Howard Fannie F   Wife M Oct 9 1880 20
Howard William R M   Son S Aug 4 1900 8 mos

> **Letter from Clare McGinnis, 1960s:** *"My Aunt Fannie, Mrs. James Howard, lived in St. Catharines for many years. On Berryman Ave and Church St. She may be in the Oddfellows Lodge Home in either Barrie or Orillia if she is still alive. She was born in 1880, same year as your grandmother"*

169. Dan McGinnis 1880-1937 married Maggie Olive Hatten 1893-1971

Ontario, Canada Births, 1869-1907, Dan McGinnes born Puslinch Twp Wellington Co. 21 Nov 1880 Male Alexander McGinnes father Harriet King mother. Alexander, a farm servant, living Arkell.

WW1 Canadian Expeditionary Force (CEF) database, Dan McGinnis signed up 5 Nov 1914 in Kingston Ontario. date of birth crossed out. Gives next of kin as Mother, Harriet McGinnis, 64 Kent St, Guelph Ontario. He is a blacksmith, born Wellington County

170. Henry McGinnis 1887-1968 married Eunice Cole ca 1894-?

Registers of Church of Our Lady, Guelph Ontario, Born 2 Apr 1887, baptised 4 June 1887. Henry McGinnis s/o Alexander McGinnis & Harriet King of Puslinch.

Sponsors Richard Lowry & Mrs. Jos. McGinnis.

Mother Protestant.

Detroit Border Crossings and Passenger and Crew Lists, 1905-1957
Name: Eunice Mc Ginnis
Arrival Date: 21 Sep 1917
Age: 23
Birth Date: abt 1894
Birthplace: Charlotte Mi
Gender: Female
Race/Nationality: English
Port of Arrival: Detroit, Michigan
Departure Contact: Husband Henry Mcginniss, 64 Kent St, Guelph Ontario
Arrival Contact: Sister Sarah Burglaund   1054 4th St, Detroit Michigan
was in USA from 1894-1907, in Jackson Michigan
5' 4" medium complexion, brown hair, blue eyes
Microfilm Roll Number: M1478_59

Woodlawn Cemetery, Guelph Ontario
Henry and Eunice are buried in Woodlawn Cemetery, Guelph Ontario Block D2

Ontario, Canada Births, 1869-1909
Name: Henry McGinnis
Date of Birth: 2 Apr 1887
Gender: Male
Birth County: Wellington
Father's Name: Alexander McGinnis
Mother's Name: Harriet King
Birth registered Sept 18, 1951 by sister Mary Ann Sheward. Both parents listed as deceased, Henry's place of birth given as Arkell.
Roll Number: MS930_7

171, 172, 173. Mary Christina King 1874-?, Eliza King ca 1877-?, Bertha King 1880-? married John Hayward

Three daughters of John King & Susanna Fife: Mary Christina, Eliza & Bertha

Bertha King Hayword aka Hayworth & daughter Kate

175. Hannah May King 1887-? married Thomas Rodgers

All photos on this page courtesy of David Rodgers

176. William Robert King 1891-? 177. Lillian King 1898-? married Frank Quance ca 1893-?

William Robert King & his third wife Flo

Lillian Quance & her brother William Robert King

possibly William Robert King ca 1918

All photos on this page courtesy of David Rodgers

184. George Edward King 1879-1912 married Sarah A. Jackson 1880-?

1901 Census of Canada Province: Ontario
District: Nipissing District Number: 92
Sub-District: Cooks Mills Sub-District Number:
R-1 Family Number: 20 Page: 2
Household Members: Name Age
George E King 21, b 13 Sept 1879 Ontario.
Methodist. Mill Man, English origin
Sarah A King 21
Grace E King 2
David Jackson 47 father-in-law

1911 Census of Canada, Province: Ontario
District: Algoma East, District Number: 54,
Sub-District: Blind River, Sub-District Number:
63, Page: 21
Household Members: Name Age
King George E Sept 1879, millwright
Sarah Feb 1880 Quebec
Grace Sept 1899
Edna Apr 1904
Hazel Apr 1906
Lloyd March 1908

Ontario, Canada Births, 1869-1909
Name: Lloyd George Elgin King
Date of Birth: 27 Mar 1908
Birth County: Algoma District
Father's name: George E King
Mother's name: Sarah A Sands [sic]

184. George Edward King 1879-1912 married Sarah A. Jackson 1880-?

1901 Census of Canada Province: Ontario
District: Nipissing District Number: 92
Sub-District: Cooks Mills Sub-District Number:
R-1 Family Number: 20 Page: 2
Household Members: Name Age
George E King 21, b 13 Sept 1879 Ontario.
Methodist. Mill Man, English origin
Sarah A King 21
Grace E King 2
David Jackson 47 father-in-law

1911 Census of Canada, Province: Ontario
District: Algoma East, District Number: 54,
Sub-District: Blind River, Sub-District Number:
63, Page: 21
Household Members: Name Age
King George E Sept 1879, millwright
Sarah Feb 1880 Quebec
Grace Sept 1899
Edna Apr 1904
Hazel Apr 1906
Lloyd March 1908

Ontario, Canada Births, 1869-1909
Name: Lloyd George Elgin King
Date of Birth: 27 Mar 1908
Birth County: Algoma District
Father's name: George E King
Mother's name: Sarah A Sands [sic]

www.ingramcontent.com/pod-product-compliance
Lightning Source LLC
Chambersburg PA
CBHW060759270326
41926CB00002B/32